Belief,
Justification,
and Knowledge

The Wadsworth Basic Issues in Philosophy Series
Edited by James Sterba

Belief, Justification, and Knowledge
An Introduction to Epistemology
Robert Audi

Basic Issues in Aesthetics
Marcia M. Eaton

Philosophy of Religion
William J. Wainwright

Belief, Justification, and Knowledge

An Introduction to Epistemology

Robert Audi

University of Nebraska, Lincoln

Wadsworth Publishing Company
Belmont, California
A Division of Wadsworth, Inc.

Philosophy Editor: Ken King

Editorial Assistant: Dorothy Paneri

Production Editor: Gary Mcdonald

Managing Designer: Julia Scannell

Print Buyer: Karen Hunt

Designer: John Osborne

Copy Editor: Pat Tompkins

Compositor: Better Graphics, Inc.

Cover: John Osborne

© 1988 by Wadsworth, Inc. All rights reserved. No part of this book may be reproduced, stored in a retrieval system, or transcribed, in any form or by any means, electronic, mechanical, photocopying, recording, or otherwise, without the prior written permission of the publisher, Wadsworth Publishing Company, Belmont, California 94002, a division of Wadsworth, Inc.

Printed in the United States of America   19

1 2 3 4 5 6 7 8 9 10—92 91 90 89 88

Library of Congress Cataloging-in-Publication Data

Audi, Robert, 1941–
  Belief, justification, and knowledge.

  (Wadsworth basic issues in philosophy series)
  Bibliography: p.
  Includes index.
  1. Knowledge, Theory of.   2. Justification
(Theory of knowledge)   I. Title.   II. Series.
BD161.A78   1988   121   87-14270
ISBN 0-534-08400-1

To Malou

Contents

P A R T   T W O

The Development and Structure of Belief, Justification, and Knowledge

PART THREE

The Nature and Scope of Knowledge and Justification

Preface

This book is a brief introduction to epistemology, conceived as the theory of knowledge and justification. The book is not elementary, but it presupposes no background in philosophy and is usable, at least in part, in selected courses offered as introductions to philosophy in general. Parts of it might serve as collateral reading in the study of a number of philosophers often discussed in introductory or middle-level philosophy courses, especially Descartes, Locke, Berkeley, Hume, Kant, and Mill, but also parts of Plato, Aristotle, Aquinas, and, of course, twentieth-century writers in epistemology. The book might facilitate the study of moral philosophy, such as the ethics of Kant and Mill, and it bears directly on topics in the epistemology of religion, some of which are discussed in Chapter 8.

My main focus is the body of concepts, theories, and problems central in understanding knowledge and justification. Historically, justification has been as important in epistemology as knowledge itself. This is surely so at present. In many parts of the book, justification and knowledge are discussed separately; but they are also interconnected at many points. The book is not historical, yet it does discuss selected major positions in the history of philosophy, particularly some of those that have greatly influenced human thought and culture. Moreover, even where major philosophers are not mentioned, I try to take their views into account. For one of my primary aims is to facilitate the reading of those philosophers, especially their epistemological writings. It would take a long book to discuss even a few historically important epistemologies in detail, but a short book can provide some of the tools for understanding them. That is one of my main purposes.

In keeping with the purposes of this book, the writing is intended to be as simple as possible for a philosophically serious introduction, and a Foreword addressed primarily to undergraduates is included in the hope that it will help to explain some of the wider benefits, including non-academic values, of studying epistemology and, even more, philosophy in general. Some of the ideas in the Foreword are based on a guide for undergraduates which I wrote for the American Philosophical Association; the guide has proved useful to students in a number of philosophy programs, and I am grateful to the APA for allowing me to draw on it.

To aid concentration on the main points, and to keep the book from becoming longer and more complicated, footnotes are not used, though parenthetical references are given in some places, and there is also a short selected bibliography with thumbnail annotations. Technical terms are explained briefly when introduced and avoided when they can be. But some I consider indispensable: they are not mere words, but tools. Moreover, while this book is an introduction to the *field* of epistemology and not to the *literature* of epistemology, I do want to help readers prepare for a critical study of that literature, contemporary as well as classical. For that reason, too, some special vocabulary is introduced.

The order of topics is designed to introduce the field in a natural progression: from the genesis of justification and knowledge (Part One), to their development and structure (Part Two), and thence to questions about what they are and how far they extend (Part Three). In a way, the reader is encouraged to *do* epistemology before talking *about* it, for instance before discussing what sort of epistemological theory, say normative or naturalistic, best accounts for knowledge. My strategy is, in part, to discuss myriad cases of justification and knowledge before approaching analyses of what they are, or the skeptical case against our having them.

In one way, my approach differs markedly from that of many epistemological books. I leave the assessment of skepticism for the last chapter, though remarks at earlier points indicate that skeptical problems lie in the background. Unlike some philosophers, I do not think that discussion of skepticism is needed to motivate the study of epistemology. Granted, historically skepticism has been a major motivating force; but it is not the only one, and epistemological concepts are of independent interest. Moreover, in assessing skepticism I use many concepts and points developed in earlier chapters; if it were treated early in the book, I would have to delay assessing it and in returning to it would waste space in reformulation. There is also a certain risk in posing skeptical problems at or near the outset: non-professional readers may tend to be distracted, even in discussing a conceptual question concerning, say, what knowledge *is,* by a desire to deal with skeptical arguments against there being any knowledge. There is some risk of underplaying skepticism in proceeding as I do; but there may be no wholly neutral way to treat it, and on balance I believe my approach to it can be adapted to varying degrees of skeptical inclination. An instructor who prefers to begin with skepticism can do so by taking care to explain some of the ideas introduced earlier in the book. The first three sections of Chapter 9, largely meant to introduce and motivate skepticism, presuppose far less of the earlier chapters than the later, evaluative discussion; and most of the chapter is understandable on the basis of Part One, which is probably easier reading than Part Two.

My exposition of problems and positions is meant to be as nearly unbiased as I can make it, and where controversial interpretations are unavoidable I try to present them cautiously. In many places, however, I offer my own view. Given the brevity of the book, I cannot provide a highly detailed explanation of each major position discussed, or argue at length for my own views. I make no pretense of treating anything conclusively. But in some cases—as with skepticism—I simply do not want to leave the reader with no idea of where I stand, or perhaps unwarrantedly doubting that there is any solution to the problem at hand. I thus propose some tentative positions for critical discussion.

Acknowledgments

This book has profited from my reading of many articles and books by contemporary philosophers, and from many discussions I have had with them and, of course, with my students. I cannot mention all of these philosophers, but particularly since I use no footnotes it is appropriate to cite many. I am sure that my debt to those I will name—as well as to some I do not, such as some whose journal papers I have read but have not picked up again, and some I have heard at conferences—is incalculable. Over some twenty years, I have benefited greatly from discussions with William Alston, as well as from reading his works; and I am much indebted to him for his advice, and his detailed critical comments, on the manuscript. My reading of books and articles by Roderick Chisholm, and a number of discussions with him, have also substantially helped me in the past fifteen years. More recently, I have learned steadily from the participants in the National Endowment for the Humanities Summer Seminars and Summer Institute I have directed. Both Alston and Chisholm (in different years) gave illuminating epistemological papers in those NEH series. I also benefited much from the papers and discussions given to the Seminars by Laurence BonJour, Hector-Neri Castañeda, Fred Dretske, Alvin Goldman, Jaegwon Kim, and John King-Farlow, with all of whom I have been fruitfully discussing epistemological topics for many years. I have learned immensely from many other epistemologists, including Robert Almeder, David Armstrong, John A. Barker, Richard Brandt, Panayot Butchvarov, Richard Feldman, Roderick Firth, Richard Fumerton, Carl Ginet, Alan H. Goldman, Gilbert Harman, Risto Hilpinen, Peter Klein, Hilary Kornblith, Keith Lehrer, Alvin Plantinga, John Pollock, Lawrence Powers, W. V. Quine, Nicholas Rescher, Frederick Schmitt, Wilfrid Sellars, Robert Shope, Ernest Sosa, the late Gail Stine, Marshall Swain, and James Van Cleve. In most cases I have not only read some of their epistemological work but also discussed one or another epistemological problem with them in detail.

I owe special thanks to the philosophers who generously commented in detail on early versions of the manuscript: Frederick R. Adams, Edward Averill, Laurence BonJour, Carol Caraway, Albert Casullo, Wayne A. Davis, Richard Foley, Robert M. Gordon, Jay Harker, John Heil, Dale Jacquette, Ross Mandel, Paul Moser, Andrew Naylor, George Pappas, Thomas Vinci, and Nicholas Wolterstorff. These philosophers not only helped me eliminate errors but also gave me constructive suggestions and critical remarks that evoked both clarification and more substantive improvement. Additions and many other changes have been made after they read the book, and I hope that the final product is closer to meeting the difficulties they discerned. To my colleagues at the University of Nebraska, Lincoln, I am specially grateful; those with whom one discusses one or another topic in a book so regularly play a unique role in its development. I am also grateful to Elizabeth Bilynskyj for editorial comments and help in preparing the index; and, for advice and help at several stages in the development of the book, I want to thank Kenneth King and the production staff at Wadsworth Publishing Company.

Foreword

Since this book could be among the first philosophical works which some readers come to know, it is appropriate to say something about the values of studying philosophy. Epistemology—the theory of knowledge and justification—is such a large part of philosophy, and so intertwined with the other parts, that most of what applies to the value of studying philosophy in general also holds for the pursuit of epistemology. For that reason (and to keep the book short), I am not going to speak specifically about epistemology here. But given what can be said about philosophy in general, many of the special values of studying epistemology will be quite plain to anyone who reflects on this book as a whole.

In talking about the values of studying philosophy, I want to make two sorts of points. Some concern its *intrinsic value*, that is, the value that studying philosophy has in itself, quite apart from what it leads to, such as knowledge of some of the deepest problems in the history of thought. The other points concern the *instrumental value* of studying philosophy, that is, the value it has through what it leads to. It would be nice if, having said this, I could explain in a nutshell just what philosophy *is*. But it is too rich and varied for that. We might roughly characterize the field of philosophy as the critical and theoretical study of ideas and issues. But what kinds of ideas and issues? And what is a critical and theoretical study?

The answer to the first question is that any kind of idea or issue *can* be studied philosophically. It is typical of philosophy, however, to pursue questions not only in epistemology but also in metaphysics, which concerns the nature of reality, in ethics, which treats questions of right and wrong, in logic, which concerns the assessment of reasoning, and in the history of philosophy itself. Historically, philosophers have addressed questions of all these sorts, as well as related problems about the nature and fundamental concepts of other fields, such as art, mathematics, religion, and the sciences—biological, physical, and social. There is a branch of philosophy for each of these fields, as well as for subfields of the broader philosophical areas; the philosophy of mind, for instance, is a subfield of metaphysics. All of the fields are interconnected. Epistemology, for example, is closely related to metaphysics: if we have knowledge of a kind of thing, say mental processes, it must be real; and if something exists in reality, such as what people see in a hallucination, epistemology must consider what can be known about it. Some connections between epistemology and metaphysics will be explored in the chapter on perception; the relations of epistemology to ethics, philosophy of religion, and philosophy of science will be discussed in the chapter on the scope of knowledge; and throughout the book philosophical method, as an approach to intellectual problems, will be exhibited.

The second question, concerning what constitutes a critical and theoretical study, is harder than the first, but we may say at least this. A critical study of an idea or issue clarifies it, interprets it, and offers a reasoned evaluation of it or at least of one or more positions regarding it; and a critical study is theoretical to the extent that these activities are anchored in an explanatory account of the nature of whatever is under study: knowledge or justification, ethics or science, mind or matter. Fortunately, this book itself should help in answering both questions. For its main business is the critical study of a large set of related ideas and issues.

It might be thought that only intellectuals can appreciate the intrinsic value of studying philosophy: for instance, the distinctive stimulation, pleasure, and excitement that philosophical activity yields to many who pursue it. But that is not so. We all have the capacity to reflect, and we seem by nature to enjoy exercising our rational capacities once we learn to do it. Nearly everyone can get excited about some philosophical problems; and once philosophical problems become intriguing in themselves, it is possible to find great pleasure in reading and discussing philosophy, quite apart from any further rewards, such as the intellectual training so characteristic of philosophical studies, or the understanding of human life philosophy can provide. Yet many people never discover their capacity to enjoy philosophical topics. Many do not have the opportunity, which for most people requires someone to help by presenting and discussing philosophical concepts, problems, and texts. Some people apparently lack the patience or will, for it usually takes a bit of work to get started. Philosophy is a field of knowledge, not a domain of loose speculation with no ground rules, where one can have an easy romance with ideas, and simply admire one's own creativity as one's phrases begin to seem profound. In any event, a nodding acquaintance is not a romance.

The instrumental values of philosophy, those realizable through what philosophical activity leads to, are too numerous to list. But I can cite a few of the valuable uses of philosophy, uses of a kind so basic that serious work in a course that covers this book, such as an introduction to epistemology, might be expected to contribute something to them. The values I cite can be grouped in three areas: the broadest uses of philosophy; its uses in one's education; and its uses in one's career. In describing these values, I am speaking of the benefits of philosophy for *individuals*. But it will be obvious that if enough individuals reap these benefits, that will be valuable for *human culture*: for the strength of its social and political institutions, for the vitality of the arts, for the depth of our mutual understanding as citizens in a shared world.

First among the instrumental values of the study of philosophy is this: it contributes to our general *ability to solve problems*. I mean problems in virtually any area, not only intellectual ones but, for instance, moral and religious problems. For philosophy clarifies what is at stake when a problem arises, helps us sort out different solutions, and—particularly through epistemological methods—aids us in weighing reasons for and against the various solutions. Second, philosophy helps us develop *communication skills*. For instance, it enhances our ability to formulate our points, to construct convincing examples, to understand other people, and to correct misinterpretations of what we have said before the mistakes cause trouble. Third, as one would expect from the first two points, philosophical training tends to strengthen our *persuasive powers*: we learn to state our views more convincingly; we learn something about how to back a view up with arguments; and we acquire the ability to meet objections from others, either by counterargument or—as is often possible—by showing that the apparent inconsistency between their view and ours disappears with proper interpretation of one or the other. Fourth, since all three points apply directly to *writing skills*, the study of philosophy can aid us in developing these skills. In writing as in speech, philosophy can help us to formulate, illustrate, explain, and defend our views, in clear, well-ordered terms.

In academic tasks, the study of philosophy is useful in at least two general respects. First, it helps us in *understanding other disciplines*. Not only are there branches of philosophy that concentrate on other subjects—such as the philosophy of art, philosophy of religion, and philosophy of science—but philosophy in general, and particularly epistemology, considers the methods of discovery and the standards of evidence used in other fields. Philosophy also explores interrelations among other disciplines, for instance biology and psychology, economics and history, literature and art. My second point here is that studying philosophy contributes to developing *sound methods of research and analysis*. In learning to state problems clearly, we learn what sorts of information we need in order to solve them and how to separate out the irrelevant. In learning to interpret what is complex or unclear, and to analyze the relations among different ideas or problems, we can begin to develop an ability to understand and resolve issues in any field, whether in the humanities, the sciences, or some other area.

The usefulness of philosophy in pursuing a career is suggested by the points already made. For all the instructional values cited can contribute at least indirectly to one's success in virtually any occupation. The capacities mentioned apply to just about any kind of subject matter or problem. They are sometimes called *transferable skills*, and leaders in business and the professions have often complained that capacities of these kinds are missing even in employees prepared for the jobs in question by specially tailored programs. There is now increasing recognition that the study of basic fields like philosophy is indispensable for really good career preparation. One must not lose sight of this in the attempt to get ready for what one sees as one's first job. Even if a narrow education were the best way to ensure getting some *job* immediately upon graduation, it is a poor way to prepare for a good *career*, even in areas far-removed from academic pursuits.

None of what I have said about the values of philosophy implies that at each step in learning philosophy one can *see* its application to other pursuits. Sometimes one cannot. But to be always looking for its external applications would be rather like playing a sport or an instrument for relaxation and, instead of concentrating on playing the game or the music well, regularly asking oneself if one is getting relaxation. Moreover, one can play a game *both* for the intrinsic value—say, the enjoyment value—of playing and for the instrumental value of playing, for instance, the relaxation it produces. The same holds for doing philosophy. Philosophy contributes distinctively to broadening and sharpening the mind; it nourishes an appetite for ideas and discussion; and it is one of the best and most direct routes to the development and spontaneous exercise of our human capacities.

Belief,
Justification,
and Knowledge

Introduction

On a hillside before me, some thirty yards away, I see a blue spruce tree. It has the shape of a cone, except that its lower branches lie parallel to the slope of the hill and it is topped by two parallel shoots of almost equal height. It is a full tree and mostly light blue. Birds perch near it, and I hear their songs. A mild breeze brings the smell of freshly cut grass. From a coarse mug I sip hot coffee. Its taste is slightly bitter. I am alert, the air is clear, the scene is quiet. My perceptions are quite distinct.

I have described some of what I *perceive*: some of what I see, hear, smell, feel, and taste. I have also expressed some of what I *believe*: that there is a blue spruce before me, that there are bird songs, that there is a smell of freshly cut grass, that the mug is rough to the touch, and that the coffee is slightly bitter. It seems altogether natural for me to believe these things, and I think I quite *justifiably believe* them. By that I mean above all that the beliefs I refer to are *justified*. This is not because they have been through a *process of being justified*, as where one defends a controversial belief by giving reasons for it. They have not: the question whether they are justified has not come up. No one has challenged them, or even asked me why I hold them. But these beliefs are justified because there is something about them in virtue of which, unlike wild guesses I may make in charades, they are warranted—in this case, they are justified simply through their arising in the normal way they have from my perceptions. Roughly, the beliefs are justified in the sense that they are quite in order from the point of view of the standards for what I may reasonably believe.

In saying that I justifiably believe there is a blue spruce before me, I am implying something else, something that is quite different, though it sounds very

1

similar, namely, that I am *justified in believing* there is a blue spruce before me. To see the difference, notice that I could be justified *in* believing something without believing it at all, quite as one can be justified in doing something, such as punishing a child, yet not do it. For example, I might be justified in believing that I can do a certain difficult task, yet fail to believe this until someone encourages me. Moreover, simply by taking stock of the size and texture of the spruce, I am justified in believing that it has more than 289 needles; but I did not actually believe that until the subject of its needles arose as I thought about the tree. Thus, I was justified in believing it before I actually did believe it.

The two notions are intimately related, however: if one justifiably believes something, one is also justified in believing it. But, as our example of the needles shows, the converse does not hold, since there are many things one is justified *in* believing which one does not actually believe. Let's call the first kind of justification—justifiably believing—*belief justification*, since it belongs to actual beliefs. Let's call the second kind—being justified in believing—*situational justification*, since it is based on the situation one is in, including one's background knowledge, such as that there are hundreds of needles on each branch. One's situational justification for believing something may or may not be accompanied by one's having an actual justified belief that it is so. In a way, we have more situational justification than we need.

Without situational justification—such as the kind arising from my seeing the blue spruce—there would be no belief justification. I would not, for instance, justifiably believe that there is a blue spruce before me. Without belief justification (or something very much like it), however , there would be no knowledge. If I did not have the kind of justified belief I do—if, for instance, I were wearing dark sunglasses and could not see the difference between a green spruce and a blue one—then, on the basis of what I now see, I would not know that there is a blue spruce before me.

How does knowledge come into the picture here? Surely I could have maintained, regarding each of the things I have said I believed, that I knew it. And don't I know these things on the same basis on which I justifiably believe them, for instance seeing and hearing? This is very plausible. But notice that if I know these things, then, of course, they are *true*, whereas I can justifiably believe something that is false. If a normally reliable friend decided to trick me into believing something false, say that he has just lost my car keys, I could justifiably believe that he lost them even if it were not true. We may not assume, then, that everything we learn about justified belief applies to knowledge. We must look at each independently to discern their differences, and we must consider them together to appreciate their relationship.

I said that I *saw* the blue spruce and that my belief that there was a blue spruce before me arose from my seeing it. If the belief arose, in the normal way, from my seeing the tree, then the belief *was* true. To be sure, if the tree had been cut down since I last saw it, and there were now a perfect artificial copy standing there, then while I might think I know the blue spruce is there, I would only falsely believe I know this, though I would still justifiably believe it. But such a bizarre happening is extremely improbable. It is not, however, impossible. One might now wonder, as skeptics do, whether I then *know* even that it is improbable. Moreover, am I at least justified in my belief that it has not happened? And suppose I do not know or at least justifiably believe that it has not happened. In that case, *am* I justified in believing that there is a blue spruce before me? If I am not justified in believing this, how can I be justified in believing what appear to be far less obvious truths, such as that my house is secure against the elements, my car safe to drive, and my food free of poisons? And how can I know the many things I need to know in life, such as that my family and friends are trustworthy, that I control my behavior and can thus partly determine my future, and that the world I live in at least approximates the structured reality which science and common sense portray? These are difficult and important questions. They indicate how insecure and disordered human life would be if we could not suppose that we have justified beliefs and knowledge. Much later, in discussing skepticism, I will take up such questions at some length. Until then I will assume the commonsense view that beliefs which arise in the way my belief that there is a blue spruce before me does are not only justified but also constitute knowledge.

Let us turn to some different kinds of circumstances in which beliefs arise in such a way that they are both justified and constitute knowledge. In doing this, I want to consider how our beliefs are related to our memory, our perceptions, our consciousness, and our reasoning.

As I look at the spruce, I *remember*, with some amusement, that I planted it twice, once at the base of the hill, where it somehow did not stand out, and later on the hillside. Again, I justifiably believe that I planted it twice. I believe I also know that I did this. But here I confess to being less confident than I am of the justification of my belief, held in the radiant sunlight, that there is (now) a blue spruce before me. As my memories become less vivid, I am correspondingly less sure that my beliefs apparently based on them are justified. Still, I distinctly recall the two plantings. The terrain was rocky; the ground was hard; the planting was difficult. Both times I needed a crowbar. By contrast, I have no belief about whether the second planting was in the fall, as was the first, or in the spring. I *entertain* the proposition that it was in the spring; I *consider* whether it is true; but all I can do is *suspend judgment*. I thus neither believe it nor disbelieve it, and I do not try to force myself to resolve the question.

As I think about planting the tree, it occurs to me that I am vividly imaging that first planting. I can still see the bale of peat moss, the readied hole, and the sapling with its burlapped roots. I have turned my attention inwards to my own imagery. The object of my attention, my own imaging of the scene, seems internal, though *its* object is external and long gone by. But clearly, I believe that I am imaging the sapling; and there is no apparent reason to doubt that I justifiably believe this and know that it is so.

The season has been dry, and it now occurs to me that the tree will not grow well without a good deal of water for its roots. But this I do not believe simply on the basis of perception. I learned it from repeated *observation*. I might also have learned it from *testimony*, as I learned from the tree specialist (after a gypsy moth infestation) that to grow well such a tree needs a leader, a shoot growing upright at the top. I needed perception to *learn* these things, and I need memory to *retain* them. Yet they do not arise from perception in the way my visual beliefs do, or emerge from memory in the way my beliefs about past events do. But do I not still justifiably believe that the tree will not flourish without water for its roots? Surely I do, and apparently I also know this.

I now look back at the tree and am impressed by how utterly vertical it stands. What is the angle, I wonder, at which its trunk intersects the slope of the hillside? The angle formed by the trunk and the upper slope looks like seventy degrees. If so, I reason, and the surface of the hill around the tree is flat, then the lower angle is 110 degrees. Now here I believe something different in kind from the other things I have cited so far: I believe that if the hillside forms a straight line beneath the trunk and the upper angle is seventy degrees, then the lower angle is 110. This is a geometrical belief. I am imagining that the hillside is a perfect plane of the kind postulated in Euclidean geometry, that the tree makes a straight line intersecting it, and that the two angles on the upper and lower sides of the tree add up to 180 degrees. I don't believe this on the same sort of basis I have for the other things I said I believed. My conception of geometry as applied to ideal lines and surfaces seems to be the crucial basis here. On that basis, my belief seems to be justified and to constitute knowledge.

I notice that the spruce is taller than the nearby hawthorn, and, looking further up the hill, I see that the hawthorn is taller than the neighboring birch. I now realize that the spruce is taller than the birch. My underlying belief here is that if one thing is taller than a second and the second taller than a third, then the first is taller than the third. And, perhaps even more than the geometrical belief, this one seems to arise simply from my grasp of the concepts in question, above all the concept of one thing's being taller than another.

The examples I have given represent what philosophers call perceptual, memorial, introspective, inductive, and a priori beliefs. My belief that the mug is coarse is *perceptual*, arising as it does from touch—tactual perception. My belief that I planted the tree twice is *memorial*, since it is stored in my memory and held on that basis. My belief that I am imaging is called *introspective* because it is conceived as arising from "looking within" (the etymological meaning of 'introspection'). My belief that the tree will not grow well without water for its roots is called *inductive* because it is formed on the basis of generalization from similar experiences with trees. Those experiences "lead into" the generalization about trees, to follow the etymological meaning of 'induction'. Finally, consider my belief that if the spruce is taller than the hawthorn and the hawthorn is taller than the birch, then the spruce is taller than the birch. A belief like this is called *a priori* (roughly, based on what is prior to observational experience) because it apparently arises not from experience of how things actually behave but simply from reasoning about, or from a rational grasp of, the key concepts one needs in order to have the belief, such as the concept of one thing's being taller than another.

Each kind of belief is *grounded* in the source from which it arises. Our examples illustrate at least three important kinds of grounding. Consider my belief that there is a blue spruce before me. It is *causally grounded* in my experience of seeing the spruce because that experience produces the belief. It is *justificationally grounded* in that experience because the experience, or at least some element in the experience, justifies my holding the belief. And it is *epistemically grounded* in the experience because in virtue of that experience my belief constitutes knowledge that there is a blue spruce before me. These three kinds of grounding very often occur together, and I will thus usually speak simply of a belief as *grounded* in a source, such as vision, when what grounds the belief does so in all three ways.

Each kind of grounding goes with a very common kind of question about belief. Causal grounding goes with 'Why do you believe that?' An answer to this question, asked about my belief that there is a blue spruce before me, would be that I see it. Justificational grounding goes with 'What is your justification for believing that?' (though 'Why do you believe that?' can be asked with this same force). Again, I might answer that I see it. And epistemic grounding goes with 'How do you know that?' Once again, saying that I see it will answer the question. Clearly the same sorts of points can be made for the other four cases: memorial beliefs are grounded in memory, introspective beliefs in introspection (or "consciousness"), inductively based beliefs in experience, and a priori beliefs in reason.

There is a great deal more to be said about each of these four sources of belief, justification, and knowledge and about what it is for them to ground what they do ground. The next four chapters will explore, and in some cases compare, these different sources. In the light of what we find out in those chapters, we can go on to discuss the development and structure of knowledge and then proceed to consider what knowledge is and what kinds of things can be known.

The Sources of Belief, Justification, and Knowledge

Perception

As I look at the blue spruce before me, I believe not only that there *is* a blue spruce there but also that I *see* one. And I do see one. I visually perceive it, just as I tactually perceive the coarseness of the mug in my hand. Both beliefs, the belief that there is a blue spruce there, and the self-conscious belief that *I* see one, are grounded, causally, justificationally, and epistemically, in my visual experience. The same sort of thing holds for the other senses. For instance, I believe not only that the mug is coarse, but also that I feel its coarseness; and both beliefs are grounded in my tactual experience. I could believe any of these things on the basis of someone else's testimony. My beliefs would then have a quite different status. For instance, my belief that there is a blue spruce before me would not be *perceptual*, but only a belief *about a perceptible*, that is, about a perceivable object. My interest here is not in beliefs that are simply about perceptibles but in perception and perceptual beliefs. Moreover, since vision and visual beliefs are a good basis for discussing perception and perceptual beliefs, I will concentrate on them and mention the other senses only occasionally.

There are at least four elements in perception, all evident in our example: the perceiver, me; the object, the spruce; the sensory experience, my visual experience of colors and shapes; and the relation between the object and the subject, commonly taken to be a causal relation by which the object seems to produce the sensory experience in the perceiver. Some accounts of perception add to this list; others subtract from it. To understand perception we must consider both kinds of account and how these elements are to be conceived in relation to one another. First, however, it is essential to consider various examples of perception.

THREE MODES OF PERCEPTION

I see, hence perceive, the blue spruce. I also see that it is straight. Thirdly, speaking in a less familiar way, I see it to be a full tree. Perception is common to all three cases. The first is one of *simple perception*, (visual) perception taken by itself. It is simply seeing the tree, and this is parallel to hearing a bird, touching a mug, smelling freshly cut grass, and tasting coffee. The second case is one of *perception that*, since it is seeing that a particular thing is so, namely, that the tree is straight. The third case is one of *perception to be*, since it is seeing something to be so: I see the tree to be full. The latter two cases imply corresponding kinds of beliefs: seeing that the tree is straight implies believing that it is, and seeing it to be a full tree implies believing it to be a full one.

We can begin to understand how perception occurs in all three cases if we consider how both kinds of beliefs are related to it. In the second and third cases, my visual perception issues in beliefs which are then grounded in it and can thereby constitute visual knowledge. In the first case, my simply seeing the tree provides a basis for both kinds of beliefs even if, because my mind is entirely occupied with a paper I am writing, no belief about the tree actually arises in me. But what kinds of beliefs are these, and how are they specifically perceptual?

Many of my beliefs correspond to perception *that*, say to seeing that something is so. I believe that the spruce is lighter toward the tips of its branches where there is new growth, that it is conical in shape, and that it is taller than the nearby hawthorn. But I also have many beliefs about it that are of the second kind; they correspond to perception *to be*, for instance to seeing something to be a certain way. Thus, I believe the tree to be blue, to be symmetrical, to be straight, and so on. The difference between these two kinds of belief is significant. As we shall see, it corresponds first of all to distinct ways I am related to the objects I perceive and, secondly, to different ways of assessing the truth of what, on the basis of my perceptions, I believe.

The first kind of belief is *propositional*, since it is belief *that* the spruce is (say) conical. The belief is thus true or false depending on whether the proposition that the tree is conical is true or false. In holding the belief, moreover, in some way I think of what I see *as a tree* which is conical: in believing that *the tree* is conical, I conceive what I take to be conical *as* a tree. The second kind of belief might be called *objectual*, since it is a belief *of* (or regarding) an object, say the tree, an object *of* which I believe that it is (for instance) straight. In holding this objectual belief I need *not* think of what I see as a *tree*; for I might mistakenly take it to be a tepee, yet still believe it to be straight. Indeed, if I had grown up in the desert and somehow failed to acquire the concept of a spruce, I could still believe, regarding the spruce I see—and perhaps think of as a blue tepee—that *it* is conical, whereas

I could not believe that *the spruce* is conical. Similarly, a two-year-old—Susie, let us say—who has no notion of a tachistoscope can, upon seeing one and hearing it work, believe it to be making noise; but Susie cannot believe, and would not say, that the tachistoscope is making noise. Her propositional belief, if any, would be, say, that that thing on the table is making noise. This would be true.

Unlike propositional beliefs, objectual beliefs are best not viewed as true without qualification; they are accurate or inaccurate, depending on whether what one believes of the object (such as that it is straight) is or is not *true of* it. It is true of the spruce, and I believe it to be true of this tree, that it is straight. But perhaps Susie could, at least for a moment, believe of a tachistoscope that it is making noise, yet not believe any proposition about it: she attributes noise-making to it, yet does not conceptualize it in the way required for having a propositional belief about it, the kind of belief expressed in a complete declarative sentence such as 'The tachistoscope is making noise.' She would then have no belief about the instrument that should be unqualifiedly called true, such as that the tachistoscope is making noise. Still, if she attributes noise-making to it, she does truly believe, *of* it, that it is making noise. If it is making noise, then in believing it to be doing so Susie is *right about it*, and this holds even if she has no specific concept of what it *is* that is making the noise.

Corresponding to the two kinds of beliefs I have described are two ways of talking about perception. I see *that* the tree is straight. This is (visual) *propositional perception*: perception that. I also see it *to be* straight. This is (visual) *objectual perception*: perception to be. The same distinction apparently applies to hearing and touch. Perhaps, for example, I can hear that a piano is out of tune by hearing its sour notes, as opposed to hearing the tuner say it needs tuning. As for taste and smell, we speak as if they yielded only simple perception; we talk of smelling mint in the iced tea, but not of smelling it to be minty. Such talk is, however, quite intelligible on the model of seeing that something is so, and we may thus take the distinction between perception *that* and perception *to be* to apply in principle to all the senses.

It is useful to think of perceptual beliefs as *embedded* in the corresponding mode of perception, roughly in the sense that they are essential to perceiving in that mode. Thus, my belief that the spruce is straight is embedded in my seeing that it is, and Susie's believing the tachistoscope to be making noise is embedded in her hearing it to be doing so; in each case, without the belief, there would not be perception in that mode. Moreover, in both kinds of cases, the belief is grounded in simple perception: if I don't see a thing at all, I don't see it to be anything, or see that it has any particular property. Depending on whether perceptual beliefs are embedded in propositional or objectual perception, they may differ in the kind of knowledge they give us. Propositional perception normally yields knowledge both of *what* it is that we perceive, and of some *property* of it, for instance of the tree's being straight. Objectual perception may give us knowledge only of a property of what we perceive, say that it is blue, when we do not know what it is, other than, perhaps, that blue thing. It may thus give us information about unconceptualized objects, or at least objects of which we have only a very general conception, say 'that noisy thing.' This is important. We could not learn as readily from perception if it gave us information only about objects we conceive in the specific ways in which we conceive most of the familiar things we see, hear, touch, taste, and smell.

SEEING AND BELIEVING

Both kinds of perceptual beliefs are quite commonly grounded in perception in a way that assures their truth. For instance, my visual belief that the tree is conical is so grounded in my seeing it that I propositionally see that it is conical; my visually believing it to be straight is so grounded in my seeing it that I objectually see it to be straight. Admittedly, I might visually believe something to be straight under conditions poor for judging it, as where I view a stick half submerged in water (it would then look bent whether it is or not). My belief might then be mistaken. But such a mistaken belief is not embedded in seeing that the stick is straight; I do *not* see that it is: if the stick is not straight, I cannot see that it is. As this suggests, there is something special about both perceiving *that* and perceiving *to be*. They are *veridical*, that is, they imply truth. If I see that the tree is straight, or see it to be straight, then it truly is straight. Thus, if I have the corresponding (the embedded) perceptual beliefs—if I believe that it is straight when I see that it is, or believe it to be straight when I see it to be—I am correct in so believing.

If perceiving *that* and perceiving *to be* imply (truly) believing something about the object in question, we should ask whether simple perception, which is required for either of these kinds of perception to occur, does too. Very commonly, simple perception, perception *of* something, implies truly believing something about it. But there is reason to doubt that it *must* produce *any* belief. This may seem to fly in the face of the adage that seeing is believing—though properly understood that may apply just to propositional or objectual seeing. In any case, how could I see the tree and believe nothing regarding it? Must I not see it to be something or other, say, blue? And if so, would I not believe, of it, *something* that is true of it, even if only that it is a blue object some distance away?

Imagine, however, that you and I are talking excitedly and a bird flies quickly across my path. Could I not see it, yet form no beliefs about it? There may be no decisive answer. For one thing, while there is much we *can* confidently say about seeing and believing, 'seeing' and 'believing' are, like most philosophically interesting terms, not precise. No dictionary definition or authoritative statement can be expected either to tell us precisely what they mean or, especially, to settle every question about when they do and do not apply. Still, we should try to resist concluding that vagueness makes any significant philosophical question unanswerable, and a negative response to the question whether seeing entails believing might be supported as follows. Suppose I merely see the bird but pay no attention to it because I am utterly intent on what we are discussing. Why must I form any belief about the bird? Granted, if someone later asks if I saw a blue bird, I may assent, thereby indicating a belief that the bird *was* blue. But this belief is not perceptual: it has visual content, but is not grounded in seeing. Moreover, it may have been formed only when I recalled my visual experience of the bird. Recalling that experience in such a context may produce a belief even if my original experience did not. For plainly a recollected sensory experience can produce beliefs about the object that caused it, especially when I have reason to provide information about that object.

It might be objected that genuinely seeing an object is different and must produce beliefs: how else, one might ask, can perception guide our behavior, as it does where, on seeing a log in our path, we step over it? But not everything we see, including the bird which flies by as I concentrate on something else, demands a response. If I am cataloging local birds, the situation is different. But where an unobtrusive object I see has no particular relation to what I am doing or thinking, perhaps my visual impressions of it are simply a *basis* for forming beliefs about it should the situation call for it, and need not produce any belief if my concerns and the direction of my attention give the object no significance.

Despite the complexity of the relation between seeing and believing, clearly we may hold what is epistemologically most important here. *If* I can see a bird without believing anything about (or of) it, I still *can* see it to be something or other, and my perceptual circumstances are such that I might *readily* both come to believe something about it *and* see that to be true of it. Suppose that someone suddenly interrupts a conversation to say, 'Look at that beautiful bird!' If I see it, I am in a position to form some belief of it, if only that it is swift, though I need not actually form any belief about it, at least not consciously. Imagine I am alone and see the bird in the distance for just a second, mistakenly taking it to be a speck of ash. If there is not too much color distortion, I may still both know and justifiably believe it to be dark. Granted, I would misdescribe it, and I might falsely believe that it is a speck of ash. But I could still know something about it, and I might point the bird out under the misleading but not incorrect description, 'that dark thing out there.' It *is* that thing I point at; and I can see, know, and justifiably believe that there is a dark thing there. My perception of the bird gives me a ready basis for this much knowledge and justification, even if the perception occurs in a way that does not cause me to believe (say) that there is a *bird* before me. Seeing *is* virtual believing, or at least potential believing.

Suppose, then, that simple perception need not produce belief, and objectual perception need not always yield propositional perception. Still, the third is clearly not possible without the first and, I think, the second as well: I cannot see *that* the bird is anything, for example dark, if I do not see it at all, and apparently I must also see it to *be* something, say a speck of blue. Thus, simple perception is fundamental: it is required for objectual and propositional perception, yet does not clearly entail either. And since objectual perception seems possible without propositional perception, but not conversely, the former seems more nearly fundamental than the latter. We have a hierarchy: propositional perception depends on objectual perception, which in turn depends on simple perception. Simple perception is basic, and it commonly yields, even if it need not yield, objectual perception, which, in turn, commonly yields, even if it need not yield, propositional perception.

I conclude that even if simple perception does not always produce at least one true belief, it characteristically does put us in a position to form at least one. It gives us *access* to perceptual information, perhaps even *records* that information in some sense, whether or not we conceptually register the information by forming perceptual beliefs of either kind. But we may say more. Perception also normally gives us situational justification: even if I could be so lost in conversation that I do not form any belief about the passing bird, I am, as I see it pass, normally justified *in believing* something about it, concerning its perceptible properties, for instance that it glides. There may perhaps be nothing specific that I am justified in believing, say that it is black or large or swift. But if I really see it—as opposed to its merely causing in me a visual impression too indistinct to qualify me as seeing it—then there is something or other that I may justifiably believe about it.

SEEING, SEEING *AS*, AND PERCEPTUAL GROUNDS OF JUSTIFICATION

What is it that explains why seeing the bird justifies me in believing something about what I see, that is, gives me situational justification for such a belief? One plausible answer is that if I see it at all, I *see it as* something, say black or large or swift, and I am justified in believing it to be what I see it as being. But consider two points. First, might the sort of distinction we have observed between situational and belief justification apply to seeing itself? Specifically, might my seeing the bird only imply that I am in a *position* to see it *as* something, and not that I *do* see it as something? Second, supposing that seeing the bird does imply seeing it *as* something, clearly that *need* not be something one is justified in believing it to be (and perhaps it need not be something one believes it to be at all.) Charles might see a plainly black bird as blue, simply because he so loves birds of blue color and so dislikes black birds that (as he himself knows) his vision plays tricks on him in bird-watching. He might then not be justified in believing that the bird is blue. It *may* be that seeing implies seeing *as* and that typically seeing *as* implies (at least objectual) believing; but seeing something as having a certain property does not always give one situational justification for believing it to have that property.

In any case, even if seeing does not imply seeing *as*, it still normally puts one in a position to form at least one justified belief. Suppose I see the bird so briefly and distractedly that I do not see it as anything in particular; still, my visual impression of it has some feature or other by which I am justified in believing something of the bird, if only that it is a moving thing. Even Charles would be justified in believing something like this. Suppose, however, that for hours he has hallucinated all manner of unreal things, and he knows this. Then he might not be justified in taking the bird he sees to be *anything* real, even though it is real. Thus, the best conclusion here is that *normally* seeing an object gives one situational justification for believing something or other about it.

If seeing is typical of perception in (normally) putting us in a position to form at least one justified belief, then perception in general normally gives us at least situational justification, which implies that we have justification *for* forming a belief. As we have seen, however, it does not follow that every perceptual belief *is* justified. Some perceptual beliefs are not. As with the biased bird-watcher, belief can be grounded in perception under conditions that prevent its being justified by that grounding. Nevertheless—and here is *a principle of justification*—when a visual belief arises in such a way that one believes something in virtue of *seeing that* it is so, normally the belief is justified. If I see that the tree is straight and, in virtue of seeing that it is, believe that it is, then (normally) I justifiably believe that it is. I say *normally* because one's justification can be overridden. Thus, Charles might see that a bird is blue and believe on that basis that it is, yet realize that all morning he has been seeing black birds as dark blue and thus mistaking the former for the latter. Until he verifies his first impression, he does not justifiably believe that the bird is blue. (We could say that he has some justification for believing this, yet better justification for not believing it; but to simplify matters I am ignoring degrees of justification.)

Suppose, on the other hand, that Charles has no idea that he has been hallucinating. Then, even when he does hallucinate a blue bird he may be justified in believing that there is one before him. This suggests a related principle of justification, one applicable to visual experience whether it is seeing or not: when, on the basis of an apparently normal visual experience, such as the sort we have in seeing a bird nearby, one believes something of the kind the experience seems to show (for instance that the bird is blue), normally this belief is justified. Similar principles can be formulated for the other senses.

SEEING AS A GROUND OF PERCEPTUAL KNOWLEDGE

Some of what holds for the justification of perceptual beliefs also applies to perceptual knowledge. Seeing the spruce, for instance, normally yields knowledge as well as justified belief about it. This suggests another principle, which might be called an *epistemic principle* since it states a condition for the visual generation of knowledge: normally, if I see that a tree is conical, I (visually) know that it is, and if I see it to be symmetrical, I know it to be. Similarly, if, on the basis of an apparently normal visual experience, I believe a proposition of the kind the experience seems to show, then normally my belief of that proposition constitutes knowledge. But in special circumstances perhaps I can see that something is so, believe on that basis that it is, and yet not know that it is. Charles's case *seems* to show this. For if, in the kind of circumstances he is in, he often takes a black bird to be blue, then even if he sees that a certain blue bird is blue and, on that basis, believes it is blue, he apparently does not know that it is (if seeing that it is blue *does* imply knowing that it is, then he does not see that it is, though he does see its blue color).

There is, however, an important difference here between knowledge and justification. If Charles is making errors like this, then even if he has no idea that he is and no reason to suspect he is, he does not *know* that the bird is blue. But even if he has no idea that he is making errors, or any reason to suspect he is, he may still justifiably believe the bird is blue. The main difference may be this: he can have a true belief which does not constitute knowledge because there is something wrong for which he is in no way criticizable (his errors might arise from a handicap which he has no reason to suspect, such as a sudden color blindness); but he cannot have a true yet unjustified belief without being in some way criticizable. This difference must be reflected in the kinds of principles that indicate how justification, as opposed to knowledge, is generated. Justification principles need not imply that the relevant basis of a belief's justification assures its truth; but since a false belief cannot be knowledge, epistemic principles must rule out factors that may produce a false belief (or at least have a significant chance of producing one).

On the basis of what we see, hear, feel, smell, and taste, we have a great many beliefs, propositional and objectual. Typically, these perceptual beliefs are justified. Very often they are true and constitute knowledge. But what is perception? Until we have a good understanding of this, we cannot see what it is about perception that grounds belief, justification, and knowledge. These problems cannot be fully resolved in a short book, but we can work toward partial resolutions. I want to discuss what perception is first and, later, to illustrate further how it grounds what it does. Let's start by considering some of the major theories of the nature of perception. Again, I concentrate on vision, and I want to discuss mainly simple perception, the fundamental kind.

| SOME COMMONSENSE VIEWS OF PERCEPTION

One natural thing to say about what it is for me to see the blue spruce is that I simply see it, at least in that I see its facing surface. It is near and squarely before me. I need no light to penetrate a haze or telescope to magnify my view. I simply see the tree, and it is as it appears. This sort of view—thought to represent untutored common sense—has been called *naive realism*. It is naive because it ignores problems of a kind to be described in a moment; it is a form of realism because it takes the objects of perception to be real things external to the perceiver, the sorts of things that are there to be seen whether anyone sees them or not.

A more thoughtful commonsense view retains the realism without the naivety. It is quite commonsensical, for instance, to say that I see the tree *because* it is before my open eyes and stimulates my vision, thereby *appearing* to me as a blue, conical shape. Stimulating my vision is a causal relation: the tree, by reflecting light, causes me to have the visual experience that is part of my seeing that very tree. Moreover, the tree apparently *must* cause my visual experience if I am to *see* it. For suppose I am looking at it and, without my noticing, someone instantaneously drops a perfect picture of the tree right in front of it. If the picture is shaped and textured right, my visual experience might not change—the scene might appear to me just as it did—yet I no longer *see* the tree. Instead, I see a picture of it. (I do see the tree *in* the picture, but that is secondary seeing and not the kind I am talking about.) Examples like this suggest that *perception is a kind of causal relation* between whatever is perceived and the perceiver. This is a plausible and very important point, though it of course does not tell us precisely what perception *is*, and I call any theory of perception which incorporates the point *a causal theory of perception*. Most theories of perception are causal. I have not stated naive realism as incorporating this causal view, but a naive realist could consistently adopt it.

We can now better understand the four elements I have described as among those crucial in perception: the perceiver, the object perceived, the sensory experience in which the object appears to the perceiver, and the causal relation between the object and the perceiver, by virtue of which the object produces that experience. Thus, if I see the tree, there is a distinctive way, presumably through light transmission to my eyes, in which the tree produces in me the visual sensory experience—of a blue, conical shape—characteristic of my seeing it. If a picture of the tree produces an exactly similar visual experience in the same way, it is the picture I see, not the tree. Similarly, if I hear a piano piece, there is a special way in which it causes me to have the auditory sensations of chords and melody and harmony that go with that particular piece. It is difficult, though fortunately not necessary for a general understanding of perception, to specify precisely what these ways are. Not just any causal chain is the right sort for perception. Suppose the piano sounds cause a special machine to produce in me both temporary deafness and a faithful auditory hallucination of the piece. Then I do not *hear* it, though my sensory experience, the auditory experience I live through in my own consciousness, is just what it would be if I did hear it. Nor do I hear it if, though the sound waves reach my brain and cause me to believe a piano is playing, I have no auditory experience. Such inner silence is not musical. Different theories of perception tend, as we shall see, to give strikingly different accounts of how these four elements figure in perception.

ILLUSION, HALLUCINATION, AND APPEARANCE

Why is naive realism naive? Suppose there is a gray haze and the blue spruce looks gray. Or suppose the book I am holding appears, from a certain angle, as if it were a parallelogram rather than a (right) rectangle, or feels warm only because my hand is cold. These are perceptual *illusions*. Now imagine that the tree burns down. I miss it, and on waking from a slumber in my chair I have a *hallucination* in which my visual experience is just as it would be if the tree were recreated and I were seeing it. Illusions and hallucinations are possible for the other senses too. When they occur, we do not "just see" the object. Either we do not see it as it is or (perhaps) do not see anything at all. So even if in some cases naive realism is right in saying that things are as they appear, this is not true of perception in general.

Philosophers often distinguish between appearance and reality, and one way to deal with illusion and hallucination is to stress that things need not really be as they appear. In an illusion, then, one sees something, but it does not appear as it really is, say rectangular. In a hallucination, what appears to one is in reality even less what it appears to be, or not what it appears to be at all: instead of a spruce's appearing blue to me, for instance, perhaps the conical section of space where it stood appears "bespruced." The sense in which the space appears blue to me is roughly that I *see it as* blue. This sort of account of perception has been called *the theory of appearing*: it says (as I interpret it) that perceiving an object is simply its appearing to one to have one or more properties, such as being conical. Thus, one perceives it—in this case sees it—*as* conical. The theory also accounts for sensory experience, including the sort one has in hallucination as opposed to normal perception: that, too, is something appearing to one to have a set of properties; the object that appears is simply a different kind: it is hallucinatory.

The theory of appearing is initially quite plausible. For one thing, it incorporates much reflective common sense. It includes, for instance, the view that if one sees something then it appears to one in some way, say as a visually experienced conical bluish patch. It also does justice to the view that things are not always as they appear. Moreover, it can explain both illusion and hallucination. On the other hand, it says nothing about the need for a causal relation between the object and the perceiver, though quite consistently with its commonsense motivation one could just stipulate that the crucial relation—appearing to the perceiver to have a property, say to be conical—is or implies a causal relation. In addition to the question of how the theory can do justice to the causal element in perception, it faces a problem in accounting for hallucinations in which there apparently *is* no object to appear to the person at all. I could, after all, hallucinate a blue spruce when I see nothing physical at all, say because it is pitch dark or my eyes are closed. In such an *empty hallucination*, as we might call it, what is it that appears blue to me? There is a plausible answer; but it is associated with a quite different theory of perception. Let us explore that contrasting view of perception.

THE SENSE-DATUM THEORY OF PERCEPTION

Once we seriously think about illusion and hallucination, we begin to question not only naive realism but also any kind of *direct realism*, any view which, like the theory of appearing, says that we see (or otherwise perceive) external objects directly rather than *through* seeing (or visually experiencing) something else. Hallucination illustrates this most readily. Imagine that when I vividly hallucinate the tree just as it would be if it were before me, my visual experience—roughly, what I go through in my visual consciousness—is exactly like the one I have when I see the tree. Does it not seem that the difference between ordinary seeing and visual hallucination is simply in what *causes* the visual experience and not in what I directly see? When I see the tree, *it* causes my visual experience. When I hallucinate it, something else (such as my deep desire to have it back) causes my visual experience. But apparently what I directly see, that is, the immediate object of my visual experience, is the same in both cases. This point presumably explains why my visual experience is the same whether I am hallucinating the tree or really seeing it.

We might develop these ideas by considering *an argument from hallucination*, consisting of two connected arguments as parts. The first constituent argument attempts to show a parallel between hallucination and ordinary perception. (1) A perfectly faithful (visual) hallucination of a tree is intrinsically indistinguishable from an ordinary experience of seeing that tree, that is, not distinguishable from it just in itself as a visual experience, as opposed to being distinguishable through verifying one's visual impression by touching the things around one. Hence, (2) what is *directly* seen, the immediate object of one's visual experience, is the same sort of thing in a perfect hallucination of a tree as in an ordinary experience of seeing a tree. But—and we now come to the second constituent argument, which builds on (2)—(3) clearly, what is directly seen in a hallucination is not a tree. Hence, (4) what is directly seen in an ordinary experience of seeing a tree is not a tree either. That is, when we ordinarily see a tree, we see it through seeing something else *directly*: something not seen *by* seeing anything else. What we see directly might be an image, and one may prefer (as some philosophers do) to say that we do not *see* such things but are only visually acquainted with them. To simplify, however, let us just bear this alternative in mind, but use the more natural term 'see'.

Just what *is* directly seen when one sees a tree, then, and how is the tree *in*directly seen? Why not say that what is *directly* seen is a two-dimensional object (or perhaps even three-dimensional item) consisting of the colors and shapes one sees in the hallucinatory experience? After all, nothing, not even (physical) light, intervenes between me and them; there is no "space" for intermediaries, hence no intermediaries can misrepresent these special objects. These objects are apparently internal to me: as traditionally conceived, they could exist even if I were a disembodied mind in an otherwise empty world. Yet I do see the tree *by* seeing them, hence see it indirectly. Moreover, the tree causes the colors and shapes to arise in me in a way that fully accords with the view that perception is a causal relation between something external and the perceiver. Perception is simply a *mediated*, hence indirect, relation between external objects I perceive and me: the object produces the mediating colors and shapes that appear in my visual field, and through seeing them I see it.

The theory I am describing is a version of *the sense-datum theory of perception*. It is so called because it accounts for perception by appeal to a view of what is directly *given in*, hence is a *datum* (a given) for, sense experience—the sort of thing one is visually aware of in hallucinating a tree. This sense-datum theory (unlike the phenomenalist sense-datum view to be discussed later in this chapter) is a realist view; but its realism, by contrast with that of naive realism and the theory of appearing, is indirect. It might be called *representative realism* because it conceives perception as a relation in which sense-data represent perceived external objects to us. John Locke (1632–1704) held a view of this kind (and presented it in *An Essay Concerning Human Understanding*, especially Books II and IV); and sense-datum theories have had brilliant defenders down to the present time. The theory has also had powerful opponents. To appreciate it better let's examine it, beginning with the way in which it takes perception to be indirect.

Sense-datum theorists might offer several reasons to explain why we do not ordinarily notice the indirectness of perception. For one thing, normally what we directly see, say colors and shapes, corresponds roughly to the physical objects we indirectly see by means of what we see directly. For another, we do not normally *infer* what we believe about external objects from what we believe about the colors and shapes that we directly see. Perception is not inferential, and for that reason (perhaps among others) it is not *epistemically indirect*, in the sense that knowledge of, or belief about, external objects is based on knowledge of, or belief about, sense-data. I know that the spruce is blue through *having* blue sense-data, not through *inference from* propositions about them. Perception is not, then, inferentially indirect, but causally and objectually indirect. Let me describe a bit differently how the sense-datum view conceives this indirectness.

Perception is causally indirect because perceived physical objects cause sensory experience, say of colors and shapes, *by* causing the occurrence of sense-data, with which we are directly (and presumably non-causally) acquainted in perceptual experience. Perception is objectually indirect because we perceive external things, such as trees, *through* our acquaintance with other objects, namely, sense-data. Roughly, we perceive external things through perceiving internal things. But we normally do not use sense-data to arrive at perceptual beliefs inferentially, say by an inference from my directly seeing a blue, conical shape to the conclusion that a blue spruce is before me. Ordinarily, when I look around I form beliefs about the external environment and none at all about my sensory experience. That experience causes my perceptual beliefs, but what they are about is the external things I perceive. It is when the colors and shapes do not correspond to the external object, as where a rectangular book appears as a parallelogram, that it seems we can understand our experience only if we suppose that the direct objects of sensory experience are internal and need not match its external, indirect object.

Let us explore the sense-datum theory further, focusing squarely on the argument from hallucination, whose conclusion suggests that what is directly seen in visual perception of external objects is a set of sense-data. Suppose I do have a hallucination that is intrinsically just like the normal experience of seeing a tree. Does it follow that what is directly seen in it is the same sort of thing as what is directly seen in the normal experience? There are at least two problems that confront the sense-datum theory here.

First, why *must* anything be seen at all in a hallucination? Imagine that you see me hallucinate the burned-up tree. I might get up, still half asleep, and cry out, 'It's back!', pointing to the spot. You would probably conclude that I *think* I see the tree again. My own initial reaction to realizing I had hallucinated the tree might be that, hallucination or no, I *saw* it. But I might as easily slump back in my chair and mumble that I wish I had seen it. We might agree that I saw it (vividly) *in my mind's eye*. But suppose I did see it in my mind's eye, and again suppose that the hallucination is intrinsically just like the ordinary seeing. Does it follow that what I directly see in the hallucination is the same, namely, something in my mind's eye? It does not. The notion of seeing in one's mind's eye is metaphorical, and such seeing need not imply that there is any real thing seen, in or outside the mind. In any event, there is further reason to resist the conclusion that something must be directly seen in hallucinations.

This brings me to a second, quite different point. If my seeing a tree is a causal relation between a sensory experience in me and the tree, then nothing follows about my seeing the tree, which is external, from the similarity of the internal elements in question, the hallucinatory experience and the ordinary sensory experience. It certainly does not follow that ordinary seeing of the tree is indirect. Consider an analogy. Two perfect ball bearings can be intrinsically indistinguishable—have the same diameter and constitution—yet one be on my left and one on my right. Their intrinsic properties can thus be identical, while their *relations* (to me) differ: one is left of me, the other right of me; hence they *do* differ in their relational properties. Similarly, the hallucination of a tree and the ordinary visual experience of a tree can be intrinsically indistinguishable, yet differ in their relations. One may be an element in a perceptual relation to the tree and the other not. Thus, for all the argument from hallucination shows, the ordinary seeing might be a relation—namely, direct seeing—to an object, say the tree, while the hallucinatory experience bears no relation to the tree or even to any other object, such as a sense-datum.

The two points just made (among others) indicate that the argument from hallucination is not sound. Its first premise, (1), does not entail the conclusion drawn from it, (2). Nonetheless, the argument poses serious problems for alternative theories. What account of hallucinations and illusions besides the sense-datum account might we adopt? To see what some of the alternatives are, it is best to begin with illusion rather than hallucination.

Recall the book viewed from an angle. The sense-datum theory says that we directly see a parallelogrammic shape and indirectly see the book. The theory of appearing, however, can also explain this: it reminds us that things need not be what they appear and says simply that the book can appear parallelogrammic, even if it is rectangular. Moreover, one could combine the causal element in the sense-datum theory with the direct realism of the theory of appearing and say that the book causes us to see it directly, rather than through producing sense-data in us, yet (because of our angle of vision), we see it as *if* it were parallelogrammic. To avoid suggesting that anything in one's experience need *be* parallelogrammic, one could take this to mean that the book visually appears parallelogrammically to us. Here 'parallelogrammically' describes a *way* we visually experience the book; it does not imply that there is an object that appears to us and *is* parallelogrammic. (The book does not appear to us *to be* parallelogrammic if we realize its shape cannot be judged from how it visually appears at an angle, but that is a different point.) Let us explore this idea in relation to the theory associated with it.

THE ADVERBIAL THEORY OF PERCEPTION

It should now be clear why we need not grant (what sense-datum theorists sometimes seem to assume) that in order for an object to appear a given way to us there must *be* something we see that *is* that way, for instance a parallelogrammic sense-datum. Moreover, it is not only the theory of appearing that makes use of this point. Suppose that one says simply that the book appears parallelogrammically, using this adverb to designate the *way* it appears, or (speaking from the perceiver's point of view) *how* one visually experiences it: parallelogrammically. On the basis of this move, one can construct what is called *the adverbial theory of perception*. Unlike the theory of appearing, which takes perception to be a relation in which things appear to us to have one or more properties, the adverbial view conceives perception as a *way* of experiencing things. Both theories are, however, direct realist views, though they reject the idea that we just see things, as naive realism holds. Other similarities (and some differences) between the two theories will soon be apparent.

The adverbial theorist stresses that we see (or otherwise perceive) things in a particular way and that they thus appear to us in that way. Often they appear as they are; sometimes they do not. In either case they are seen directly, not through intermediaries. Even if I do not see the book as rectangular, I do see *it*: it is seen directly, yet appears parallelogrammically. So far so good, perhaps. But what about hallucinations? Here the adverbial theory again differs from the theory of appearing. Unlike the latter, it denies that all sensory experience is *of* some object. The importance of this denial is not immediately apparent, perhaps because we suppose that usually a person visually hallucinating does see *something*. Consider Macbeth, distraught by his murder of Duncan, hallucinating a dagger that seems to him to hover in midair. Presumably he sees something, say the wall behind "the dagger" or at least a chunk of space where it hovers. The adverbial theorist might thus find an object, if only the space where the "dagger" seems located, for Macbeth to experience "daggerly." Somehow this space might play a role in causing him to have daggerish visual sensations, just as, for the theory of appearing, that space—despite being immaterial and transparent—might somehow appear to him to be a dagger. Indeed, in this case what the adverbial theorist calls experiencing "daggerly" might be roughly equivalent to what the theory of appearing calls having something appear to one to be a dagger.

Supposing we accept this adverbialist account, what happens if it is pitch dark and Macbeth's hallucination is empty? Then, whereas the theory of appearing posits something like a sense-datum to serve as what appears to be a dagger, the adverbial theory denies that there is *any* kind of object appearing to him and seeks some other account of his "bedaggered" visual experience, such as the influence of drugs. But is it really plausible to hold, with the adverbial theory, that in this instance Macbeth saw nothing at all? Can we really explain how the normal and hallucinatory experiences are intrinsically alike without assuming they have the same direct objects?

In the light of the special case of empty hallucination, then, the sense-datum theory may seem the most plausible of the three. It provides an object of Macbeth's visual experience in utter darkness, whereas the adverbial theory posits no objects at all to appear to one in empty hallucinations. Moreover, the sense-datum view postulates the same sort of direct object for ordinary perception, illusion, and hallucination, whereas the theory of appearing does not offer a uniform account of their direct objects and must explain why entities like sense-data do not occur in normal perception as well as in empty hallucination.

Perhaps, however, the hallucination problem seems more threatening than it should to the adverbial theory because hallucinations are felt to be *perceptual* experiences and hence expected to be *of* some object. But as we have seen, while hallucinatory experiences can be intrinsically indistinguishable from perceptual ones, all that can be assumed is that they are *sensory* experiences. Hallucinatory experiences, on the adverbial view, are simply not cases of perceiving, at least not in a sense requiring that any object appear to one. Thus, nothing at all need appear to one in hallucinations, though *it may appear to the subject* that there is something there. The hallucinator may then be described as having a visual sensory experience, but—since nothing is perceived—not a normal perceptual experience.

ADVERBIAL AND SENSE-DATUM THEORIES OF SENSORY EXPERIENCE

If a sensory experience need not be a normal perceptual experience, though a perceptual experience is always sensory, it is important to consider the debate between the adverbial and sense-datum theories as applied to sensory experience. For both theories take such experience to be essential to perception, and both offer accounts of sensory experience as well as of perception.

While the most natural thing for adverbial theorists to say about hallucinatory experience is that it is not genuinely perceptual, but only sensory, they might instead say that where a perceptual experience is hallucinatory, it is not one of seeing (except perhaps in the mind's eye, or perhaps in the sense that it is seeing colors and shapes conceived abstractly as properties and not as belonging to sense-datum objects). The theory suggested by these responses to the hallucination problem might be called the *adverbial theory of sensory experience*. It says that having a sensory experience, such as hallucinating a blue spruce, is experiencing in a certain *way*, for example visually experiencing "blue-sprucely." Most such experiences are genuinely perceptual; they are of, and thus caused by, the external object perceived. But some sensory experiences are neither genuinely perceptual nor externally caused. People having them are in a visionlike state, and what is going on in their visual cortex may be the same sort of process that goes on when they see things; yet they are not seeing, and their visual experience typically has an internal cause, such as an abnormal emotion.

May we, then, regard the sense-datum theory of perception as refuted by the points just made in criticism of the argument from hallucination and on behalf of the adverbial theory and the theory of appearing? Certainly not. We have at most seen how one major argument for that sense-datum theory fails and how alternative theories of perception can account for the apparently central elements in perception: the perceiver, the (ordinary) object perceived, the sensory experience, and the causal relation between the second and third.

Indeed, supposing that the argument from hallucination fails to show that sense-data are elements in normal perception of external objects, sense-data might still be needed to account for non-perceptual sensory experience. In this limited role, a *sense-datum theory of non-perceptual sensory experience*, according to which such experience is simply direct acquaintance with sense-data, may seem preferable to the adverbial theory of sensory experience. For one thing, there is something unsatisfying about the idea that even in a visual hallucination so vivid that, if one did not suspect error, one would stake one's life on the presence of the hallucinated object, one sees nothing, except either metaphorically in one's mind's eye, or in a sense of 'see' that does not require an object. Still, perhaps there is such a sense of 'see', or perhaps one can experience colors and shapes in a visual way without seeing anything.

There is another aspect of the controversy. It concerns the *metaphysics* associated with adverbial and sense-datum theories of any kind, specifically, the sorts of things they require us to take as fundamental realities. In this respect, the adverbial theories of perception and sensory experience have a definite advantage over the counterpart sense-datum theories: the former do not posit a *kind* of object we would not otherwise have to regard as real. From the adverbial perspective, the objects that perception and sensory experience involve are simply perceivers and what they perceive. These are quite familiar entities which we must recognize and deal with anyway. But sense-data are quite different. They are presumably mental, or at least they depend for their existence on the mind of the subject; yet they are unlike some mental phenomena in that no good case can be made for their being really phenomena in the brain, since they have properties, for instance green color and perfect rectangularity, not normally found in the brain (which normally has neither green nor rectangular parts). Moreover, there are difficulties in the way of fully understanding sense-data in any terms. Is there, for instance, even a reasonable way of counting them? Suppose my image of the blue spruce gradually gets greener. Is this a sense-datum changing or a new one replacing an old one? There seems to be no way to tell. If there is no way to tell, how can we ever be sure we learn more about a sense-datum than what initially appears to us in experiencing it: how can one distinguish learning something about *it* from learning about something *new*?

Problems like these also affect the theory of appearing insofar as it must posit sense-data or similar entities to account for hallucinations. Granted, such problems can beset our understanding of ordinary objects as well, but apparently less seriously. They may be soluble for the case of sense-data, but they at least give us some reason to prefer a theory that does not force us to regard sense-data as the only objects, or even among the objects, we are directly aware of when we see, hear, touch, taste, and smell.

PHENOMENALISM

If some philosophers have thought perception can be understood without appeal to sense-data, others have conceived it as understandable in terms of sense-data alone as its objects. Think about the book you see. It is a perceptual object. Now, granted one might conceive a real perceptual object as one that is as it is independently of what we think it to be; but real perceptual objects, such as tables and chairs and books, are also plausibly conceived to be, by their very nature, *knowable*. Indeed, it is doubtful that real objects of this sort *could* be unknowable, or even unknowable through the senses if lighting and other perceptual conditions are good. Now suppose we add to these ideas the assumption that we have genuine, certain knowledge only of what appears to us—what would be as it is even if we should be hallucinating. What more does appear to us besides the colors and shapes of perceptual objects? Further, how do we know that this book, for example, could even exist without someone's perceiving its color and other sensory properties? Certainly we cannot *observe* the book existing unperceived. If you observe it, you perceive it.

Moreover, if you imagine subtracting the book's sensory properties one by one—its color, shape, weight, and so on—what is left of it? This is not like peeling an apple, leaving its substance; it is like stripping layer after layer from an onion until nothing remains. Should we not conclude, then, that the book simply *is* a stable set of sensory properties, a collection of visual, tactile, and other sense-data which in some sense *recur* in our experience, say confronting us each time we have the sense-data corresponding to a certain bookcase in our home? Similarly, might it not be that to see the book is simply to be visually acquainted with such a stable set of sense-data?

George Berkeley (1685–1753) argued from a variety of angles that this is indeed what a perceptual object is. The view (which Berkeley developed in detail in his *Treatise Concerning the Principles of Human Knowledge*) is a version of what is called *phenomenalism*, since it constructs external objects out of phenomena—which, in this use of the term, are equivalent to sense-data. Phenomenalism, in this form, retains the sense-datum theory of sensory experience, but not the sense-datum theory of perception, which posits external objects as causes of the sense-data experienced in ordinary perception. Using the adverbial theory of sensory experience, one might also formulate an *adverbial phenomenalism*, which constructs physical objects out of sensory experience alone and says that to see a tree (for instance) is to experience "treely" in a certain vivid and stable way. On this view, perception does not require even sense-data, only perceivers and their properties. The sense-datum version of phenomenalism, however, has been more often discussed by philosophers, and I will concentrate on that.

Whereas the sense-datum theory is an indirect realism, phenomenalism is a *direct irrealism*: it says that perceptual objects are directly perceived, but denies that they are real in the sense that they exist independently of perceivers. It does not deny that physical objects exist in the sense that they are both stable elements of our experience and governed by causal laws, such as those of physics. Nor does it deny that there can be hallucinations, as where certain sense-data, like those constituting Macbeth's dagger, are too unstable to compose a physical object, or are perceivable only in one mode, such as vision, when they should have tactile elements as well, such as a cool smooth surface. What phenomenalism denies is that physical objects are real in the classical sense implying existence independent of perceptual experience.

Berkeley did not neglect to consider what happens to a book when we leave it in an empty room. His answer has been nicely put in a limerick:

There was a young man who said, "God
Must think it exceedingly odd
If he finds that this tree
Continues to be
When there's no one about in the quad."

Reply:

Dear Sir:
Your astonishment's odd:
I am always about in the quad.
And that's why the tree
Will continue to be,
Since observed by
Yours faithfully,
God.

A phenomenalist need not be a theist, however, to account for the stability of external objects. John Stuart Mill (1806–1873), writing in the same epistemological tradition as Berkeley, called external objects "permanent possibilities of sensation." When no one is in the room, to say that the book is in there is to say that there is an enduring possibility of the sensations one would have if one perceived such a book. If one enters the room and looks in the appropriate direction, that possibility should be realized. A phenomenalist can, however, be more radical and take objects not to have *any* kind of existence when unperceived.

Unlike the sense-datum theory of perception, phenomenalism is not often currently defended. But it has had major influence. Moreover, compared with the sense-datum theory, it is more economical and in that way simpler: instead of perceivers, sense-data, and external objects, it posits, as the things figuring in perception and sensory experience, just perceivers and sense-data. Indeed, adverbial phenomenalism does not even posit sense-data, though it does appeal to a special kind of property, that of experiencing in a certain way.

As a theory of perception, then, phenomenalism has fewer objects to analyze and interrelate than do the other theories we have discussed. In addition, phenomenalism appears to bridge the most important gap between sensory experience and perception of objects: since the objects are internal and directly experienced, it seems natural to say that they must be as they appear to be—we see all there is of them, or at least of the surface we see. On the other hand, for the external objects of common sense, whose reality is independent of perceivers, phenomenalism must substitute something like permanent possibilities of experience. Thus, the bare-bones appearance of the theory is illusory. Even that metaphor is misleading; for our bodies are also sets of sense-data; even the flesh itself is not too solid to melt into the sensations of its perceivers.

It is tempting to reject phenomenalism as preposterous. But if we flatly reject it, we learn nothing from it. Let me pose just one objection from which we learn something important about the relation between sense experience and external objects. The theory says that a book, for instance, is a suitably stable set of sense-data and that seeing it is being visually acquainted with them. If so, then there is a set of sense-data—perceptual items like colors and shapes in one's visual field—such that if, under appropriate conditions, these elements occur in me, then it follows that I see a book. But surely there is no such set of sense-data. No matter how vividly and stably I experience the colors and shapes appropriate to a book, it does not follow that I see one. For it is still possible that I am just hallucinating one, or seeing something else *as* a book. This remains possible even if I have supporting tactual experiences, such as the smooth feel of paper. For even the sense of touch can be stimulated in this way without one's touching a book. Thus, seeing a book is not *just* having appropriate booklike experiences, even if it is *partly* this, and even though, as phenomenalists hold, there is no experienceable difference between a sufficiently stable set of bookish sense-data and an independently real material book. Still, if seeing a book is not equivalent to any such set sensory experiences, phenomenalism fails as an account of the perception of ordinary objects. If there are objects for which it holds, they are not the kind we have in mind in seeking an account of perception.

| PERCEPTION AND THE SENSES

I want to conclude this chapter by indicating some remaining problems. I have already suggested that the adverbial theory, the sense-datum theory, and the theory of appearing provide plausible accounts of perception, though I consider the first prima facie best and I leave open that some theory different from all of them may be better than any. I have also suggested that at times perceptually grounded beliefs fail to be justified, and that, even when justified and true, they can fail to constitute knowledge. There are two further kinds of problems we should explore. One kind concerns observation, the other the relation of perception to the five senses.

Observing something in a mirror can count as seeing it. Indeed, it illustrates the sort of thing ordinarily considered seeing something indirectly, as opposed to seeing it by virtue of seeing sense-data. We can also speak of seeing through telescopes and other instruments of observation, again indirectly. But what if the object is microscopic and colorless, yet appears to us through our lens as gray? Perhaps we see it, but not quite as it is. If we see it, however, there must be *some* respect in which what we see it *by* is faithful to it or at least represents it by some relation of causal dependence, as where the object's moving leftward is reflected in a movement of the image. But what we see a thing by need not be faithful in all respects. A green tree can look black at night, and we can see something move even if its color *and* shape are distorted.

Observation of faraway objects poses further problems. Consider seeing the nearest star in the night sky. It is about four light years away. Presumably we see it (if at all) only *as it was*. Suppose it exploded two years ago. Do we now see it at all, or just a trace of it (as it was)? The latter view is preferable, on the ground that if we unqualifiedly see something now, it exists now. This seems so even though we may see a thing that exists now only *as* it was. Similar points hold for ordinary seeing, since there is still some temporal gap, and for hearing. But if I can see the spruce only as it was a fraction of a second ago, presumably I can still know that it is now blue, provided there is no good reason to think its color has suddenly changed. In any event, it is plain that understanding perception and perceptual knowledge in these sorts of cases is not easy.

We normally regard seeing as intimately connected with light. But must seeing involve light? That is doubtful. Suppose you could step into a pitch-dark room and have the experiences you would have if it were fully lighted. The room would thus presumably *look* to you just as it would if fully lighted, and you could find any unobscured object by looking around for it. Wouldn't this show that you can see in the dark? Not quite. For seeing is a causal relation, and for all I have said you are just vividly hallucinating precisely the right things. But suppose you are not hallucinating. Indeed, if someone puts a coin in a box or covers your eyes, you do not see the coin. For somehow the coin affects your eyes through a mechanism other than light transmission yet requiring an unobstructed path between it and your eyes. *Now* it begins to seem that you are seeing.

Let us go a step further. Suppose Sue has lost her eyes in an accident, but we provide her with a camera that is hooked up to her brain in the way her eyes were. When she points it in a given direction in good light, she has just the visual sensations, say of color and shape, that she would have had by looking with her eyes. Might this not be seeing? Indeed, do we not think of the camera as *functioning* like eyes? If, under the right causal conditions, she gets the right sorts of sensations through her eyes *or* a functional equivalent of them, she is seeing.

But are even "eyes" (or organs functioning like eyes) necessary for seeing? What if someone who lacks "eyes" could get visual sensations matching the objects in the room by strange radiations they emit? Suppose, for instance, that the sensations are stopped by enclosing the coin in cardboard, and that moving it away from the person results in a decrease in its size as represented in the visual impression. If no part of the body (other than the brain) is required for the visual sensations, do we have seeing? If the production of visual sensations is crucial for seeing, presumably so. If seeing requires the use of an eye or equivalent organ, no—unless the brain itself is taken to be a visual organ. It is clear enough that the person would have knowledge of what we might call the visual properties of things, above all colors and shapes. One *might* call that visual knowledge. But visual knowledge in this weak sense need not be grounded in seeing, nor acquired through use of any sense organs. For these reasons, it is somewhat doubtful whether it must be a kind of *perceptual* knowledge.

One more question: can there be "blind sight," seeing in the absence of visual sensations? It is apparently possible for people to navigate among obstacles as if they saw them, while they honestly report having no visual sensations. Could this be seeing? We automatically tend to understand such behavior in terms of seeing, and there is thus an inclination to say that they are seeing. The inclination is even stronger if light's reaching the eyes is necessary for the person to avoid the obstacles. But it is not clear that we must say this, and I doubt that it is so; the most we must say is that the person seems to *know* where the obstacles are. This is possible without vision, for instance by something like sonar. Moreover, even dependence on light does not establish that the process in question is visual: the light might somehow stimulate non-visual mechanisms. Similar questions arise for the importance of sensations to perception in the other sensory modes, for instance of auditory sensations in hearing. There, too, we find hard questions for which competing answers are plausible.

It is difficult, then, to provide an overall philosophical account of just what seeing, or perception in general, is; and while all the theories we have discussed can help in answering the questions just posed, none does so in a simple and decisive way. Still, in exploring those theories we have seen many important points about perception. It is a kind of causal relation. It requires, in addition to the perceiver, both an object of perception and a sensory experience that in some way corresponds to that object. It implies that the perceiver at least normally has justification for certain beliefs about the perceived object, and it normally produces both justified beliefs about that object and knowledge of it. It may be illusory, as where something appears to have a property it does not have. It may also be hallucinatory. But both illusions and hallucinations can be accounted for without positing sense-data, and thus without adding a kind of element to the four that seem central in perception, or reducing perceptual objects to sense-data. They can also be accounted for, I think, without denying that perceptual experience normally yields belief, justification, and knowledge about the world outside the perceiver.

Memory

On the basis of memory, I believe that I twice planted the blue spruce. Because of the way this belief is apparently grounded in my memory, it seems to me to be justified and also to constitute knowledge that I twice planted that tree. In particular, it seems to me to be grounded in memory in the way that what I genuinely *remember* is grounded there. But what is memory, and what is it to remember something?

MEMORY AND THE PAST

Let us first clear away some tempting mistakes. We cannot say simply that memory is a capacity for knowledge or belief about the past. Consider the events of World War II. I know a good deal about them, but I do not remember them. I witnessed none of them. I may also know propositions about the past on a basis other than memory. Suppose I gain knowledge about the past from your present description of what you did yesterday. I could lose some of the knowledge you give me, say that you were carrying a camera, as soon as I have acquired it, just as one forgets a phone number needed only for a moment. In these instances, I have knowledge of the past, but only for too brief a time to qualify as remembering the propositions I momentarily knew.

The same example shows that *beliefs* about the past, such as those I acquire about your activities, do not necessarily represent memory. For they need not be *memorial beliefs*, that is, beliefs preserved in memory; nor need one, in holding them, remember something. Beliefs about the past need not be memorial because they can be sheer fabrications unconnected with memory capacities. Imagine, for instance, that though I have not seen you for a year, for some reason I groundlessly form the belief that precisely a month ago you were wearing the same belt I see you wearing now. This belief would not be memorial. Furthermore, beliefs about the past need not represent remembering, even if they are memorial, because they may be false or, even if true, utterly baseless and true only by lucky accident. Thus, if for a year I retain my groundless belief that you wore that same belt both times, I have a memorial belief that you did; but since it is mistaken—or just happens to be true because by chance you selected the same belt for both occasions—I do not remember that you did. At best I have retained my impression that you did.

One might think that just as a perceptual belief is caused by an object perceived, memorial beliefs are caused by a past event remembered. Some memorial beliefs are. But even if it should be true that events in the past do produce those beliefs, past events are not the only *objects* of memory. We remember, and thereby believe, general truths, such as those of mathematics. These truths are certainly not events, nor are they about the past. Moreover, even if every memorial belief is at least partly caused by a past event, a belief caused by a past event need not be memorial. This point applies even if the belief is true. Suppose that my unknowingly taking a drug causes me to feel strange later and thus to believe I was poisoned. Even if I was poisoned—by something else I did not even know I ate—and this belief is thus true, I may have no memories connected with the belief. Thus, the belief's being caused by the past event of my taking the drug need not make it a memory belief, any more than a belief caused by a flash that I do not see, but merely feel as a momentary heat, need be a visual belief, even if it is a true belief with visual content, say that a camera flashed near my hand. Similarly, a noise too faint for me to hear may cause Tom to jump, which in turn causes me to believe that he is startled; my belief that he is startled is thus (indirectly) caused by the noise, but is not auditory. It is in no way grounded in my hearing.

The analogy between memory and perception is limited, but it does get us on the right track. For surely a belief about the past is memorial *only* if it has some causal connection to a past event, just as seeing an object requires some causal connection between it and the perceiver. In both cases, it is very hard to specify just what kind of causal connection is necessary, but fortunately many points can be made about memory without knowing that.

THEORIES OF MEMORY

If we model theories of memory on the three major kinds of theories of perception discussed in Chapter 1, there is much we can discover both about the kind of causal relations required for remembering and about how memory grounds belief, justification, and knowledge. Broadly speaking, the three kinds are direct realism (including the adverbial theory and the theory of appearing as well as naive realism), representative realism, and phenomenalism. In constructing theories of memory, there are at least three different but closely related notions we must keep track of: *memory, remembering,* and *recalling.* We remember, and recall—roughly, call back to mind—in virtue of our memory, which is a general capacity: the better it is, the more and better we remember and recall. But the capacity of memory, like that of perceiving, can produce impressions that are illusory or, in a way, hallucinatory. In developing the memorial counterparts of the three kinds of theories of perception, I'll concentrate mainly on remembering, particularly on simple remembering *of* events, for instance of my planting the tree, as opposed to (propositional) remembering *that* I planted it or (objectual) remembering the planting *to be* hard. Moreover, while I assume that remembering an event is like perceiving something in that it apparently does not entail having a belief about it, I will concentrate on cases typical of those in which one does have such a belief. These cases are crucial for understanding memorial knowledge.

The memorial counterpart of naive realism is the view that when we remember an event, we just directly remember it, as if it were *present in* our memory as a cat might be present before us (except that the event is not literally taken to be occurring, as a cat one sees is literally before one). Like all the major views of memory, this one assumes that some causal chain links us to the remembered event; for example, if I remember seeing Bill a year ago, then it must be in part *because* I did see him that I believe (or am disposed to believe) that I did, and not, say, because I dreamt that I did. As a direct realist view, this position also maintains that our memory belief—our holding of which (when it is true) constitutes our remembering—is not produced by any intermediary with which we are acquainted, such as an image. To say that would imply a counterpart of the sense-datum theory.

At this point, however, the naive realist view must be revised. To begin with, the causal chain must be in a sense *unbroken.* To see why, consider a broken chain. Imagine that you saw me plant the tree and you remember my doing so. The planting is then the causal ground of your memory belief, as it is of mine, and we both remember my planting it. But suppose I had forgotten the event and thus no longer believed I planted the tree, then later came to believe, solely on the basis of your testimony, that I planted it. There is still a causal chain from my present belief back to the planting; for the planting produced your belief, which in a way produced your testimony, which in turn produced my present belief. But the memorial chain in me was broken by my forgetting. I may still have knowledge of the planting; but I do not remember it. My knowledge of the event no more represents remembering than my knowledge—based solely on your testimony—that there is a radiant sunset visible from the front porch represents my seeing it, when I am inside reading.

The realist view seems correct, then, in requiring an unbroken causal chain. But as stated so far the view is deficient in some of the ways that naive realism about perception is. For one thing, memory is subject to illusion. I might remember an event, such as meeting you, but not quite as it was, just as you might see white paper in yellow light, and thus not see it as white. Here I do not simply remember; I remember incorrectly, for example in remembering the meeting as in New York when it was in fact in Chicago. Secondly, there is the counterpart of hallucination: I may have a vivid image of having mailed a letter, and might believe I remember doing it, yet be quite mistaken. We must, then, account for memorial illusion and similar problems.

The territory may begin to look familiar, particularly if we recall the sense-datum theory of perception. For instance, we might suppose that there are memory images, and that they are genuine objects which stand to remembering rather as sense-data are thought to stand to perceiving. These images might even *be* sense-data if they are vivid enough, but normally they are more like the images of fantasy. Perhaps, then, we remember an event when we have at least one true belief about it suitably grounded in a memorial image of it, that is, an image of it which, by a suitable unbroken chain, derives from our experience of it and represents the event correctly in at least some respect. Let us call this *the representative theory of memory*.

Like the sense-datum theory of perception, the representative theory of memory is an indirect realism. It construes our remembering as mediated by memory images (though not as based on inference from facts about such images). The view is also like the sense-datum theory in readily accounting for memorial illusion and similar problems. To remember incorrectly, as opposed to simply having a false belief about the past with no basis in memory, is to be acquainted with a memory image which, despite its being sufficiently faithful to the remembered event to ground one's remembering it, has some aspect which produces a false belief about the event, say that it was in New York rather than Chicago. The counterpart of hallucination occurs when one has an image that is intrinsically like a memorial one, but not linked to a past event by a suitable causal chain, just as, in perceptual hallucinations, the sense-data are not produced by the object (or are produced by it in an abnormal way).

Unfortunately, the representative theory of memory has many of the difficulties of the sense-datum theory and some of its own. Consider the similar difficulties first, particularly in relation to remembering. Remembering an event surely does not require acquaintance with an image of it. It is not impossible for me to reel off, from memory, some details of a news report I heard a week ago, even if I have no images, even auditory ones, of the report or what it concerned. Moreover, misremembering an event does not require acquaintance with something, such as an image, which actually *has* the property one mistakenly remembers the event as having had, as a sense-datum representing a book viewed from a certain angle is supposed to have (say) the property of being parallelogrammic. I can misremember meeting you by remembering the meeting as being in New York, when it was actually in Chicago, even if the correct aspect of my memory is not accompanied by an image that is of our actual meeting in Chicago. I may simply remember the occasion with its animated conversation, yet have the false impression that it was in New York. That false impression does not require, for instance, my imaging the skyscrapers of Wall Street. Moreover, in retrospective imagination, I can vividly experience our meeting even if I am acquainted with no object that represents it for me in the way that, in hallucinations, sense-data are supposed to represent physical objects. I can apparently imagine past events without having direct acquaintance with memorial pictures of them, just as I can apparently hallucinate an object without having direct acquaintance with a sense-datum representation of it.

A further difficulty for the representative theory arises when we consider a disanalogy between remembering and perceiving. I can remember our meeting now and describe it to someone from memory even if I have *no* images or imagelike experiences at all, whereas I apparently cannot see a tree if I have no visual sensations. Remembering, even of events that one has perceived, is neither a sensory process nor necessarily an *imaginational* one. So there need not be, in every case of remembering, even the *makings* of a representative theory to which images are crucial.

For similar reasons, the memorial counterpart of phenomenalism is not plausible. On the most plausible phenomenalist account of memory, remembering an event is understood in terms of the imaginational content of present experience. To remember an event is (roughly) to have a suitable set of images representing it, on the basis of which, in a certain way, one believes (or is disposed to believe) something about that event. But this will not do. Remembering simply does not require a set of images analogous to the sense-data from which phenomenalists try to construct physical objects (or even a set of imaging experiences such as an adverbial phenomenalist might posit). And just as no set of sense-data is such that its existence implies perception of an external object, no set of images (even apparently memorial images) is such that, in having a belief about the past grounded on those images, one must be remembering something. No matter how vivid my images of talking with you beneath the skyscrapers of Wall Street, I may not remember our talking there, and my belief that we did talk there (or anywhere) may be mistaken.

If these difficulties are as serious as they seem, then if we are to change course and construct a plausible counterpart of the adverbial theory of perception, we must take account of them. First, such a theory will not claim that remembering is *temporally* direct, since it will not construe past events as present; but it will take remembering to be epistemically direct, since memorial beliefs are not inferential. Moreover such a theory must not say that (actively) remembering an event, such as planting a tree, is memorially imaging in a way suitably caused by that past event, as perceiving an object is sensory stimulation suitably caused by the thing perceived. For no such imaging need occur (though it typically does). One can describe a past event to others, and in doing so actively remember it, even if one is imaging nothing but the faces one sees.

Positively, the adverbial view, applied to remembering events, should be expressed as something like this. First, *actively (occurrently) remembering* an event is realizing a memorial capacity towards it, where this capacity is linked to the event by an unbroken causal chain. The typical realizations are imaging processes concerning, and formations of beliefs about, the event; but there may be others. Second, *passively (dispositionally) remembering* an event is having this capacity unrealized, as where, though I can (and have a disposition to) recall the planting if I want to, my mind is wholly on other things.

Propositional remembering, remembering *that*, can be construed similarly. On the adverbial view, to remember that an event occurred is a memorial way of believing that it did, roughly, to have one or more true beliefs about it which are suitably linked by an unbroken chain to past experience and represent the event as having a certain character, say as happening in bright sunlight. Most of what we propositionally remember is dispositional, roughly, recorded in dispositional beliefs. When these beliefs are called up in active propositional remembering, as where I describe how I planted a tree, one is experiencing in a memorial *way*, as opposed to being acquainted with imagistic memorial objects. One may, but need not, image memorially, as where one actually calls up the remembered experience and recalls its features in one's imagination. Moreover, whether one images a remembered event or not, it need not be entirely *as* one remembers it. One can remember a meeting as being in the wrong city, thus remember it in the wrong way geographically, just as one can see a rectangular book as paral-lelogrammic. In neither case, moreover, need one be fooled. Typically, if I remember something as having a certain quality, say a conversation as being rushed, I believe it was like that; but I can remember it *as* such, yet know from independent evidence (such as having transacted the business in question) that it was not. On the other hand, if one really remembers some object or event, then one is right about at least some aspect of it, or is at least in a position to form some true beliefs about it on considering the matter.

Will this direct realist view stand scrutiny? Here is one nagging doubt. When I am remembering an event I typically *do* have some related image. I mean active remembering, as opposed to my remembering of events that are now far from my mind which I *could* actively recall if the subject came up. The first kind of remembering is *occurrent*, since it is in part a matter of something's occurring in me. The second kind is *dispositional*, since it is a matter of my being disposed (roughly, tending) to remember actively (occurrently) *provided that* something, such as a question about the event, activates my memory. Thus, while yesterday's concert may be far from mind while I write a letter, if someone asks me how I liked the Chopin then my dispositional memory may be activated; and, as I recall it, thereby occurrently remembering it, I may say I thought it inspiring. It is occurrent remembering that is analogous to perception and is my main concern now; and it is occurrent remembering that is closely associated with imaging. Does occurrent remembering require some sort of imagery after all, even if not images as sense-datum objects?

Here is a natural way to answer. Consider one of your memories of an event, for instance meeting someone for the first time, in such a way that you take yourself to be actively remembering that event. Second, ask yourself whether now you are imaging. When I do this, I image. Here, then, remembering involves imaging. But notice what has happened: I have called up a memory and inspected the results of my effort. If I am imaging, perhaps that is because of the *way* I evoked the remembering, or because I scrutinized the process of my calling up the meeting. This procedure, then, is defective as a way to determine whether remembering requires imaging. But the procedure does show something. For suppose that what I have done is *recall* a past event. Perhaps recalling, which is calling to mind, *does* require imaging if it is a recalling *of* an imageable event, as opposed to, say, a theorem. There is some reason to think this is so. If no imaging of our meeting comes into my consciousness, how can I have recalled it? Sometimes, moreover, we say that we cannot recall someone, meaning not that we do not know who the person is, but that we cannot image the person. There recalling seems to imply some sort of imaging.

Even if recalling should imply imaging, remembering does not. Why, then, does that idea persist? For one thing, when we collect specimen memories in order to examine remembering, we often do it by recalling things. Further, what we cannot recall we often *believe* we cannot remember. This is natural, on the adverbial view; for inability to remember is lack of a capacity, and, understandably, we may think we lack a capacity when, under normal conditions, we cannot exercise it. But imaging is only *one* exercise of memorial capacity, important though it is. Hence, inability to image does not imply absence of the capacity. We can see, then, both why there is a tendency to think that remembering requires imaging and why we should not accept this view.

If imaging seems more important for remembering than so far granted, consider another case. Suppose I can neither recall nor image Jane. I can still remember her; for *on seeing her* I might recognize her and might remember, and even recall, our last meeting. This would suggest that my memory simply needed to be "jogged." In adverbial terms, before I see her again I can dispositionally know in a certain memorial way—objectually remember—even though I cannot imagistically experience in that memorial way—recall. I choose the example of remembering a person because it is easy to show that one does remember someone by creating the right occasion. We cannot as easily do this with past events, since they cannot be literally brought back. But it is doubtful that the relation between recalling and remembering is different with events.

It is important to see that the way I am now considering the relation between recalling and remembering is direct and non-introspective. I am exploring what is possible and what it would show. Now it is possible for me to have no image of planting the spruce, yet give an account of the planting that is both remarkably accurate *and* grounded by a suitable causal chain in the original experience of the planting. To be sure, my *beliefs* about what events I remember may depend on what I can recall, which may be largely dependent on what I can image. But what events I *do* remember is a matter of how my memorial capacities are grounded in the past. I need not rely on my images or even my ability to image, though in fact retention of images no doubt aids remembering. The representative theory of memory, then, seems mistaken, and some analogue of direct realism regarding perception is apparently preferable. The suggested adverbial view of remembering is a good position from which to work; but I leave some important questions about memory unexplored, and I do not present that view as clearly correct.

THE EPISTEMOLOGICAL ROLE OF MEMORY

We can now see some points about memory as a source of belief, knowledge, and justification. Obviously our memory, as a mental capacity, is a source of beliefs, at least in the sense that it *preserves* them and enables us to *call them up*. It also enables us to *draw on our beliefs to supply premises* in reasoning, as where we solve mathematical problems using memorized theorems. When these memory beliefs are of propositions we remember to be true, they constitute knowledge. If you remember we met, you know we did. Similarly, if you remember me, you know me (at least in the sense of knowing who I am—which is not to say you can recognize me in person). So memory, when it is a source of what is remembered, yields both knowledge *that* and knowledge *of*. The analogy to perception is significant here too.

Is memory also a source of justification? Surely what justifies much of what I believe about the past is my memory. For instance, my belief that I twice planted the blue spruce is justified because of the way it is preserved in my memory. It has, for example, a special kind of familiarity, confidence, and connection with other things I seem to remember. Moreover, it appears that if I remember that I met you, I am justified in believing I met you. It thus seems that where memory yields genuine remembering it yields justification. Certainly this normally holds. Perhaps, however, I could remember that I met you, yet *fail* to be justified in my belief because (in fun) you convince me, by good arguments, that I am confusing you with someone else. Still, if my belief remains properly grounded in my actual memory of having met you (perhaps because the memory is so clear that the belief is almost unshakable), I may nonetheless genuinely remember that I met you. Yet if your arguments are good enough, I may properly reproach myself for still holding the belief that I met you, and my belief may perhaps cease to be justified. If this case is possible, then if remembering that something is so entails knowing it is so, knowing that something is so does not imply justifiably believing it. (In Chapter 7, I return to the relation between knowledge and justification, but it is important here to see that the domain of memory provides a challenge to understanding that relation.)

Furthermore, if the case is possible and one *can* remember that something is so, yet fail to be justified in one's believing that it is so, then we might question whether memory yields justified beliefs after all. Fortunately, the example by no means rules this out. Quite apart from cases of genuine remembering, memory often yields justified belief. If I have a vivid and confident belief that I met Jane, and this belief seems to me to arise from a memory of the occasion, I may, simply on that basis, be justified in the belief. Surely this is, after all, just the sort of belief that usually does represent remembering, and I have no reason to question its credentials. Memory can justify a belief even where that belief does not constitute knowledge or rest on actual remembering. If I do not in fact remember meeting Jane, perhaps the only reason why I do not is that it was her identical twin—of whose existence I had no idea—whom I met. A justification principle suggested here is this: normally, if one has a clear and confident belief that one experienced a given thing, and this belief seems to arise from one's memory, then the belief is justified. A still broader principle may perhaps be true: normally, clear and confident memorial beliefs with any subject matter are justified provided they do not conflict with other beliefs one holds. With both principles the degree of justification may not be great, particularly if there is no corroboration, such as apparently recalling a sequence of related events. But these and similar principles help to describe how memory is a source of justification.

There is, however, a very important difference between the way memory is a source of knowledge and the way it is a source of justification. To see this, we must take account of several points. Memory is a *preservative* capacity with respect to both belief and knowledge. When you first come to believe something you do not (yet) remember it. And you cannot remember something unless you *previously* knew or at least believed it, for instance perceptually. Memory *retains* belief and knowledge. It does not generate them, except in the sense that, by *using* what you have in memory, you can acquire beliefs and knowledge through inference (or perhaps through other processes that themselves yield belief and knowledge). This is not to deny that memory is sufficiently connected with knowledge to figure in an epistemic principle. Normally, a true memorial belief, supported by a vivid, steady experience of recall that is in turn corroborated by other memory experiences, represents knowledge. But if this principle is correct, that is *because* such beliefs are of a kind that ordinarily constitute knowledge originally, say when one learned through perception the truth that the spruce is taller than the hawthorn.

Thus, memory is not a *basic source* of belief or knowledge, one which generates them other than through dependence on some different source of them. But it *is* a basic source of justification. We can be justified in believing something either simply on the basis of remembering, or of our having a clear and confident memorial belief, that it is so. This holds even if we have no associated images. But in accounting for what justifies memorial beliefs, images do have a significant if restricted role. We are better justified in a memorial belief supported by imagery, especially vivid imagery, than in memorial beliefs not thus supported (other things being equal). Perhaps the reason is that there is less likelihood of error if both imagery and beliefs point in the same direction, say to my having met you two years ago. But we need not ascertain the basis of the point to see that it holds.

For all the analogy between memory and perception, then, there are important differences. Both, however, are to be causally conceived, and both are sources of belief, justification, and knowledge, propositional as well as objectual. But perception is a basic source of all three: it can produce them without dependence on another belief-producing capacity, such as reasoning. Memory, being a capacity for the preservation, and not the creation, of belief and knowledge, is not a basic source of them. But it is a basic source of justification. That, however, is a vitally important epistemological point. And as we shall see, the role of memory in our knowledge in general is also of great epistemological importance.

Introspection

So far, I have talked almost entirely about beliefs regarding things outside myself. But there is much that I believe about what is internal to me. I believe that I am *thinking* about self-knowledge, that I am *imaging* quiet blue waters, and that I *believe* I am a conscientious teacher. In holding these three beliefs, I am attributing rather different sorts of properties to myself: thinking, imaging, and believing. What sorts of properties are they, and how do our beliefs about them give us justification and knowledge? Let's start by describing the properties.

THREE KINDS OF MENTAL PROPERTIES

Thinking is a kind of process and involves a sequence of events. Imaging, which is more commonly called having an image, is (I assume) being in a certain state and does not absolutely require the occurrence of any events. Imaging can be static. I could image something for a time without any *change* whatever in my imaging, and hence without the occurrence of any event that might be part of the imaging. (The same holds even if having an image is standing in a relation to, say, a sense-datum.) Believing may also be called a state; but if it is one, it differs from imaging in at least two ways. First, it need not enter consciousness. I have many beliefs which, unlike my belief that I am now writing, I cannot call to mind without making an effort. Second, believing need not in any sense be "pictorial." Consider a belief present in consciousness, in the way my belief that I am now thinking is. This belief is present because I have called it to my attention. Even a belief present in consciousness in this way *and* about something as readily picturable as the Statue of Liberty need not involve anything pictorial in the way my imaging must. Without picturing anything, I can entertain my belief that the Statue of Liberty has a majestic beauty, whereas my imaging quiet blue waters requires my picturing a blue surface.

It will help in sorting things out if we observe a distinction that has already come up. Let's call mental states (or properties) like beliefs *dispositional* and mental processes like thinking *occurrent*. The basic idea is this. To be in a dispositional state is to be disposed—roughly, to tend—to do or undergo something under certain conditions, but not necessarily to be actually doing or undergoing something or changing in any way. Thus, my believing that I am a conscientious teacher is, in part, my being disposed to say that I am one, under conditions that *elicit* that sort of verbal manifestation of my belief, such as your asking me whether I am carefully reading my students' papers. Yet I can have this belief without doing or undergoing anything connected with it. I can have it in dreamless sleep. By contrast, to have an occurrent property *is* to be doing, undergoing, or experiencing something. Thus, if you are thinking about mental phenomena you are doing something, even if you are in an armchair; and if you are imaging my blue spruce, you are experiencing something, at least in the sense that your imaging the tree is now present in your consciousness, as a feature of your experience. Such imaging, however—as opposed to *calling up* an image—is not a process as, for example, silently talking to oneself is. We might call occurrent properties like thinking *process properties* and occurrent properties like imaging *phenomenal properties* to mark a difference between them. But clearly both differ from dispositional properties. All three kinds of mental properties are important for understanding the epistemological role of introspection.

INTROSPECTION AND INWARD VISION

If we take a cue from the etymology of 'introspection', which derives from the Latin *introspicere*, meaning 'to look within', we might construe introspection as attending to one's own consciousness and—when one's mind is not blank— thereby achieving a kind of inner seeing. If it does produce inner seeing, we can draw on what we know about perception. For instance, we can explore introspectional counterparts of some theories of perception and sensory experience. But one limitation of that procedure is apparent the moment we reflect on the dispositional mental properties, for instance believing, wanting, and having a fear of cancer. We do not "see" such properties. It is true that by introspection, say in thinking about what one wants, one can come to know one has a want (if one does not already know it); but wants are not even seen in our mind's eye, as an image of quiet blue waters apparently can be.

The analogy to vision might, however, still apply to introspection regarding occurrent properties. But if it does, it presumably applies only to the phenomenal ones, like imaging. For surely thinking is not seen. It need not even be heard in the mind's ear. Granted, I may hear my silent recitation of Shelley's "Ozymandias," but thinking *need* not occur in inner speech, certainly not speech of that sort. Perhaps it is only pictorial mental properties that we see through inner vision; and perhaps it is only *sensory* properties, such as inner recitations, tactual imagings (say, of the coarseness of a mug), and the like that seem accessible to inner analogues of perception: hearing in the mind's ear, touching in the tactile imagination, and so on. It is doubtful, then, that we can go very far conceiving introspection as producing inward seeing. Still, how might the analogy hold up even for the one important case of pictorial properties?

SOME THEORIES OF INTROSPECTION

Suppose that introspecting such things as images of quiet blue waters does produce a kind of inner seeing. Are we to understand this seeing on realist lines? One might think that the sense-datum view simply cannot be extended to introspection. For on the introspectional counterpart of that view, seeing (in one's mind's eye) an image of quiet blue waters would require something like *another* image, one that represents the first one in the way sense-data represent a physical object seen by virtue of the perceiver's acquaintance with them. Call it a *second-order image*, since it is an image of an image. What would such things be like? If I try to have an image of my image of quiet blue waters, I either get that very image all over again, or an image of something else, or something that is not an image at all, such as a *thought* of my original image. But this does not show that there could not be an image of the first one. Perhaps there could be second-order images that are less vivid than the original ones they picture, just as my imaginational image of quiet blue waters is less vivid than the sensory image I have in actually seeing those waters.

Perhaps. But a defender of an adverbial theory of sensory experience might argue that even when a perceptual imaging is later "copied" in retrospective imagination, there is really just *one* kind of imaging process and that it occurs more vividly in perception than in imagination. Thus, imaging blue waters is simply imaginationally, rather than perceptually, sensing blue-waterly. Since the adverbial view does not conceive imaging as a relation to an object, there *is* no image as an object to be copied. There is thus no place for second-order images, and the less vivid imagings which might seem to represent images are best construed as less vivid occurrences of the original imaging process. These points would not show that there *cannot* be second-order images. But they reduce the inclination to think there are by giving a plausible alternative account of the facts that originally seemed to demand second-order images for their explanation. Chief among these facts is that in recalling an image, one may have a less vivid image which apparently stands to it as an imaginational image of a scene stands to the sensory image of it from which the imaginational image seems copied. The adverbial theory of sensory (and other phenomenal) experience might explain this by interpreting the recalled image—say, of blue waters—as recollectively sensing blue-waterly, where this is like visually sensing blue-waterly, but less vivid.

Given these and other points, it seems doubtful whether any realist theory of introspection of images can justify a strong analogy between that kind of introspection and ordinary viewing. For it is by no means clear that there *is* any object introspected to serve as the counterpart of an object of ordinary vision. Moreover, recall that seeing is a causal relation between the object of perception and the perceiver. If, contrary to the sense-datum theory, there are no images as objects in their own right, but only *processes* of *imaging* things, then there *are* no images to cause one to have introspective experiences or introspectively grounded beliefs that one has an image. Imaging processes are properties of persons; they are not relations between persons and objects of immediate, inner perception. Thus, if introspective viewing is causal, it differs significantly from seeing in what does the causing. This is not to say that introspection has no object *in the sense* of something it is *of* (or about), such as an image of blue waters. But on the adverbial view of introspection, this kind of object expresses the content of the introspection—what it is about—and is not a thing with its own colors and shapes.

Supposing the adverbial account of introspection is true, however, introspection may still be like simple perception in two ways. First, introspection may imply some kind of causal relation between what is introspected in it and the introspective consciousness of that. Secondly, it may imply a causal relation between what is known introspectively and the beliefs constituting this knowledge. How can we tell if these analogies hold? In answering, I want to concentrate mainly on introspective beliefs. The main question is how we can tell whether, in introspecting something, as when we concentrate on our own imaging, the beliefs we thereby form about what we are concentrating on are produced by that very thing, or by some aspect of it, such as its imagined blue color. Many considerations are relevant here, but let me cite just two sorts.

First of all, it is surely *because* I am imaging quiet blue waters that, when I introspectively consider what I am conscious of, I believe I am imaging them (and am conscious of my imaging). It is natural and apparently reasonable to take this 'because' to express a causal relation. If the cause is not some inner object seen, it is presumably the state or process of imaging. This is, in any event, how the adverbial theory of sensory experience would view the causal relations here. Similarly, if I introspectively believe that I am thinking about introspection, I believe this because I *am* thinking about it: the thinking process itself is what causes me to believe that it is occurring. In both cases the introspective belief is produced by inner processes; and while some inner processes are *like* seeing an object, they can all be understood without presupposing that there really are special inner objects seen by the introspective eye.

A second point is this. Suppose my believing that I am imaging quiet blue waters is *not* caused by my imaging them. The belief is then *not* introspective at all. It is *about* what is introspectible, but it is not grounded in introspection, any more than a belief merely about a perceptible, such as the rich red in a painting in a faraway museum, is a perceptual belief. It may seem that the case described is impossible. But suppose I have been asked to image quiet blue waters, yet I hate the water and anyway have a lot on my mind. Still, if I want to be cooperative, then even though my mind is mainly on my problems, I may call up an image. Since I am not concentrating on calling up the image, however, the image that I actually get might be only of a blue surface, not of blue waters. I might now inattentively assume (and thereby come to believe) that I have called up the requested image of quiet blue waters. This belief is produced by a combination of my calling up the wrong image, which I do not attentively introspect at all, and by non-imaginational factors such as my desire to cooperate. The belief is neither true nor introspective.

This example suggests that even a true belief about one's conscious states or processes would not be introspective without being causally connected with them. Other examples support the same point. Imagine that my task is to think about introspection for a solid hour. I monitor myself and introspectively conclude from time to time that I am thinking about introspection. As I reflect on my topic, I continue to believe that I am thinking about introspection. Now when I truly believe this simply because I have repeatedly confirmed it and am confident of steady concentration, and *not* because I am still monitoring myself introspectively, my belief, though perfectly true, is not introspective. The best explanation of this seems, again, to be that the belief is not caused (in the right way, at least) by the thinking. It is a retained belief about my ongoing mental activity; it is not produced by that activity as a focus of my introspective attention. It is a propositional belief *that* I am presently thinking about introspection, but it is not an objectual belief, regarding my present thinking, to the effect that it is about introspection. It is not grounded in my *present* thinking at all, any more than my belief about the rich red in a painting in a distant museum is grounded in seeing it. Thus, while there may be no objects—such as sense-data or imaginational copies of them—which we introspect, introspection still seems causal: like perception and, though in a different way, recalling, it produces something like a sensory impression and, at least typically, beliefs. The causes of introspective beliefs, however, are apparently processes and events in the mind; they are not, or need not be, objects that reside therein.

INTROSPECTION AND PRIVILEGED ACCESS

In the light of what has been said, let us suppose that introspection is a causal process, though with limited similarities to viewing. Still, if it is a causal process, then we should ask some of the same epistemological questions about it that we asked about perception. For instance, is it subject to counterparts of illusion and hallucination? And if it is, in what way might it still be a source of justification and knowledge? Let's start with the issue of illusion and hallucination.

One might think that the inner domain, which is the subject of introspective beliefs, is a realm about which one cannot make mistakes. If it is, one might conclude that neither illusion nor hallucination regarding this domain is possible. Indeed, David Hume (1711–1776) maintained that since the contents of the mind are known by "consciousness" (by which he meant something at least much like introspection), they must appear in every respect what they are, and be what they appear (*A Treatise of Human Nature*, Part IV, Section II).

Hume's statement suggests two far-reaching theses about self-knowledge. The first is a thesis of *infallibility*: one cannot be mistaken in a belief to the effect that one is now in an occurrent mental state (such as imaging) or that one is undergoing a mental process (such as thinking) or that one is experiencing something (such as pain). The second is a thesis of *omniscience* with respect to the contents of one's present consciousness: if one *is* in an occurrent mental state, undergoing a mental process, or experiencing something, one cannot fail to know that one is. Together, these two theses constitute a *strong doctrine of privileged access*. The first says that our access to what is (mentally) occurring in us is so good that our beliefs about its present makeup are infallible; there is no risk of error. The second says that our access to it is so good that we cannot fail to know what (mentally) occurs in us; there is no risk of ignorance.

Suppose for the sake of argument that both the infallibility and omniscience theses are true. Would that rule out inward counterparts of illusion and hallucination? Not necessarily. For having illusions and hallucinations does *not* imply having false beliefs or being ignorant of anything. Looking from an angle, you can see a book as having the shape of a parallelogram, without believing that it does; and I can hallucinate the blue spruce without believing it is before me. In both cases, we may know the facts.

On the other hand, if there *are* no inner objects, such as blue, watery images, to appear to us to have properties they do not possess, such as wavy surfaces, then illusions of the kind we have in perception, in which an object appears to have properties it actually lacks, cannot occur. As for hallucinations, even if there are inner objects we see when we image, what would be the difference between hallucinating an image of, for instance, a loved one, and just *having* that image? The hallucinatory image might be less vivid or unstable. But it might also be just like a normal image, and we thus may not say that the former simply *is* a less vivid or unstable version of a normal image. Suppose, however, that in order to be a genuine image of a loved one, an image *must* be caused by, say, seeing that very person. We could then make a simple causal distinction between hallucinatory and genuine images. But through detailed description and good luck I could have an accurate image of Susie that is in a sense *of* her, even if I have never seen her. There are certainly different kinds of images and various ways they can mislead, but the analogy between perception and introspective consciousness does not extend in any simple way to the possibility of inner illusions and hallucinations.

It might be, however, that quite apart from illusion or hallucination, we can have false beliefs, or suffer some degree of ignorance, about what (mentally) occurs in us. I think this is clear for dispositions like believing, wanting, and fearing. We can mistakenly believe that we do not have a certain ignoble desire, particularly if it is important to our self-image that we see ourselves as having only righteous desires. For the same reasons, we can fail to know that we *do* have the desire. One can also discover a fear which, previously, one quite honestly disavowed because it was at odds with one's sense of oneself as courageous. But dispositions should probably not be conceived as *occurring* in us, and in any case it is the occurrent mental phenomena to which philosophers have tended to think we have the kind of privileged access expressed in the theses of infallibility and omniscience. Can we be mistaken, or at least ignorant, about our occurrent mental states or processes?

Consider first the possibility of mistake. Could one believe one is thinking about introspection when one is only daydreaming? It would seem so, provided one does not attend closely to what is occurring within oneself. But suppose the infallibility thesis is restricted to beliefs based on attentive introspection, where this implies "looking" closely at the relevant aspect of one's consciousness. Call this the *restricted infallibility view*. If I carefully consider the proposition that I am thinking about introspection, and believe it on the basis of attentive introspection (that is, on the basis of my focusing on the relevant aspect of my consciousness), could this belief be mistaken? This seems doubtful. But is it impossible? Suppose I desperately want to believe that I am thinking. Could this not lead me to take my daydreaming to be thinking and even to have an attentive introspective belief that I am thinking? I think so. Similarly, I could believe, on the basis of attentive—but imperfect—introspection, that I am imaging an octagon and then, concentrating harder and counting sides, discover that the figure has only seven.

If it is possible to be mistaken in believing that one is now in an occurrent mental state (such as thinking), then the omniscience thesis of privileged access should also be abandoned, even if it, too, is restricted, as it should be, to cases in which I carefully attend to (introspect) my consciousness. The easiest way to see this is to note that if I know every truth about—am omniscient about—my consciousness, then I cannot believe any falsehood about it, and so am infallible about it—unless I can *both* know all the truths about it, yet be inconsistent and also believe a falsehood about it. It is at best unlikely that both these things occur, leaving one omniscient, yet inconsistent and fallible, regarding one's own consciousness. Thus, if I am fallible, I am surely not omniscient. But such inconsistency is not clearly impossible. Let's be more concrete: our daydreaming example casts doubt on the restricted thesis of omniscience. In that example, while I am in fact daydreaming, I would presumably not know that I am. If I did know that I am daydreaming, I would believe this, and then it is very doubtful that I would *also* believe I am thinking about introspection. These points do not imply that I might be ignorant of *every* truth about my daydreaming. Since I (objectually) believe it to be thinking about introspection, I presumably at least know my daydreaming to involve words or colors or shapes. But I would still not know that I am daydreaming and thus would not be omniscient regarding the processes occurring in me.

It may help to point out that there could someday be a source of significant evidence against at least the strong doctrines of privileged access. For it could turn out that every occurrent mental phenomenon is uniquely correlated with some distinct brain process. Then someone could devise a "cerebroscope" for viewing the brain and read off what is occurring in consciousness from the cerebroscopic data. It seems possible that we could cerebroscopically discover the unique pattern for, say, believing on the basis of attentive introspection that one is imaging quiet blue waters, at the same time we discover the pattern for imaging a field of blue-green grass. It would be natural here to suppose the subject is mistaking the grassy image (or imaging process) for a watery one.

But there is a problem with this reasoning. How could one *establish* the unique correlations except by relying on the accuracy of people's introspective beliefs? Wouldn't it be necessary to start by *asking* people what they are, say, imaging, to assume they are correct, and only *then* record the associated brain state? And if learning the correlations would depend on the accuracy of introspective reports, how could the correlations show such reports to be mistaken?

A possible reply is this. Suppose that learning the correlations would depend on the accuracy of introspective reports. Still, neuroscientists would not have had to rely on the accuracy of precisely the introspective belief being shown to be mistaken, and perhaps not even on the accuracy of highly similar beliefs. Imagine, however, that they did have to rely on just the sorts of belief we are examining, together with evidence regarding these beliefs' reliability which we already have independently of the cerebroscope. Would this imply that the cerebroscope could not provide powerful evidence against introspective beliefs?

Consider an analogy. We might use a mercury thermometer to construct a gas thermometer. We might calibrate a container of gas with a piston that rises and falls as the gas is heated and cooled. The new temperature readings might correlate perfectly with mercury readings in many instances: in measuring water temperature, air temperature, and other cases. The gas thermometer might then be used for the same jobs as the mercury thermometer *and* might gauge temperatures that the mercury thermometer cannot measure, say because they are above the boiling point of mercury. Could we not use a gas thermometer to correct a mercury thermometer in some cases, or perhaps to correct all mercury thermometers in restricted ways? We could. This seems so even if we had originally taken the mercury thermometer to be infallible in measuring temperature, perhaps because we thought of its readings as partly definitive of what temperature *is*. Similar points might hold for beliefs about what is presently occurring in one. If the analogy does extend this far, then even the restricted omniscience view fares no better than the restricted infallibility view. For even when one is attentive to what is occurring internally, a cerebroscope could indicate that one does not believe (hence does not know) that a certain thing is occurring, such as a frightening image which one thinks one has put out of mind.

INTROSPECTION AS A SOURCE OF JUSTIFICATION AND KNOWLEDGE

It is important not to overextend our criticism of various claims of privileged access. After all, even the restricted infallibility and omniscience views are very strong claims of privileged access. They can be given up quite consistently with holding that we do have a very high degree of privileged access to what is occurring in us. Nothing I have said suggests that our beliefs about what is now occurring in us are not *normally* true. The difficulty of finding reason to think they even *could* be false confirms that they should be considered at least very likely to be correct. Similarly, provided we are attentive to what is occurring in us, if something (knowable) is occurring, such as a favorite melody in our mind's ear, *normally* we know that it is, or at least are in a position to know this simply by forming the belief that the melody is going through our mind.

Granted, our "access" to our dispositional states is not as good as our access to what is occurring in us. After all, the very existence of one's imagining (or of an image if there are such objects) *is* simply its place in consciousness. But beliefs and other mental dispositions need not even enter consciousness, nor ever be a subject of our thoughts or concerns. Nevertheless, our beliefs to the effect that we now want (fear, intend, believe) something are normally justified; and normally, when we have a want (or fear, intention, belief, or similar disposition) we are in a position to know this. (We very commonly do *not* know it, however; for such things may not enter consciousness at all, and there is often no reason to take any notice of them or form any beliefs about them.)

There are a great many issues and details I have not mentioned; but if what I have said is correct, we can now generalize about introspection in relation to belief, justification, and knowledge. Plainly, many beliefs arise from introspection, and the points that have emerged suggest the epistemic principle that normally, beliefs grounded in attentive introspection are true and constitute knowledge. Moreover, normally, if I attentively focus introspectively on something going on in me, I know that it is going on, under at least some description: I may not know that I am humming the slow movement of Beethoven's *Path-*

étique Sonata, but I do know I am humming a melodic piano piece. The corresponding justification principles seem at least equally plausible: normally, beliefs grounded in attentive introspection are justified; and normally, if I attentively focus on something going on in me, I am justified in believing that it is going on in me. To be sure, some are better justified than others, and even some that are not attentive are justified. There are many possible principles, and many possible qualifications of the two stated. But those two principles are sufficient to suggest the power of introspection as a source of justification and knowledge. The examples I used to argue that introspection is fallible do not show that the apparently false introspective beliefs were *unjustified* or that true ones are not knowledge. A false belief, particularly if it is of a kind usually justified, can still be justified; and a true belief of a kind that can sometimes be false may itself constitute knowledge.

There is, however, a danger of overestimating the strength of introspective justification. From our examples, it might be thought that attentive introspection, even if not absolutely infallible, generates a kind of justification that *cannot* be defeated. How could I fail to be justified in believing that I am imaging quiet blue waters, if my belief is grounded in attentive introspection? It seems to me that I could not be *unless* I could have good reason to believe I may be mistaken—as perhaps I could *if* I had sufficient evidence for believing this, such as repeated cerebroscopic results indicating that I have been mistaken in quite similar cases. It is far from obvious that I could have sufficient evidence of this sort. In any case, plainly beliefs grounded in attentive introspection, such as my belief that I am now imaging blue waters, are normally justified to a very high degree. Moreover—and here we have another justification principle—normally, my simply being engaged in attentive introspection also yields situational justification even where it does not yield belief. If I somehow "notice" my imaging blue waters yet do not form the belief that I am doing so, I am nonetheless justified *in* believing that I am.

If we now ask whether introspection—"consciousness" in one sense—is a *basic* source of belief, justification, and knowledge, the answer should be evident. It is. In this, as in many other respects, it is like perception. But it may well be that the degree of justification which introspection generates is greater than that generated by perceptual experience, other things being equal. Furthermore, we can introspect at will, though we may also do it quite spontaneously; and there is no limit to how many things we can come to know by so doing. But we cannot perceive at will; and what we can know through perception is limited by what there is outside us to perceive, jut as what we can know through remembering or recalling is limited by what has actually happened (or remains true). Thus, introspection, unlike perception and memory, enables us to *acquire* knowledge whether external circumstances cooperate or not.

There is a tradeoff, however. Through perception we acquire (primarily) justified beliefs and knowledge about the external world; through introspection we acquire (primarily) justified beliefs and knowledge only about the internal world. But the internal world is of great importance; without good access to it we would have little if any self-knowledge and, for that reason, probably at best shallow knowledge of others. Moreover, self-knowledge is an important resort when questions arise about one's justification or knowledge regarding external objects, as where, confronted with a strange object, one carefully considers the stability, coherence, and variations of one's perceptual experience in order to rule out hallucination. Both perceptual and introspective knowledge are vital, and both, as we shall soon see, can be extended far beyond their beginnings in our experience.

CHAPTER 4

Reason

I see the blue spruce and I believe that it is there before me. I look away, and I believe that I am now imaging it. I remember its shape, and I believe that one of its upright shoots is taller than the other. These are beliefs grounded in my experience: perceptual, introspective, and memorial. But I also believe that *if* the spruce is taller than the hawthorn and the hawthorn is taller than the birch, then the spruce is taller than the birch. On what basis do I believe this? Certainly it is on the basis of perception that I believe *each* of the three comparative propositions; it is easy to see, for instance, that the spruce is taller than the hawthorn. But I do not believe on the basis of perception that *if* the spruce is taller than the hawthorn and the hawthorn is taller than the birch, then the spruce is taller than the birch. Apparently, as a rational being I just grasp, and thereby believe, this truth. It is evident to reason, one might say. Such truths are often called *self-evident*, because they are obvious in themselves: if one comprehendingly considers them, one believes and knows them. One need not consult one's experience, nor even reflect on such propositions, to grasp—roughly, to understand—them and thereby to believe that they are true.

There are many truths we readily grasp and thereby immediately believe, in the way just illustrated. That is, we believe them immediately in the sense that we see their truth without having to infer them from anything else, or even having to understand them on the basis of believing something else. The point is not that we grasp them instantly, though we may. What is crucial is that our belief exhibits *epistemic immediacy*: it is not based on inference or on a further, evidential belief. If it were, it would be mediated by (and thereby at least partly grounded in) the set of premises from which we infer (or through which we believe) the proposition, as my belief that the spruce is taller than the birch is mediated by the other two comparative propositions which are part of the basis of the belief.

My belief of the truth that if the spruce is taller than the hawthorn and the hawthorn is taller than the birch, then the spruce is taller than the birch, may or may not exhibit *temporal immediacy*. When I consider this proposition, it may or may not take me a moment to see its truth; but when I do see it, my belief of that truth will be epistemically immediate, not inferential. Similar points apply to the propositions that all vixens are female, that nothing is red and green all over (at one time), that if some dogs are pets, then some pets are dogs, and that if all human beings are mortal and Socrates is a human being, then he is mortal. How might we understand the justification of our beliefs of such propositions? And how do we know them?

THE CLASSICAL VIEW OF THE TRUTHS OF REASON

The best-known answers to these questions, and probably the only ones we might call *the classical answers*, derive largely from Immanuel Kant (1724–1804). He discussed both the truth of the kinds of propositions in question and how we know them. (He gives a short presentation of his views on these matters in the Preamble to his *Prolegomena to Any Future Metaphysics*.) What he said is complex and difficult to interpret precisely, and I am simply going to lay out a version of the classical account which may correspond only roughly to Kant's views. Moreover, I am interested mainly in our justification and knowledge regarding these *truths of reason*, as we might call them, but I will also talk about the basis of these truths themselves where that is useful in discussing our beliefs of them.

Take the proposition that all vixens are female. I easily grasp its truth, and I immediately believe it; I need no premises or evidence. There *was* a time when I did not know the word 'vixen'; I might then have looked at the sentence 'All vixens are female' and not known what proposition it expressed, much less seen the particular truth (true proposition) it does express. But this does not show that one does not immediately believe that truth when one (comprehendingly) considers it. It shows only that encountering a sentence expressing a truth does not *enable* one to consider that truth unless one *understands* the sentence. We can see, moreover, that when one does consider the truth that all vixens are female, one does not (or at least need not) know it on the basis of beliefs about the sentence 'All vixens are female'. For we can consider that same truth by using some other sentence to express it, and perhaps without using a sentence at all. If, however, we think about the basis of the truth of the proposition, we may discover something which in turn helps to explain why we so readily understand and believe it.

Consider what a vixen is. It is a female fox. Indeed, the concept of a vixen may be analyzed in terms of being female and being a fox. So in saying that a vixen *is* a female fox, one could be giving an analysis of the concept of a vixen. Now suppose that (like Kant) we think of an analysis of a concept as indicating what the concept contains. We can now say that the concept of being female is part of the concept of a vixen, and that being female is thus an element in being a vixen. In the light of all this, we might call the truth that all vixens are female an *analytic proposition*: what it predicates of a vixen (any given vixen), namely, being female, can be analyzed out of the concept of its subject, that is, out of the concept of a vixen. The same sort of thing holds for the propositions that all bachelors are unmarried, that all triangles have three angles, that all sound arguments have true premises and true conclusions, and so on.

This way of looking at our example helps to explain something else that is true of the proposition that all vixens are female: it *cannot* be false. Try to imagine a non-female vixen. Since the concept of a vixen is analyzable as (and hence equivalent to) that of a female fox, one is in effect trying to imagine a non-female female fox. This would be something that is and is not female. We would have a contradiction. Thus, there cannot be such a thing, on pain of contradiction. It is absolutely impossible that there be a non-female vixen. Analytic propositions are, for this reason, thought to be—and sometimes even *defined* as—true on pain of contradiction; that is, their falsity entails a contradiction, and hence they can be false only if a contradiction is true. That is absolutely impossible. Analytic propositions are therefore regarded as *necessary truths*, truths that hold in *any* possible situation (though other kinds of truths may also be considered necessary).

Now if analytic propositions are true by virtue of the sort of conceptual containment relation we have been exploring, might we not know them in virtue of grasping that relation? In considering the proposition that all vixens are female, one in some way grasps the containment relation between the concept of a vixen and that of being female. It might be objected that the correct account is instead this. One quickly or subconsciously reasons: the concept of a vixen is analyzable as that of a female fox; *being female* is contained in that analysis; hence all vixens are female. A defender of the classical view would reply that this is how one might *show* one knows that all vixens are female, not how one *knows* it, at least not if one just grasps its truth. One perhaps *could* come to know the proposition that way. But one need not come to know it thus, and believing it in virtue of grasping the crucial conceptual relation does not require coming to know it in that way.

We can now see how the classical account might apply to apparently non-analytic truths that are directly grasped. Think about the proposition that nothing is both red and green all over (at one time). Can we analyze *being non-red* out of the concept of being green, or *being non-green* out of the concept of being red, so that in saying that something *is* red and green all over at once someone could be shown to be implying that it is red and non-red, or green and non-green?

This is doubtful. For one thing, it is not clear that we can analyze the concept of being red (or the concept of being green) at *all* in the relevant sense of 'analyze'.

We *can* scientifically clarify what being red is by appeal to facts about light. But on the classical view, such clarification helps us understand certain facts about red *things* and perhaps about the property of being red, rather than telling us what the *concept* of a red thing is equivalent to. Compare analyzing the concept of a vixen with making scientific discoveries about vixens. One could discover that they have a unique tracking system, but not that they are male. On the classical view, we cannot identify anything as a vixen—say, for experimental purposes—except under the assumption that it is female. Thus, the possibility of discovering anything inconsistent with its being female is ruled out from the start. This does not make analytic truths more important than scientific truths. The former are simply of a different kind: they are not open to scientific verification or falsification, but they also do not compete with scientific truths.

Could one analyze the concept of being red as equivalent to the concept of having a color other than green and blue and yellow and so on, where we list all the remaining colors? Even if we could list all the other colors, the concept of being red is simply not equivalent to a *negative* concept of this sort. Moreover, an analysis does not merely provide an *equivalent concept*, that is, one which (necessarily) applies to the same things to which the concept being analyzed does. An analysis of a concept must meet at least two further conditions. First, it must exhibit a suitable subset of the elements that constitute the concept; secondly, it must do so in such a way that one's seeing that they constitute it can (to some significant degree) yield *understanding* of the concept. The concept of being red is surely not constituted by that of being a color that is not green, not blue, and so on; and one could not understand what it *is* for something to be red simply in terms of understanding that long list. Indeed, one could presumably understand the list of other colors quite well even if one had never seen or imagined redness, and one *had* no perceptual, imaginational, or other concept of it at all. It is arguable, in fact, that the concept is *simple* in the sense that, unlike that of a vixen, it is not analyzable into elements of any kind.

Even if the concept of being red is not analyzable into elements of any sort, we can still immediately and rationally grasp that nothing is red and green all over. Truths like this are called *a priori propositions* (propositions knowable "from the first") because they can be *known a priori*, that is, simply through reason as directed toward them and toward the concepts occurring in them, at least if reason is used extensively enough and with sufficient care. But since these propositions are not analytic and seem to assert something beyond what analysis of the relevant concepts can show, they are also called *synthetic propositions*. They bring together or "synthesize" concepts and properties, even if in a negative way (as by linking redness with non-greenness). They do not, even in part, analyze concepts. It is noteworthy that while analytic propositions are characterized roughly in terms of *how they are true*—by virtue of conceptual containment (or, on a related account, on pain of contradiction)—a priori propositions are characterized in terms of *how they are known*, or can be known: through reason. (This allows that they can *also* be known through experience, say through testimony, at least if the testifier's knowledge is, directly or indirectly, grounded in reason.) It should perhaps not be surprising, then, that the categories of the analytic and the a priori are not identical.

The other synthetic truths, those that are not a priori, as well as the negations of these truths, are called *empirical (or a posteriori) propositions*. This means, roughly, that the propositions in question (or their negations) can be *known only empirically*, that is, are knowable only on the basis of experience, as opposed to reason—above all on the basis of perceptual or introspective experience (in the ways described in Chapters 1 and 3). Empirical propositions, on the classical view, include all truths known perceptually, such as those about the colors and shapes of things around us and all truths known scientifically, such as generalizations linking the temperature and the volume of gases. (The term 'empirical', unlike 'a priori', is often used to refer to falsehoods as well as truths, but my main examples of empirical propositions will be truths.)

Analytic truths, as well as certain synthetic ones, are called a priori because analytic truths are knowable through the use of reason. But analytic truths appear to be knowable—or at least are showable—through a different use of reason than is appropriate to the synthetic a priori truths. It may be that I know that nothing is red and green all over by virtue of simply grasping, as a rational creature, a kind of incompatibility between the concept of being red (at a time and place) and the concept of being green. But I apparently do not know it by virtue of grasping a *containment* relation between being red (or green) and anything else. If this does not illustrate two different uses of reason, it at least does indicate a different kind of application of reason to different kinds of relations of concepts.

Since my knowledge of the proposition that nothing is red and green all over is not based on grasping a containment relation, it differs from my knowledge of the analytic truth that all vixens are female. Yet in both cases the relation between the concepts involved in the truth seems to be the basis of that truth. In both, moreover, I apparently know the truth through rationally *understanding* that relation: analytic containment in one case, mutual exclusion in the other. I may need experience to *acquire* the concepts in question, for instance to acquire color concepts or the concept of a fox. But once I have the needed concepts, it is my grasp (roughly, my understanding) of the conceptual relations, and not whatever experience I needed to acquire the concepts, which is the *basis* of my knowledge of analytic and other a priori truths. In part because of these similarities, as well as because the falsity of such propositions seems absolutely inconceivable, the classical view takes synthetic a priori truths as well as analytic truths to be necessary. It may not be contradictory to say that something is red and green all over, and no one has proved that this proposition is contradictory, in the sense that it entails that some proposition—say, that the object in question is colored—is and is not true; but on the classical view it is nonetheless absolutely impossible that something be red and green all over. We need only reflect on the concepts to realize this: being red excludes being green.

THE EMPIRICIST VIEW OF THE TRUTHS OF REASON

The classical view of the nature of what I am calling a priori truths—truths of reason—and of our knowledge of them has been vigorously challenged. To appreciate the epistemological significance of reason as a source of justification and knowledge, and of truths of reason themselves, we must consider some alternative accounts of these truths.

John Stuart Mill held that ultimately there are only empirical truths and that our knowledge of them is based on experience, for instance on perception (see especially his book *A System of Logic*, particularly Book II, Chapters 5–7). We might call this sort of view *empiricism about the truths of reason*, since it construes apparently a priori truths as empirical, though it need not deny that reason has *some* role in giving us justification and knowledge. Reason may, for example, be crucial in extending our knowledge by enabling us to prove geometrical theorems from axioms. But the sort of view I want to explore—without following Mill in particular—denies that reason grounds justification or knowledge other than in experience.

Before we consider Mill's thesis in detail, we should contrast it, from the most general epistemological point of view, with Kant's. Kant's position on the truths of reason might be called rationalist, Mill's empiricist. These terms are used too variously to make precise definition wise. Very roughly, however, *rationalism* in epistemology takes reason to be far more important in grounding our knowledge than empiricism allows, and rationalists virtually always assert or imply that, in addition to knowledge of analytic truths, there is synthetic a priori knowledge. Very roughly, *empiricism* in epistemology takes experience to be the basis of all of our knowledge except possibly that of analytic propositions and purely logical truths, such as the truth that if all whales are mammals and no fish are mammals, then no whales are fish. (For both empiricists and rationalists, analytic propositions are typically taken to include logical truths.) Even if such logical propositions are not true by virtue of containment relations, they are in an important respect like those that are. Their negations entail contradictions, for instance that some whales are and are not fish. They are therefore paradigms of truths of reason; for the use of logic alone, which is perhaps the purest use of reason, can show that they can be false only if a contradiction is true—which is impossible.

Thus, analytic propositions are sometimes given a broader characterization than I gave and are taken to be those whose negations entail a contradiction. In any case, a *radical empiricist*, like Mill, takes *all* knowledge to be grounded in experience. A *radical rationalist* (which Kant was not) takes all knowledge to be grounded in reason, for instance to be intuitively grounded in a grasp of self-evident propositions or deductively based on inference from a priori truths that are intuited.

Empiricism about the truths of reason is most plausible for the synthetic ones, so let us sketch it with reference to an apparently synthetic a priori proposition. Mathematical truths, particularly truths of simple arithmetic, are often regarded as synthetic a priori. Consider the proposition that $7 + 5 = 12$. It is easy to say that one just knows this, as one knows that nothing is red and green all over. But how does one know it? Here we cannot readily find a good analogy for the simple exclusion relation we grasp in the case of red and green. Could it be that from experience with objects, say with counting apples, combining two sets of them, and recounting, we learn our first arithmetic truths and then use reason to formulate general rules, such as those for calculating larger sums?

Viewed in this way, arithmetic develops rather as a scientific theory is often thought to, with observations crucial at the base, generalizations formulated to account for them, and broader principles being postulated to link all the observations and generalizations together. And do we not *first* learn to add by counting physical things, or by counting on our fingers? To be sure, we cannot imagine how the number 7 added to the number 5 could fail to equal the number 12. But the world *could* go haywire so that when (for instance) five apples and seven oranges are physically combined the result of counting the new set is *always* eleven. If that happened, would we not begin to think that arithmetic must be revised, just as Einstein's work showed that the physics of the incomparable Sir Isaac Newton needed revision? Perhaps the crucial epistemological consideration is what overall account of our experience is most reasonable; and if the best overall account should require rejecting a proposition now thought a priori and necessary, so be it.

Several points can be made in defense of the classical view. One concerns the distinction between two related but quite different things: the *genesis* of one's beliefs—what produces them—and their *justification*, in the sense of what justifies them. A second point concerns the question whether arithmetical propositions can be tested observationally. The third focuses on the possibility of taking account of what looks like evidence against arithmetical truths, so that even if one's final epistemological standard *is* meeting the demands of the best overall account of experience, these truths can be preserved in *any* adequate account.

First, granting for the sake of argument that our arithmetic *beliefs* arise from physical counting, is the experience that *produces* them what *justifies* them? The genesis of a belief—what produces it—is often different from what justifies it.

The testimony of someone I realize is unreliable might, when I am off guard, produce my belief that different brands of aspirin do not, as aspirin, differ chemically; my belief would at that point be unjustified and might become justified only later when I learn that aspirin *is* simply acetylsalicylic acid. Moreover, regardless of what produces our arithmetic beliefs initially, when they are justified in the *way* my belief that 7 + 5 = 12 now is, it does not appear that experience *is* what justifies them. For instance, I do not, on careful reflection, see how the truth of the proposition might be grounded in the behavior of objects when they are combined; and I would not try to justify it, as opposed to *illustrating* it, by citing such behavior.

This brings us to the second point: I do not even think of the proposition that 7 + 5 = 12 as *testable*, say by examining how objects combine, though it is *exemplifiable* in that way. The empiricist might reply that this by no means shows that the proposition is, as the classical view insists, necessary. Indeed, it does not. But let us look closely at the idea that it might be tested, and thereby disconfirmed, by our discovering that when sets of five objects are combined with sets of seven, we then find just eleven.

We come now to the question how one might deal with repeated and systematic counterevidence. Classical theorists will argue that it is surely possible for the world to alter in such a way that this combination procedure results in one item's disappearing, or in our failing to see it. They will also argue that this is a better interpretation of the strange cases described than saying that it has turned out to be false that 7 + 5 = 12. Thus, instead of saying that an arithmetical principle has been falsified, we say that the world no longer exemplifies it. I confess, indeed, that I do not really understand how the purely arithmetical principle could be false: the number 7 plus the number 5 equals the number 12, regardless of how apples and oranges behave. The principle is apparently not *about* apples and oranges, though (so far as we know) their behavior exemplifies it. For the classical view, at least, it is about *numbers*, which, unlike the arabic or roman or other *numerals* we use to express them linguistically, are abstract and non-physical.

By contrast with the classical view, Mill denied that there *are* abstract entities and so, believing that mathematical propositions are about something, he naturally viewed them as generalizations about the behavior of physical objects. We must certainly grant that if physical things did not exemplify the proposition that 7 + 5 = 12, the proposition would be of far less *value* to us. But this would not entail that it is false. If the physical world went haywire, it could turn out to be false that when seven apples are placed together with five more and the total collection is counted, the count yields twelve. But this is a *physical* principle. It is not, and does not even follow from, the purely mathematical proposition we are discussing.

The empiricist view of the a priori can also be applied to analytic propositions and even to self-evident logical truths. Suppose that we discover that vixens have certain characteristics we think of as male, such as certain hormones. Imagine that gradually these discoveries mount up so that the female foxes in our laboratory begin to seem better classified as male than as female. Could not a time come when we begin to doubt that vixens are female after all? And what about the logical principle of the excluded middle, which says that every proposition is either true or false? Consider the proposition that John is bald. Must this proposition be either true or false no matter what the quantity or distribution of hair on his head?

Again, there are difficulties with the examples. For one thing, particularly over a long time, we can begin to use a term in a different sense from the one it now has. Thus, the discoveries about vixens could result in our someday using 'vixen' to mean not 'female fox' but 'fox with female external sexual characteristics and of the kind we have in the lab'. Then, when we utter such words as 'Vixens are not really female', we are not denying the analytic proposition now expressed by 'All vixens are female'. Our experience might in this way result in our someday no longer asserting that vixens are female; but it certainly does not follow that it might falsify the proposition we *now* assert when we say that. Given what we now mean by 'vixen', in saying that all vixens are female we do not rule out that *those* "vixens" in the lab could turn out to have internal biological and chemical characteristics in the light of which *they* ultimately need not be considered female.

Regarding the principle of the excluded middle, I would stress that Aristotle (384–322 B.C.) plausibly argued against it in relation to certain instances, and some contemporary logicians do, too. Consider the common case of vague statements, for instance that Tom (who has lost much of his hair) is bald. Must this be either true or false? There is not now, and there is some reason to think there never will be, an uncontroversial answer to the question whether it *must* be. The principle of the excluded middle is surely a poor example to make the empiricist case, though it is often used to suggest that even logical truths are not necessary. When standard examples of simple logical truths are used, the effect seems very different. Consider the proposition that if Ann is coming by bus or she is coming by plane, and she is not coming by bus, then she is coming by plane (which exemplifies the general logical truth that if at least one of two propositions is the case and the first is not, then the second is). Is there any plausibility in the view that this might be false? I find none; and while nothing I have said proves that empiricism about the a priori is mistaken, it appears less plausible than the classical account.

THE CONVENTIONALIST VIEW OF THE TRUTHS OF REASON

There is another important approach to understanding the truths of reason and our justification and knowledge regarding them. To see how it goes, suppose that analytic propositions may be said to be *true by definition*. One can now make moves parallel to the classical ones that are expressed in terms of concepts. Thus, 'vixen' is definable as meaning (the same thing as) 'female fox'; 'female' is part of that phrase; hence, by grasping a definition (even if we do not call it to mind) we can *see* how the proposition that all vixens are female is true. The predicate, 'female', is part of the meaning of the subject, 'vixen', just as the concept of being female is part of the concept of a vixen. By *appeal* to this definition, we can *show* that the proposition that all vixens are female is true. Granted, in the case of synthetic truths of reason, we cannot make the same moves; but we can still speak of truth by virtue of *meaning*, in the limited sense that it seems to be a matter of the meanings of, say, the terms 'red' and 'green', that if one of them applies to something at a time and place, the other does not.

What terms mean is a matter of convention. It depends entirely on agreement, usually tacit agreement, among the users of the relevant language, on the proper application of the term. We could have used 'vixen' differently, and we would have if the history of our language happened to differ in a certain way with respect to that term. Moreover, even now we could decide to use 'vixen' differently. The suggested account of the truths of reason—*conventionalism*—grounds them in conventions, especially definitional conventions, regarding meaning, and it conceives our knowledge of them as based on our knowing those conventions. Since knowledge of conventions is reasonably taken to be empirical knowledge based on suitable observations of linguistic behavior, conventionalism (as I am interpreting it) is a kind of empiricism regarding the truths of reason, and it has been held by a number of philosophers in the empiricist tradition.

Some of the points made by conventionalism are quite plausible. In grasping the definition of 'vixen' as meaning the same thing as 'female fox', perhaps we can see that all vixens are female; and by appeal to the definition perhaps we can show this. But if these points hold, that may well be because in grasping the definition we understand the *concepts* involved and thereby see a containment relation between the concept of a vixen and that of being female. Furthermore, it seems possible to grasp the relevant conceptual relations, and thereby know the analytic truth, even if one does not know any such definition. Hence, knowledge of analytic truths apparently does not depend on knowledge of conventions.

Conventionalism also fails to give a good account of what grounds the *truth* of analytic propositions. It is not *because* 'vixen' means the same thing as 'female fox' that all vixens are female. For, as we saw in assessing the empiricist view, this analytic truth does not depend on what 'vixen' means. This truth holds whether there is such a word or not. It could be expressed in some other language or by other English terms. It could be so expressed even if the word 'vixen' never existed, or if, while 'vixen' had always meant the same thing as 'female fox', *both* terms had meant something else, for example 'wily creature'.

Moreover, while one *can* come to know that all vixens are female through understanding definitions of terms that express this truth, one cannot know it wholly on the basis of the truth of those definitions. To know that all vixens are female by virtue of knowing that, say, 'vixen' has the same meaning as 'female fox', I need a bridge between knowledge of convention and knowledge of vixens. Consider one thing such a bridge requires. I must be justified in believing a general principle something like this: that a proposition expressed by a subject-predicate sentence such as 'All vixens are female' is true if its predicate—here 'female'—expresses something contained in the concept designated by its subject term—here 'vixen'. But this principle seems analytic; if it is, then apparently one can know an analytic truth by knowing conventions only if one *assumes* some other analytic truth. In any case, to know, in the light of this principle, that all vixens are female, I must take the relevant sentence—'All vixens are female'—to be an instance of the principle, that is, to have a predicate expressing something contained in the concept designated by its subject. I am in effect using logic to discern something about a particular sentence by bringing that sentence under a generalization about sentences. But how can conventionalism explain how I am justified in believing the logical truths I thereby depend on, such as that if all sentences of a certain kind express truths, and this sentence is of that kind, then it expresses a truth? I cannot respond by doing the same thing all over again with this logical truth; for that would presuppose logic in the same way, and the procedure would have to be repeated. The problem would arise yet again, and no finite number of steps would explain my justification. We could thus never account for a given logical truth without presupposing one. Since conventionalism presupposes (at least) logical truths of reason, in order even to begin to account for analytic ones, it cannot show—and provides no good reason to believe—that either every truth of reason, or all knowledge of such truths, is grounded in convention.

These criticisms should not be allowed to obscure a correct conventionalist point. The meaning of 'vixen' *is* crucial for what proposition is expressed by the sentence 'All vixens are female', that is, for what one is stating when (in the normal way) one uses this sentence to make an assertion. Thus, if 'vixen' came to mean the same as 'wily creature', that sentence would express a falsehood, since there are plenty of wily males. But from the fact that change in what our terms mean can result in our saying different things in uttering the same words, nothing at all follows regarding whether *what* we say in using these words is necessarily true, or true at all. Those matters depend on what it *is* that we say.

There is, however, an underlying insight in conventionalism: truths of reason are associated with meanings, can be known when meanings are grasped, and can be shown through pointing out relations of meanings. But important though these points are, they do not support the conventionalist view that either the truths of reason themselves, or justification or knowledge regarding those a priori propositions, are *based* on what words mean or on our conventions for using them. For all that these points establish, our understanding of word meanings is simply a route to our grasping of concepts and shows what it does about the truths of reason only because of that fact.

SOME PROBLEMS FOR THE CLASSICAL VIEW

Of the accounts just considered, then, the classical view of the truths of reason and our knowledge of them stands up best. But there are other accounts and many variants on the ones discussed here. Moreover, I have sketched only the main lines of the classical view. There are also difficulties for it. Recall the problem of vagueness. Perhaps the concept of being red, as well as the term 'red', is vague. Is it, then, an a priori truth that nothing is red and (any shade of) orange all over? And how can we tell? One answer is that while words are by and large vague, concepts are not, and what *is* red (instantiates the concept of redness) is never orange even though we have no non-arbitrary way of precisely specifying the limits of colors. Thus, we might confront a sentence, say 'That painting has a patch that is at once red and orange', which we cannot assess until we see whether it implies the necessary falsehood that the patch is two different colors at once or, because of the vagueness of its terms, expresses the possible truth that the patch has a single color as appropriately considered red as orange. But this answer is only the beginning of a solution to the problem of how to deal with vagueness and is less plausible for highly complex concepts such as that of an artwork. For the more vague our terms, the harder it is to discern what propositions are expressed by sentences using those terms, and thus the harder it is to decide whether these sentences express truths of reason. None of this implies, however, that there are not some clear cases of synthetic a priori truths.

A related problem for the classical view emerges when we consider the close relation (which some consider an equivalence) between what a term means and the concept it expresses. With this relation in mind, notice too that meaning can change gradually, as where we discover things about vixens a little at a time and thereby almost imperceptibly come to mean something different by 'vixen'. A point may then come at which it is unclear whether the term 'vixen' expresses the concept it now does or not and, correspondingly, whether what is then expressed by 'All vixens are female' is analytic or not. This does *not* give us reason to doubt that what that sentence now expresses is analytic; but it does show that it may be difficult to *decide* whether or not we have before us an analytic proposition. That difficulty may drastically limit the usefulness of the notion of the analytic in understanding philosophical and other problems.

It might be argued, moreover, that on reflection the distinction between meaning change (semantic change) of the kind illustrated and falsification of the proposition we started with simply does not hold. This point is especially likely to be pressed by those who think that the basic epistemological standard is what is required for an overall account of our experience. Consider the following states of affairs: (a) scientists' discovering that despite appearances vixens have such significant male characteristics that they are *not* really female—an outcome the classical theory says is impossible—and (b) scientists' making discoveries about vixens so startling that we come to use 'vixen' in a new sense, one such that, while scientists deny that "vixens" in this new sense are female, what they are thereby saying provides no reason to doubt that what we *now* mean by 'All vixens are female' is true. Is there really a clear difference between (a) and (b)? Classical theorists take (b) to be possible and tend to hold that it is only because possibilities like (b) are not clearly distinguished from (a) that (a) *seems* possible. They regard the difference between (a) and (b) as clear enough to sustain their view and tend to conclude that what may seem to be falsification of an analytic proposition is really only a change in meaning that leads us to substitute for an analytic truth what looks like a proposition inconsistent with it, yet is actually compatible with it. Other philosophers think that the difference is not clear at all and that future discoveries really can weigh against what the classical view calls analytic propositions.

It is difficult to doubt, however, that there are *some* truths of reason, such as elementary logical principles, and such simple analytic propositions as that all vixens are female, which are both knowable a priori and necessarily true. Whether some truths of reason are also synthetic is more controversial, but it looks as if some of them are. Whether, if some of them are, those synthetic truths are also necessary is also very controversial. I see no good reason to deny that they are necessary, but there may be no decisive argument to show this. If synthetic truths of reason are necessary, perhaps one must simply see that this is so by reflecting on the examples. In any case, our capacity of reason, our rational *intuition*, as it is sometimes (perhaps misleadingly) called, is a source of beliefs of simple truths of reason, such as the self-evident truth that if the spruce is taller than the hawthorn and the hawthorn is taller than the birch, then the spruce is taller than the birch. Moreover, reason, in the form of contemplating or reflecting on certain a priori truths, can yield both situational justification—hence justification for forming beliefs of them—and actual justified beliefs of them. Clearly, reason can also yield knowledge of them.

Reason is, furthermore, a basic source of belief, justification, and knowledge. Like introspection and unlike perception and memory, it is an *active* capacity, in that we may employ it at will; and through reflection we can acquire a vast amount of significant knowledge. Granted, reason yields no knowledge or justified belief until experience, including perception, reflection, and introspection, acquaints one with concepts sufficient for grasping a priori propositions. But despite this genetic dependence of reason on experience, in one way reason may be an even firmer basis of justification and knowledge than experience. For there may be truths of reason that are so simple and luminously self-evident that they *cannot* be unjustifiably believed, at least at a time when one comprehendingly considers them. Could one comprehendingly consider, yet unjustifiably believe, that if Shakespeare is identical with the author of *Hamlet*, then the author of *Hamlet* is identical with Shakespeare? One could believe it partly on the basis of a bad argument; if so, there is something unjustified in the *way* one believes it. But if one believes it, one understands it, and if one understands it, apparently one is justified in believing it, at least at a time when one comprehendingly considers it. If there are propositions like this, then there can apparently be *indefeasible justification*: justification so secure that a belief possessing it, even if it is held in part on the basis of a bad argument, cannot be unjustified. If there is no indefeasible justification, however, at least our understanding of simple self-evident truths of reason gives us both very secure justification for believing them and, when we do believe them, knowledge of them. Reason, then, stands with experience as a basic source, and apparently the only other basic source, of belief, justification, and knowledge.

The Development and Structure of Belief, Justification, and Knowledge

CHAPTER 5

Inference

As I sit reading, I hear knocking. I wonder whether some-
one is at the door. I then hear extended, very rapid knocking. It now occurs to me
that it is a pecking sound, and I realize, and thereby come to believe, that there is
a woodpecker nearby. This way of coming to believe something differs from the
way I came to believe there was a knocking in the first place. That belief was
perceptual, and it arose simply from my hearing the knocking. My belief that
there is a woodpecker nearby, however, is not perceptual. It arises from my
further belief that the rapid knocking sounds like the pecking of a woodpecker. I
hear the rapid knocking, recognize its character, and come to believe that it
sounds like the pecking of a woodpecker. On the basis of this belief, I naturally
conclude that there is a woodpecker nearby. Some beliefs, then, arise from, and
are based on, other beliefs rather than directly on the sources I have described:
perceptual, memorial, introspective, and rational.

INFERENCES AS PSYCHOLOGICAL PROCESSES AND AS PROPOSITIONAL STRUCTURES

What sort of process is it by which my belief that there is a woodpecker arises
from my belief that there is a knocking that sounds like its pecking? One clue is
the naturalness of saying that, on the *basis* of my belief that the knocking is such a
pecking, I *conclude* that there is a woodpecker nearby. I *infer* that there is one
nearby from what I believe about the knocking: that it sounds like the pecking of
a woodpecker. In inferring this, I conclude something on the basis of something

else I believe. *What* I conclude—the conclusion I draw—I in some sense derive from what I believe. The concluding and the beliefs are mental. But neither what I conclude, nor what I believe from which I conclude it, is mental: these things are objects of my beliefs, as they might be of yours, and such objects of beliefs are commonly thought to be propositions.

There are, then, two sorts of things involved when I conclude something: one is the mental process of my concluding it on the basis of one or more beliefs of mine; the other is the two or more propositions which are my conclusion and my ground for it. Call the first item the *inferential process*. Call the second its *inferential content*; for it indicates what is inferred from what, and it does this in a way that shows how *my* inferring that there is a woodpecker nearby is drawing the *same* inference as you would make if you inferred this from the proposition that there is knocking which sounds like that of a woodpecker. Our inferrings are two different processes, one in me and one in you. But their content is the same. I want to talk about inference in both of these senses: as a process and as a structure of propositions.

If inferring is a process corresponding to a conclusion and one or more premises, then should we suppose that in drawing my inference I *said* to myself something like, 'Those knocks sound like a woodpecker's; hence, there is a woodpecker nearby'? This might apply to someone just learning to recognize woodpecker knocking, but not to me. I do not need to concentrate on the proposition that there are those sounds, much less to say to myself something like 'hence there is a woodpecker'. I quickly realize, through hearing the sounds—and remembering what sort of sound a woodpecker makes—that they are its sounds; I briefly entertain this proposition, and on the basis of believing it I draw my conclusion without signposting my doing so by a silent 'hence'. My inference, though it is something I do, is not self-conscious. I need not introspect my doing it. What I do instead is simply draw my conclusion when my ground for it registers in my consciousness: in response to wondering what I hear, I categorize the sounds as a pecking, and I then infer that there is a woodpecker.

Compare this with a case in which, as I am reading on an unusually still morning, a vehicle backfires. I go on reading without thinking about the noise, though I do have the thought that someone drove by after all. Now did I *infer*, while reading, that someone drove by, say on the basis of believing that I heard a vehicle backfire? Surely I *need* not have. If I am familiar with backfires, I might simply have recognized the sound as from a vehicle and, on the basis of my belief that it is, automatically formed the belief that someone drove by.

One might object that I *must* have inferred that someone drove by, from my recognition of the backfire. Granted, this recognition is a ground of my belief that someone drove by. Still, I need not *do* anything that qualifies as drawing a conclusion from it. Recall that I was quite occupied with reading and did not stop even to think about the noise, whereas, in the case of the woodpecker, I focused on the question whether someone was at the door and, when I heard the rapid knocking, listened to it in the light of that question, which I then answered by attributing the knocking to a woodpecker. Moreover, the two *contexts* differ significantly. The backfire is a kind of noise that makes it obvious that someone is driving by, whereas the pecking, far from coinciding with a flutter of wings that mark the presence of a bird, is an isolated stream of sounds in the quiet of the afternoon. Certainly there is an event of *belief formation* when I hear the bang and come to believe that someone is driving by. But I need not form this belief by drawing an inference.

TWO KINDS OF INFERENTIAL BELIEF

The contrast just drawn must not be allowed to obscure something important that is shared by the two kinds of belief formation I have described. In both cases, I believe one thing on the basis of another thing I believe; for instance, I believe that someone drove by on the basis of believing that a vehicle backfired. In both instances, then, there is an inferential *structure* corresponding to my beliefs; it consists of a proposition we might think of as a conclusion and at least one we might think of as a premise from which the conclusion is drawn. This similarity helps to explain why there is an inclination to regard my coming to believe that someone drove by as somehow inferential. Moreover, the notion of a process of inference is not sharp; and sometimes we cannot in practice get enough information about how a belief was formed even to make an educated guess about whether or not it arose from an inference.

There is a way to describe our two examples that will help to remind us of both their similarities and their differences. Call my belief that there is a woodpecker nearby *episodically inferential*, since it arises from a process or episode of inferring, of explicitly drawing a conclusion from something one believes. Call my belief that someone drove by *structurally inferential*, since it is *based on* another belief in much the *way* one belief is based on a second when the first does arise from the second by inference. Being so based implies (among other things) that my holding the second belief, the basis (or premise) belief, is at least part of what explains why I hold the first. Yet my belief that someone drove by is not episodically inferential, because it arises, not from my drawing an inference, but in an automatic way not requiring an occurrent reasoning process. In both cases there is an inferential structure (which is no doubt reflected in the brain) corresponding to my beliefs: I believe the conclusion *because* I believe the premise(s), even though the beliefs are related by an inferential episode in one case and by an automatic process of belief formation in the other. In the first case, I do something—I infer a conclusion; in the second, something *happens* in me—a belief arises on the basis of one or more other beliefs I hold.

Both beliefs, then, are structurally inferential, but only the belief that there is a woodpecker nearby is episodically inferential. To bring out what they have in common I call them *indirect*. For each case I believe one thing on the basis of, and so in a sense *through*, believing another thing. Indirect beliefs are mediated by other beliefs, whether through inference or not. We are talking, of course, about particular beliefs held by specific people at particular times. People differ in their inferential patterns, and in any given person these may also change over time. No doubt one could become so familiar with woodpecker knocks that when one hears them, one just believes they are occurring, rather as, on seeing green grass in good light, I may just believe, perceptually, that there is grass before me. Such effects of increased familiarity show that what one person believes indirectly another may believe directly, and that a kind of proposition we believe indirectly at one time we may believe directly at another. Thus, we cannot in general specify propositions which can be believed *only* in one way, or determine whether a belief is inferential by considering just the proposition believed. It would be *abnormal* to believe (wholly) *in*directly that if some dogs are pets, then some pets are dogs, or to believe directly that there are seventeen cats eating scraps of beef in my grandfather's backyard. But strange cases like these are possible.

THE INFERENTIAL DEVELOPMENT OF BELIEF, JUSTIFICATION, AND KNOWLEDGE

The examples I have given represent one way we *learn* through using our senses in combination with our rational powers. Through making inferences and through forming beliefs that are structurally inferential, we not only acquire new beliefs, but new justified beliefs and new knowledge. Indeed a great many of our justified beliefs and knowledge arise in this way. The woodpecker case illustrates how this process works. In a moment I come to believe, among other things, that no one is at the door and that there is a woodpecker nearby; and I also acquire situational justification for these beliefs, justifiably hold them, and know the truths which, in holding them, I believe. Much of life is like this: through the joint work of perception and our rational powers, particularly our inferential capacities, we acquire new beliefs, our justification is extended, and we gain new knowledge. We also forget, cease to be justified in believing certain things when we cannot remember our evidence, and sometimes infer conclusions we are not entitled to infer. But let us first concentrate on the way belief, justification, and knowledge develop.

Inference is typically a source of new beliefs, but it need not be. Recall the backfire, and suppose I am so familiar with such sounds that no categorization is necessary for me to recognize them and that I *directly*—that is, non-inferentially—believe that a vehicle backfired. But now imagine that, realizing firecrackers have lately been set off nearby, I wonder whether the sound might have been a firecracker's. I recall the sound, remember that it had a muffled, not a popping, quality, and infer from its having that quality that it was indeed a backfire. Here I infer something I already believe. My inference, then, is not a *source* of belief, though it does *change* my belief, which now becomes inferential. My inference is *confirmatory*, but not, as in typical cases, *generative*.

Even when inference is not a source of belief, however, it may still be a source of both justification and knowledge. Again, suppose I know that lately there have been firecrackers exploding nearby. I now might *not* know, or be justified in believing, that there was a vehicle backfire, until I recall the quality of the sound, rule out its being that of a firecracker, and infer in this light that a vehicle backfired. I might thus have neither justification for believing a vehicle backfired, nor knowledge that it did, until I draw the inference.

On the other hand, suppose I am not justified, and indeed am *un*justified, in believing that the muffled sound in question indicates a backfire. My situation might be this: in my whole life I have heard only one backfire; I have, however, heard many firecrackers with that sort of sound; and my belief that this sound indicates a backfire is based on testimony from someone I think is usually unreliable. Here I do not become justified, inferentially or otherwise, in believing that there was a vehicle backfire. For a crucial premise of my inference—that this kind of noise indicates a backfire—is one I am unjustified in believing. The same would hold if I had been unjustified in believing my other premise: that there was a muffled sound.

Now imagine a different case, this time regarding knowledge. Suppose I *am* justified in believing my premise that the muffled sound indicates a backfire, since my previous experience adequately justifies my believing this. But suppose that, through no fault of my own, I have somehow failed to discover that there are common firecrackers which sound to me precisely the same. Then, while I am still correct in believing my conclusion—that there is a backfire—I am *mistaken* in believing, and so do not *know*, my *premise* that such a sound indicates a vehicle backfire. Thus, I infer a true conclusion, but using a premise which, though I justifiably believe it, is false. This example shows how I may be justified (and even correct) in believing that there was a vehicle backfire, yet not *know* that.

This last case is not typical, however. Perhaps more often than not, inference on the part of rational persons yields beliefs that are both justified and constitute knowledge. If inference is often a source of justification and of knowledge, is it a *basic* source? Our example suggests that it is not. If, for instance, I am not justified in believing my premises that there was a muffled sound, and that such a sound indicates a backfire, then my inferring that there was a backfire does not yield justification for my believing this conclusion and I do not justifiably believe it. Apparently my inference justifies me in believing my conclusion only if I am justified in believing its premise (or premises) in the first place.

Points like this suggest that inference is not a basic source of justification or knowledge, but rather *transmits* them in appropriate circumstances. We can *extend* our justification and knowledge by inference. Our examples show two kinds of extension. The first is acquisition of new knowledge and new justified beliefs; the second is increase in our justification for believing something we already hold. A third kind of extension occurs when a belief arises by inference from two or more independent sets of premises, such as testimony from two independent observers. One may be better justified in believing what they jointly testify to than one is in believing any one of them alone. Moreover, our experience often leads to inferential extension of all three sorts without our making any particular effort to draw inferences. For the formation of structurally inferential beliefs, and even of many episodically inferential beliefs, occurs quite often and very naturally. But even careful and amply justified inferences do not *create* justification or knowledge where there is none to start with.

SOURCE CONDITIONS AND TRANSMISSION CONDITIONS

If inference is not a basic source of justification and knowledge, but transmits it, it must meet two kinds of conditions. First, there are *source conditions*, as our examples show: one needs justification or knowledge in the first place. To see what the second kind of condition is, suppose that I do know that the muffled sound I hear indicates a vehicle backfire and I infer that a *truck* backfired. But imagine that I really cannot tell the difference between car and truck backfires. Then I do not know, in virtue of my inference, that a truck backfired. I started with knowledge, but it was not transmitted to my belief of my conclusion, since I drew a conclusion from it which it did not warrant. There are, then, *transmission conditions*, as well as source conditions, that an inference must satisfy in order to yield knowledge. Since Chapters 1 through 4 deal with source conditions in some detail, I will say little about them here and concentrate on transmission conditions.

We can best understand transmission conditions if, as is common in the field of logic, we divide inferences into two categories, deductive and inductive. The usual basis of division (which I adopt only in part) is an interpretation of the character of the inferential structure underlying the process of inference, or at least a choice of the kind of standard appropriate for assessing that structure. We can simplify matters by calling these structures *arguments*, even though, considered in the abstract, they need not represent anyone's actually arguing *for* something or *with* anyone. In this abstract sense, there was argument involved even where, simply to assure myself that I was correct in believing that there was a vehicle backfire rather than a firecracker blast, I inferred, from reconsidering the kind of noise I heard, that there was a backfire. I used an argument even though I was not trying to convince anyone, even myself, of anything. But I was trying to justify something I believed. I did this by tapping a justified source and transmitting its justification to my belief that a vehicle backfired.

A natural interpretation of the case is this: I reasoned from the premises that (1) the noise indicates a backfire and (2) if it does indicate that, then there was a backfire, to the conclusion that (3) there was a backfire. My argument here, and hence my reasoning from its premises to its conclusion, is (deductively) *valid*; that is, it is absolutely impossible for its premises, (1) and (2), to be true and its conclusion, (3), false. For short, the premises of a valid argument (logically) *entail* its conclusion. It is of course not in general impossible for the premises to be false, as it is for some dogs to be pets, yet no pets dogs. But it is absolutely impossible that the premises are true *and* the conclusion false.

In the most common terminology, only deductive reasoning is properly said to be valid; and we might think of deductive reasoning as the sort that "aims" at validity, in the sense that it is of a kind best evaluated as valid or invalid. Thus, even though the argument from hallucination (discussed in Chapter 1) is invalid, the philosophical reasoning that employs it seems meant to be valid and is appropriately assessed as deductive. By contrast, much reasoning that is not valid simply does not appear meant to be deductive in the first place. Suppose, for instance, that my reasoning had run: (A) the noise sounds like that of a backfire; (B) the likely explanation of the noise is that a vehicle backfired; so, probably, (C) a vehicle backfired. As the word 'probably' signals, I do not take my reasoning to be valid or to be deductive at all: I simply take its premises to provide some reason to believe its conclusion. Even if I had not used 'probably', it would be inappropriate to consider the reasoning deductive. For it is obvious that a likely explanation *need* not be considered true; it would thus be a mistake to regard the reasoning—or the person using it—as aiming at validity. We *could* call the reasoning inductively valid, meaning roughly that relative to its premises it is reasonable to accept its conclusion; but to avoid confusion I simply term reasoning of that sort 'inductively good'. Note that it is reasoning processes, and not abstract structures, that I call deductive or inductive. I do not take arguments, as abstract structures, to be intrinsically of either kind, though we *speak* of them as deductive or inductive so far as they seem best assessed by deductive or inductive standards. (The intentions of those presenting them are one among many other factors determining the appropriate standards.)

I want to stress in passing that we should not conceive deductive and inductive reasoning as they have often been characterized. Deductive reasoning has often been described as "going" from the general to the particular, say from (i) all human beings are mortal and (ii) Socrates is a human being to (iii) Socrates is mortal. But our deductive backfire case, embodying the valid argument from (1) and (2) to (3), is different; it is about only particular things. Notice too, that even in the classical example about Socrates, one premise is particular, in the sense that it concerns a single individual. Moreover, even those who take deductive reasoning to go from the general to the particular should recognize that the reasoning from (a) all humans have fears and (b) all who have fears are vulnerable to (c) all humans are vulnerable is deductive (and valid). Perhaps they focus on cases in which we draw a conclusion about something or someone, say Socrates, by *subsuming* the person or thing under a generalization about similar entities, say people. If so, it is better to call such reasoning *subsumptive* (or instantial). As for inductive reasoning, it has often been said to "go from" the particular to the general, as where one bases the conclusion that everyone has fears on the enumerative premises that Abe does, Betty does, Carl does, Donna does, and so on. This characterization is good so far as it goes. But it misses the case of reasoning from the likely explanation of the noise to the conclusion that it is a backfire. Nor does it do justice to certain reasoning *by analogy*, such as my concluding that a plant probably has a property, say hardiness, because it is much like another plant that has that property. It is better, then, to think of inductive reasoning as reasoning that, first, "aims" at providing good grounds for its conclusion, but not at validity, and, second, is best evaluated in terms of the degree of probability of its conclusion relative to its premises. This conception has the further advantage of applying to all three main kinds of inductive reasoning: generalizational, explanational, and analogical.

THE TRANSMISSION OF JUSTIFICATION AND KNOWLEDGE

We can now say something about the conditions for transmission of justification and knowledge. Clearly it is partly a matter of the status of the underlying argument: the one whose premise or premises are one's basis for the belief in question. The natural thing to say initially is that justification and knowledge are transmitted in deductive inference only if the underlying argument is valid and, in inductive inference, only if the underlying argument is (inductively) good. But these views need clarification. Let's consider the two cases separately.

Suppose Joe hastily infers from the propositions that (1) all Marxists admire *Das Kapital* and (2) Adam admires *Das Kapital* that (3) Adam is a Marxist. This is invalid deductive reasoning, and even with true premises it would not transmit either justification or knowledge from beliefs of them to a belief of its conclusion. Suppose Joe then produces the better argument from (i) most Marxists admire *Das Kapital* and (ii) Adam is a Marxist to (iii) Adam admires *Das Kapital*. If we conceive his reasoning as deductive, say because Joe's underlying principle is not the expected inductive one—that if most As are Bs and x is an A, then probably x is a B—but the false one that if most As are Bs, and x is an A, then x *is* a B, then we must also say that transmission is blocked because his reasoning is invalid. He employs a mistaken (deductive) logical standard. Apparently, then, *deductive transmission requires validity*; specifically, the argument underlying an inferential belief must be valid if knowledge or justification is to be deductively transmitted to that belief from the belief(s) it is based on.

The case with inductive reasoning is more complicated. For one thing, the notion of good inductive reasoning is vague. It might seem that we could simply define it as reasoning with premises that render its conclusion more likely than not to be true. But this will not do, though such reasoning may be called *probable* to indicate that it has this specific merit. For one thing, a probability of just over .50 allows that even given the truth of the premises, the falsehood of the conclusion is almost as likely as its truth (since probabilities range from 0 to 1, with .50 representing as great a likelihood of truth as of falsehood). For another thing, judging how good the reasoning is may require assessing the conclusion in relation to more than the premises. Relative just to the premise that Dave has a certain kind of cancer, the probability of the conclusion that he will die of it may be .60, since 60 percent of its victims do; but relative to his youth, vigor, and treatment, the probability of his death may be .08. Thus, the inductive reasoning from the premise that he has the particular cancer to the conclusion that he will die of it is not good, even though the conclusion does have a probability of more than .50 relative to its premise.

Suppose we assume for a moment that good inductive reasoning has premises taking account of *all* the relevant evidence. May we then conclude that justification and knowledge are inductively transmitted only by good inductive reasoning? This view is too strong. For it may often happen that some of the relevant evidence is not needed for such inductive justification of one's belief because one's premises already contain quite sufficient evidence. Evidence may be relevant to a belief without being needed for its justification, as where testimony from a tenth witness who agrees with the rest is unnecessary. The point is important; for even if we can understand the notion of *all* the relevant evidence, we at best rarely have all the evidence relevant to a belief.

Is good inductive reasoning *sufficient* to transmit justification? Unfortunately, it may not be, particularly if the reasoning is extended through many inferences. To see why, notice first that the *degree* of justification inductively transmitted from one's premises to one's conclusion may drop, even if nothing new enters the picture, such as someone's challenging one's conclusion the moment one draws it. The degree of justification may drop because, even if one starts with excellent justification for one's premises, if they give only a probability of, say, .75 to one's conclusion, one will have much weaker justification for the conclusion than for the premises, if they are one's *only* basis for it. (I am assuming, somewhat artificially, that justification admits of degrees in the way probability does.) Roughly, one should take the chance that the conclusion is true to be only 75 percent of the chance that the premises are true. It is now apparent how good inductive reasoning, carried out through a series of inferences, can fail to transmit justification from its initial premises to its final conclusion. Even if the probability the initial premises give to the first conclusion is .90, if one went on inferring further conclusions, each being a premise for the next, then even with the same degree of probability in each case, one could eventually infer a conclusion for which one has less justification than .50. For with each case the likelihood that one's conclusion is true would be 10 percent less than for one's previous conclusion.

In some respects, the case of *knowledge* differs from that of justification. Since knowledge does not admit of degrees (at least not in the way justification does), it might be transmitted across an inductive inference without diminution in degree even if such transmission does imply some reduction in one's justification (other things being equal). If, for instance, you know that the weather is bad and you inductively infer that Jane, who is driving, will be late, you could know the latter proposition on the basis of the former even though there is a very slight chance that she left early and compensated for the weather. Your *grounds* for your premise may be better than your grounds for your conclusion and may render it only very probable, rather than entailing it; but you may still unqualifiedly know your conclusion. This knowledge may not be as good, say as securely grounded, as your knowledge of the premises; for instance, it might not be as nearly certain. But it *can* still be knowledge.

On the other hand, knowledge might not be transmitted even across an inductive inference whose premises give its conclusion extremely high probability. For example, you might know that you hold just one out of a million coupons in a fair sweepstakes which will have one winner. You may inductively infer, with very high probability, .999999, that you will lose, since 999,999 of the million coupons will. But you do not *know* you will lose. You might be lucky; and you have as good a chance to be lucky as any other holder of a single coupon. Your knowledge of your premises, then, is not inductively transmitted to your conclusion. (If we change the example so that you *deduce* the qualified statement that the probability of your losing is .999999, you may know that. But that is a different conclusion.)

We have seen some important points. Inference transmits justification and knowledge; it is not a basic source of them. It can generate them only derivatively, by transmission, from knowledge and justification already possessed. Inference can originate knowledge or justified belief in the sense that the beliefs in question are new to the believer, but not—as the basic sources of knowledge and justification can—from something other than belief, such as perception. Deductive transmission apparently requires validity; and inductive transmission apparently requires an inductive counterpart of validity, something like a strong relation of support between premises and conclusion. But even where the support is strong, the degree of justification may drop in a way that it need not drop in the deductive case.

As our examples show, to understand the transmission of justification and knowledge we must consider two sorts of conditions: those necessary for transmission of knowledge and justification, conditions such that transmission occurs *only* if they are met by an inference; and sufficient conditions, those such that if they are met by an inference, then transmission *does* occur. It is even harder to specify sufficient conditions than necessary ones. For a sufficient condition must "cover" all the necessary ones: if it does not imply that each of them holds, it leaves out something necessary, and so is not sufficient. Let me simply suggest the sort of thing we must add to what we so far have in order to arrive at sufficient conditions for inferential transmission.

This time it will help to take inductive cases first. Might we say that if, by good inductive reasoning, one infers something from premises which take account of all the relevant evidence, then if one justifiably believes (or is at least justified in believing) those premises, one is justified in believing the conclusion? *If* justification is like knowledge in this respect, the answer is negative. The sweepstakes example shows that, even when the probability is very high, the counterpart of this condition, with knowledge substituted for justification, does not hold. But the condition is plausible for justification. In that same case, for instance, one *may* justifiably believe one will lose.

Let us see what we can learn from a different example. Imagine that I enter my house and find evidence of a burglary, such as ransacked drawers. I infer that valuables have been stolen. From that I infer that the $20 in my little daughter's piggy bank is missing. And from that in turn I infer that my daughter will be upset. At each point I am justified in believing my premise and, it would seem, make a good inductive inference from it. In most such cases, my justification would carry right down the line from my initial premise to my final conclusion. But it need not. There is a chance that the bank was overlooked and a chance that my daughter will be calm, if only because she is so grateful that important things, like the teddy bears, are undisturbed. Could it not be that at each step my justification for my conclusion drops in such a way that, unlike my inference that I will lose the sweepstakes, my last inference fails to produce a justified conclusion? As one goes along, the crucially relevant evidence, the evidence one must take into account, may mount up or at least change. For instance, by the time I get to the question whether my daughter will be upset about the piggy bank, it becomes relevant to note that the teddy bears are unharmed before inferring that she will be upset, whereas this would not have been relevant if the disappearance of the piggy bank were the only disturbance in the house.

But how should we decide what is relevant, and how one's justification is affected by ignoring only some of what is relevant? This is a hard question which I can only partially answer. But one positive point is this: whether one is inferentially justified in holding a conclusion one draws depends on many factors, including some *not* expressed in one's premises. One's believing the premises may be the origin of one's belief and a source of one's justification. But there are other relevant factors—such as what one knows, or should know, about what will preoccupy the child on discovering the burglary. One's justification ultimately depends on complex relations among all the relevant factors. We might say that while justification may emerge from a straight inferential line, it will do so only if the line figures in the right kind of *pattern* of related beliefs and available relevant information.

DEDUCTIVE TRANSMISSION

Let us turn now to deductive transmission. One might think that valid deductive inference is sufficient as well as necessary for transmitting justification and knowledge. Certainly it often does transmit them, as where one learns theorems by validly deducing them in doing geometrical proofs. I do not mean that whenever *there is* a valid inference, in the sense of 'a set of propositions constituting a valid argument', from something one believes to a conclusion, then one "implicitly" knows the conclusion, or even has situational justification for believing it. If that were so, then simply by knowing the axioms of Euclidean geometry (which are quite simple), one might implicitly know, and be justified in believing, all its theorems (assuming these theorems are all within one's comprehension, since one cannot believe or, at the time, even be justified *in* believing a theorem too complex for one to understand). The main issue here is about the transmission of justification and knowledge from justified beliefs, or from beliefs constituting knowledge, to other beliefs *arrived at* by inference, not about transmission of situational justification or "implicit" knowledge to propositions that one *could* infer from those one knows or justifiably believes.

But even if we restrict our concern to transmission of knowledge across inference processes, it is at least not obvious that knowledge is always transmitted across valid deductive inferences (I mean, of course, the non-trivial kind, which have consistent premises none of which is equivalent to the conclusion). Recall our example of the backfire. Suppose that I am sufficiently acquainted with the sound to *know* that it is a backfire. Then, from what I know, it follows that it is not the sound of a firecracker with a similar muffled sound. Suppose that, aware that this follows, I infer that it is not such a sound. Do I know that it is not? What if I have no evidence that there is no one around setting off such firecrackers? At most, I can say from general experience that this is improbable. It is not clear that, simply through validly concluding it from my inferential ground, I know that the sound is not that of a firecracker with a similar muffled quality. One might now say that this just shows that I did not know in the first place that a vehicle backfired. But I do not see that we must say that. It may be equally plausible to say that because one *now* realizes that one's basis for believing this might not have been decisive, one *no longer* knows it, yet did not know it in the first place.

Consider a different case. I add a column of fifteen figures, check my results twice, and thereby come to know, and justifiably believe, that the sum is 10,952. As it happens, I sometimes make mistakes, and my wife (whom I justifiably believe to be a better arithmetician) sometimes corrects me. Suppose that, feeling unusually confident, I now infer that if my wife says this is not the sum, she is wrong. From the truth that the sum is 10,952, it certainly follows that if she says it is not, she is wrong. If it *is* the sum, then if she denies it, she is wrong. But even though I know and justifiably believe that this is the sum, can I, on this basis, *automatically* know or justifiably believe the *further* proposition that if she says that it is not the sum, she is wrong? Suppose my checking just twice is only enough to give me the *minimum* basis for justified belief and knowledge here. Surely I would then not have sufficient grounds for the further proposition that if she says the answer is wrong, she is wrong.

One way to interpret the example is this. To be justified in believing that if she says the sum is not 10,952, she is wrong, or to know or justifiably believe this about her, I need grounds good enough not to be outweighed by the supposition that she (the better arithmetician) says that 10,952 is not the sum. In inferring that if she says it is not the sum, she is wrong, I *am* making the supposition that she says it. I need not believe she will; but because I am supposing she will, I am justified in believing that if she does, she is wrong, only if my justification for believing that the sum *is* 10,952 is good enough to withstand the supposition that she denies it is the sum. This supposition is implicit in my belief that if she says this, she is wrong; but under the supposed conditions, her justification is good enough to reduce mine below the threshold which it just barely reaches.

Again, one might now object that I really do not know or have justified belief in the first place. That might be true if I have checked my sum only twice. But suppose that carefully checking three or four times is required to reach the threshold. For *any* reasonable standard of justification or knowledge, there will be a point where I *just* meet, and do not exceed, that standard, and I will then not be justified in believing the further proposition that if she says the sum is wrong, then she is wrong. This point concerns situational justification. It is also true that if I infer this further proposition without first getting *additional* grounds for my answer, I would not know *or* justifiably believe it.

The example can be varied to make the same point in a different way. If the sum *is* 10,592, then even if there are two mistakes in the calculations I made to get it, it is *still* 10,592. This may sound strange, but the mistakes could cancel each other, say because one mistake yields a 9 instead of the correct 7, and the other yields a 6 instead of the correct 8. Now imagine that again I justifiably believe that the sum is 10,592 and know this (I have been careful enough and have not actually made any errors). Perhaps simply to test my intuitions about deductive transmission, I might infer that (even) if there are two errors in my calculation, the sum is 10,592. Surely I do not know or justifiably believe this; nor did my original, minimal justification give me situational justification for believing it.

Cases of this sort strongly argue that, first, justification and knowledge *need* not be transmitted through valid reasoning from known premises, and second, situational justification is not automatically transmitted even to propositions obviously entailed by those we are justified in believing. But typically, transmission does occur in both of these cases, and it is difficult to say under just what conditions it does not. The general point, however, is that whether one is justified in believing something, or knows it, depends not only on one's specific evidence for it but also on a pattern of factors including one's relation to the proposition itself and one's specific circumstances.

MEMORIAL PRESERVATION OF INFERENTIAL JUSTIFICATION AND KNOWLEDGE

Let me conclude by introducing a further point that applies to both deductive and inductive inferential transmission. Imagine that you learn something, say a theorem, by validly inferring it from something you know, say a set of axioms. You may remember the axioms *as* your grounds; then your memory preserves both your premises and your conclusion. But eventually you may forget your grounds, for instance how you proved, and even how *to* prove, a theorem. Similarly, you forget the testimony or book from which you learned, perhaps by inductive inference partly based on the premise that the book is reliable, that the Battle of Hastings was in 1066. Can you still know and justifiably believe these things?

The answer in both cases is surely that you can. Memory can retain beliefs *as* knowledge, and as justified beliefs, even if it does not retain the original grounds of the relevant beliefs. But because it does not retain the grounds, and no new grounds need be added, it does not necessarily retain the beliefs *as* inferential. Moreover, where the grounds are not retained and none are added, one might find it at best difficult to indicate *how* one knows, beyond insisting that, say, one is sure one remembers, perhaps adding that one certainly did have grounds in the past. But so long as one did have adequate grounds and *does* remember the proposition, surely one may justifiably believe, and know, that proposition.

This example is another illustration of the point that a belief which is inferential at one time may be non-inferential at another. This may happen repeatedly with the same belief. Long after a belief, for instance a belief of a theorem, has ceased to be inferential, one could acquire new grounds for it, such as that one has a clear recollection of a mathematical friend's affirming the theorem. One could later forget the new grounds also, and simply remember the theorem. If one's memory of it is very indistinct, however, the result might be that one has only belief which not only does not constitute knowledge but also is only weakly justified if justified at all. Often, however, the new beliefs, justification, and knowledge we acquire by inference may be retained even when their inferential grounds are long forgotten. This applies, of course, to structurally inferential belief as well as to episodically inferential belief.

At any given moment in waking life, we have basic sources of belief, if only the stream of our own consciousness. As we experience the world around us and our own interactions with it, new beliefs arise, both from basic sources and inferentially. As rational beings, we are almost constantly forming beliefs on the basis of other beliefs, whether through a process of inference or only through acquiring structurally inferential beliefs. Both deductive and inductive inference are common. Both transmit justification and knowledge when they give rise to beliefs on the basis of reasoning which meets the appropriate deductive, inductive, and evidential standards. This seems to occur quite commonly, and we have a vast store of indirect and indirectly justified beliefs. False and unwarranted beliefs arise from some inferences. But from many inferences we learn something new and thereby enlarge, strengthen, and develop our body of knowledge and justified beliefs.

The Structure of Knowledge

I hear a rustling in the darkness outside my window. It is the leaves. I realize that there is a wind. My belief that there is a wind is based on my belief that the leaves are rustling. It is also justified on the basis of my belief that they are rustling. And if I know that there is a wind, I know it on the basis of my belief that the leaves are rustling. In each case one belief is inferentially based on another. For even though I need not go through a process of drawing an inference, the relation between the two beliefs is like the one which would hold between them if I considered the proposition that the leaves are rustling and, using my knowledge that this is due to wind, conclude that there is a wind. My belief that there is a wind, then, is inferential; and so is my knowledge that it is and my justification for believing that it is.

INFERENTIAL CHAINS AND THE STRUCTURE OF BELIEF

I call the kind of belief, justification, and knowledge just illustrated *indirect*. For one has such beliefs, justification, and knowledge only on the basis of, and thereby *through*, other beliefs, justification, or knowledge. That point holds whether or not there is any process of inference. The point applies to both episodically and structurally inferential beliefs. By contrast, my belief that there is a rustling sound is direct. I believe this simply because I hear the sound, not on the basis of something else I believe. To be sure, my belief of this *could* be indirect; if I am in a cautious mood, I could suspend judgment on it and then, on reflection, again believe it, but this time on the basis of believing that I have a vivid auditory impression of rustling. If it is so based, then it will be justified, and will constitute knowledge, only if the belief it is based on is justified and constitutes knowledge. Could *all* my beliefs be indirect, however? And could all justification of belief, and all our knowledge, be indirect? These are questions about the *structure* of a body of belief, justification, or knowledge, and I want to pursue them in detail.

In exploring these questions of structure, I want to talk above all about knowledge and justification, and especially about knowledge. But what we know (propositionally) we believe; and the kind of justification epistemology is chiefly concerned with is that of belief. The structure of my knowledge, then, is that of a certain body of my beliefs, namely, those that constitute my knowledge.

I am not talking about knowledge in the abstract, for instance about the body of scientific knowledge, that is, of propositions scientifically known. Some of this knowledge might be solely in books, expressed in formulas no one remembers. Thus, some scientific knowledge might be of propositions no one actually believes. This kind of knowledge can even survive the death of all its possessors, though it cannot antedate their birth. It must be discovered. But once discovered, it may remain in our records past all memory. We *can* talk about the structure of such knowledge in the abstract, say about whether all the propositions of scientific knowledge can be systematized so that some are like the axioms of a geometry and the rest like its theorems. But that is not my topic. I am exploring how people's beliefs may actually be structured.

I want to approach the question whether all our beliefs could be indirect through a simple example. When I am being very cautious, my belief that there is a rustling could be based on my belief that I have an auditory impression of rustling. Could the latter belief also be based on another one? What might that be? It was only by exercising caution that I thought of something to serve as a basis of my belief that there was rustling. Might I now believe that it *seems* to me that I have an auditory impression of rustling, and base my belief that I have that impression on this new belief? This is doubtful. I cannot base one belief on another simply because I want to.

Even if I could base one belief of mine on another at will, how far could such a sequence of beliefs go? Could I believe the involuted proposition that it appears to me that it seems to me that I have an auditory impression of rustling? I suppose I could, though not simply at will. But again, I do not see that I would now come to hold anything on the *basis* of believing this strange proposition. Suppose, however, that I did come to hold, on the basis of this proposition, that it seems to me that I have an impression of rustling. I cannot manufacture an *inferential chain* of beliefs in this way to infinity. Nor do I already have an infinite set of appropriate beliefs as raw material waiting to be brought to consciousness—if indeed I can have an *infinite* number of beliefs (particularly outside mathematics).

So far, however, I have ignored the possibility that every belief is indirect by virtue of a circle. Imagine that I could hold one belief on the basis of a second and a second on the basis of a third, and so on, until we come full circle and get to a belief I hold on the basis of the first. Then all my beliefs would be indirect, yet I need not have infinitely many beliefs. To assess this, recall my belief that there is a rustling. Might there be a circle here? For instance, could my belief that it appears to me that it seems to me that I have an auditory impression of rustling be based on my belief that there is a rustling? There is good reason to doubt this.

Suppose for the sake of argument that I do have a circular chain of beliefs, each based on the next. This raises a problem. First, there is good reason to think that (a) one belief is based on a second only if the second is at least in part causally responsible for (one's holding) the first. For instance, if I believe there is a wind, on the basis of my believing that the leaves are rustling, then I believe that there is a wind, at least in part *because* I believe that the leaves are rustling. Second, there is good reason to think that (b) if one thing is in part causally responsible for a second and the second is in part causally responsible for a third, then the first is in part causally responsible for the third. But together these two points imply that (c) in a circular chain of beliefs, each based on the next, every belief is in part causally responsible for, and thus a partial cause of, itself. That seems impossible. Let us explore how such a circle might go in a simple case.

Imagine a circle of three beliefs, each based on the next. (1) I believe there is a wind. I believe this on the basis of (2) my believing there is a rustling; I believe that there is a rustling, on the basis of (3) my believing I have an impression of rustling; and I believe that I have this impression, on the basis of believing there is a wind. This case would be a *circular causal chain*, one whose last link is connected to its first in the same way each is connected to its successor. For, given point (a), belief (1) is in part causally responsible for belief (3), and, given point (b), (3) is in part causally responsible for (1). This implies, however, given (b), that (1) is in part causally responsible for itself! That is apparently impossible. The belief would be (in part) pulling itself up by its bootstraps. If such circular causal chains are not possible, then there cannot be a circular chain of beliefs each based on the next; for the latter kind of chain implies the former, on our highly plausible assumptions, (a) through (c). (We have not assumed that the imagined chain implies that some belief must be *based* on itself, only that such chains imply a belief's being in part causally responsible for itself; the basis relation implies more than a causal connection.)

One might think that a belief of a self-evident proposition can be in part causally responsible for itself. But this seems at best an inaccurate way of saying that such a proposition is not believed because one believes something *else*; that is normally so, and normally one believes it because one grasps the appropriate conceptual relation(s). In any case, our concern is beliefs in general, not just beliefs of self-evident propositions. On balance, then, it is reasonable to conclude not only that we *have* direct beliefs, such as beliefs about colors before us and beliefs of self-evident propositions, but also that we could not have *only* indirect beliefs.

THE EPISTEMIC REGRESS PROBLEM

Is knowledge like belief in this, so that some of it is direct, or could all our knowledge be indirect, that is, based on other knowledge we have? It may seem that this is possible, and that there can be an infinite *epistemic regress*—roughly, an infinite series of knowings each based on the next. It is especially likely to appear that indirect knowledge need not always be based on direct knowledge, if one stresses that, very commonly, 'How do you know?' can be repeatedly answered, and one supposes that we stop answering only for practical reasons having to do with our patience or ingenuity. Let us explore this issue by supposing that there is indirect knowledge and seeing what this implies.

Imagine that a belief constituting indirect knowledge is based on knowledge of something else, or at least on a further belief; the further knowledge or belief might be based on knowledge of, or belief about, something still further, and so on. Call this sequence an *epistemic chain*; it is simply a chain of beliefs, with at least the first constituting knowledge, and each belief linked to the previous one by being based on it. Now it is often held that there are just four possible kinds of epistemic chain, two kinds that are unanchored and do not end, and two kinds that are anchored and do end. First, an epistemic chain might be infinite, hence entirely unanchored. Second, it might be circular, hence also unanchored. Third, it might end with a belief that is not knowledge—thus anchored in sand. Fourth, it might end with a belief that constitutes direct knowledge—thus anchored in bedrock. Our task is to assess these chains as possible sources of knowledge or justification. This is a version of *the epistemic regress problem*.

The first possibility is difficult to appreciate. Even if I could have an infinite number of beliefs, how would I ever know anything if knowledge required an infinite epistemic chain? To know, and thus to *learn*, the simplest kind of thing, such as that there is green before me, I would apparently have to know an infinite number of things. It is doubtful that, given our psychological makeup, we can know, or even believe, infinitely many things. It might seem that we can have an infinite set of arithmetical beliefs, say that 2 is larger than 1, that 3 is larger than 2, and so forth. But surely for a finite mind there will be some point or other at which the relevant proposition cannot be grasped. It would be too "long" to understand and so cumbersome that one could not even take in a formulation of it, being unable to remember enough about the first part of it when one gets to the end. What we cannot understand we cannot believe; and what we cannot believe we cannot know.

Even if we could have infinite sets of beliefs, however, infinite epistemic chains apparently do not account for all, and probably not for any, of our knowledge. In the case of some beliefs, such as that if some dogs are pets, some pets are dogs, I cannot even find *any* belief that yields another link. The proposition is self-evident, and it is difficult even to imagine a further proposition on the basis of which I could believe it. It is not clear how this belief could be grounded, as knowledge, by any chain, much less by an infinite one.

Indeed, it is not clear how infinite epistemic chains would help to account for any other knowledge (or justified belief). Notice that many kinds of infinite chains are possible. No one has provided a plausible account of what kind might generate justification or knowledge. But some restrictions are badly needed. For an infinite chain can be imagined for *any* proposition. Thus, even for a proposition one believes to be obviously false, one would find it easy to form beliefs to back it up; and though one could not continue doing this to infinity, one could nonetheless claim that one *has* the infinite set required to support the original belief. Take the obviously false proposition that I weigh at least 500 pounds. I could back up a belief of this by claiming that if I weigh at least 500.001 pounds, then I weigh at least 500 (which is self-evident), and that I *do* weigh at least 500.001 pounds. I could in turn "defend" this by appeal to the propositions that I weigh at least 500.002 pounds, and that if I do, then I weigh at least 500.001. And so forth, until the challenger is exhausted. A chain like this can be infinite; hence, no matter how ridiculous a proposition I claim to know, there is no way to catch me with a claim I cannot back up in the same way. Given such resources, anything goes. But nothing is accomplished.

The possibility of a circular epistemic chain as a basis of knowledge has been taken much more seriously. It might seem that if there cannot be a circular causal chain of indirect beliefs, each based on the next, then there cannot be a circular epistemic chain either. But perhaps my *knowledge* that there is a wind could be somehow based on my belief that the leaves are rustling, even though my *belief* that there is a wind is not based on any further belief. We would then have a circle of knowledge, but not of belief, and no causal bootstraps problem. If this is possible, it may turn out to be important. But how realistic is it?

Does any of our knowledge really emerge from circular epistemic chains? Let's try to go full circle. I know there is a wind. I know this on the basis of the rustling of the leaves. Now I think I know they are rustling because I *hear* them. But it might be argued that I just do not notice that I really know it on the basis of, say, my knowledge that I have an impression of rustling. Perhaps. But how far can this go? I do not see how to go full circle, unless I *think up* propositions I do not *originally* believe, hence do not originally know. And suppose I do think up a suitable set, come to know them, and make my way full circle. Suppose, for instance, that I get as far as knowledge that it seems to me that I have an auditory impression of rustling. Might I know this on the basis of knowing that there is a wind (the first link)? It is doubtful. I apparently know introspectively, not perceptually, that I have the impression. Moreover, there being a wind is not, by itself, even a good reason to believe that I have an impression of rustling. Other difficulties beset the circular approach. But these cast sufficient doubt on it to suggest that we consider the remaining alternatives.

The third possibility, that an epistemic chain terminates in a belief which is not knowledge, can be best understood if we recall that in discussing the transmission of knowledge, we noted both source conditions and transmission conditions. If the third possibility can be realized, then knowledge can originate through a belief of a premise which is not known. I might, for example, know that there is a wind, on the basis of believing that there is a rustling, even though I do not know that there is a rustling. The regress is thus stopped by grounding knowledge on something else, but not in the *way* it is normally grounded in experience or reason. Is this possible? In one kind of case it is not. Suppose I simply guess that the sound I hear is a rustling, but happen to be right. Might I then know there is a wind anyway, provided there is? Surely not; knowledge cannot be grounded in such guesswork, even when the guess is correct.

Imagine, however, that while I do not know there is a rustling, I do hear some sounds that might indicate rustling, and I make an *educated* guess and am thereby justified, to *some* extent, in believing that there is. If, on the basis of this somewhat justified belief that there is a rustling, I now believe that there is a wind, and there is, do I know this? The answer is not clear. But that would be no help to proponents of the third possibility who claim that knowledge can arise from belief which does not constitute knowledge. For it is equally unclear, and for the same sort of reason, whether my guess that there is a rustling is *sufficiently* educated—say, in terms of how good my evidence is—to give me knowledge that there is a rustling. If it is clear that my guess is not sufficiently educated to yield this knowledge, then I also do not know there is a wind. If it is clear that the guess is educated enough, I apparently do know that there is a wind, but my knowledge would be based on other knowledge, hence would not realize the third possibility.

Notice something else. In the only cases in which the third kind of chain is at all likely to ground knowledge, there *is* a degree—perhaps a substantial degree—of justification. If there can be an epistemic chain which ends with belief that is not knowledge only because the chain ends, in this way, with justification, then it appears that we are at least in the general vicinity of knowledge. We are at most a few degrees of justification away. The sand has turned out to be rather firm.

The fourth possibility is the one apparently favored by common sense: epistemic chains end in direct knowledge. That knowledge, in turn, is apparently grounded in experience or in reason, and this non-inferential grounding explains how it is (epistemically) direct: it arises, directly, from perception, memory, introspection, or reason. In any case, the ground-level knowledge could not be inferential; otherwise the chain would not end without a further link. To illustrate, normally I know that there is a rustling just because I hear it. Hence, the chain grounding my knowledge that there is a wind is anchored in my perception. Such experientially or rationally grounded epistemic chains may differ in many ways. They differ in composition, in the sorts of beliefs constituting them. They differ in the kind of transmission they exhibit; it may be deductive, inductive, or combine both deductive and inductive links. They also differ in their ultimate grounds, the anchors of the chains, which may be experiential or rational, and may vary in justificational strength.

Different proponents of the fourth possibility have held various views about the character of the *foundational knowledge*, that is, of the beliefs constituting the knowledge that makes up the final link of the chain and anchors it in experience or reason. Some, for instance, have thought that the appropriate beliefs must be infallible, or at least indefeasibly justified. But this is not implied by anything said here: all that the fourth possibility requires is direct knowledge, knowledge not based on other knowledge (or other justified belief). Direct knowledge need not be of self-evident (thus in a sense "self-justified") propositions, nor constituted by indefeasibly justified belief. The case of introspective beliefs shows this. The proposition that I am now thinking about knowledge is not self-evident, not even to me since I realize that my reflections can sometimes merge into daydreaming. But I do have direct knowledge of that proposition.

| THE EPISTEMIC REGRESS ARGUMENT

What we have just seen suggests a version of what is called the *epistemic regress argument*. It starts with the assumption that (1) if one has any knowledge, it occurs in an epistemic chain (possibly including the special case of a single link, such as a perceptual or a priori belief, which constitutes knowledge by virtue of being anchored directly in one's experience or reason). It then states that (2) the only possible kinds of epistemic chains are the four mutually exclusive kinds just discussed: the infinite, the circular, those terminating in beliefs that are not knowledge, and those terminating in direct knowledge. It affirms that (3) knowledge can occur only in the fourth kind of chain; and it concludes that (4) if one has any knowledge, one has some direct knowledge. Assuming knowledge requires a knower, we may also draw the more general conclusion that if there *is* any knowledge, there is some direct knowledge. A similar argument was advanced by Aristotle (in the *Posterior Analytics*, Books I and II), and versions of the regress argument have been defended ever since.

As proponents of the argument normally understand (1), it implies that any given instance of indirect knowledge depends on at least one epistemic chain for its status *as* knowledge. So understood, the argument clearly implies the further conclusion that any indirect knowledge a person has *epistemically depends on*, in the sense that it cannot be knowledge apart from, an appropriate inferential connection, via some epistemic chain, to some direct knowledge that the person has. Thus, the argument would show not only that if there is indirect knowledge, there *is* direct knowledge, but also that if there is indirect knowledge, that very knowledge is *traceable* to some direct knowledge as its foundation.

A similar argument applies to justification. We simply speak of *justificatory chains* and proceed in a parallel way, substituting justification for knowledge; and we arrive at the conclusion that if one has any justified beliefs, one has some directly justified beliefs. Similarly, if one has any indirectly justified belief, it exhibits *justificational dependence* on an epistemic chain appropriately linking it to some directly justified belief one has, that is, to a foundational belief.

FOUNDATIONALISM AND COHERENTISM

These two sets of conclusions constitute the heart of the position called *epistemological foundationalism*. The first set, concerning knowledge, may be interpreted as the twofold thesis that the structure of a body of knowledge, such as yours or mine, is foundational, and therefore that any indirect (hence non-foundational) knowledge there is depends on direct (and thus in a sense foundational) knowledge. The second set, regarding justification, may be interpreted as the twofold thesis that the structure of a body of justified beliefs is foundational, and therefore that any indirectly (hence non-foundationally) justified beliefs there are depend on directly (thus in a sense foundationally) justified beliefs. In both cases different foundationalist theories may diverge in the kind and degree of dependence they assert. A strong foundationalist theory of justification, for instance, might hold that indirectly justified beliefs derive *all* their justification from foundational beliefs; a moderate theory might maintain only that the former would not be justified apart from the latter, and the theory might allow other factors, such as coherence of a belief with others one holds that are *not* in the chain, to add to its justification.

None of the foundationalist theses I have stated says anything about the *content* of a body of knowledge or of justified belief, though proponents of foundationalism usually specify, as René Descartes (1596–1650) does in his *Meditations*, what sorts of content they think appropriate. Foundationalism thus leaves open what, in particular, is believed by a given person who has knowledge or justified belief and what *sorts* of propositions are suitable material for the foundational beliefs. I want to talk mainly about foundationalism regarding knowledge, but much of what I say can be readily applied to justified belief.

Foundationalism has been criticized on a number of points. I want to focus in particular on the most important objections that stem from the best alternative theory of the structure of knowledge, *coherentism*. There are many versions of coherentism, including some that seem mainly based on the idea that if an epistemic circle is large enough and sufficiently rich, it can generate justification and account for knowledge. But we have seen serious difficulties besetting circular chains. Let us therefore try to formulate a more plausible version of coherentism.

The central idea underlying coherentism is that the justification of a belief emerges from its coherence with other beliefs one holds. The unit of coherence may be as large as one's entire set of beliefs (though of course some may figure more significantly in producing the coherence than others, say because of differing degrees of closeness in their subject matter). This idea would be accepted by a proponent of the circular view, but the thesis I want to explore differs from that view in not being *linear*: it does not construe justification or knowledge as emerging from an inferential line going from premises to that conclusion, and from other premises to the first set of premises, and so on, until we return to the original proposition as a premise. On the circular view, no matter how wide the circle, there is a *line* from any one belief in a circular epistemic chain to any other. In practice one may never trace the entire line, as by inferring one thing one knows from a second, the second from a third, and so on, until one reinfers the first. Still, on this view there is such a line for every belief that constitutes knowledge. Thus, the kinds of problems we encountered earlier regarding circular epistemic chains must be resolved if the view is to be sustained.

HOLISTIC COHERENTISM

Coherentism need not be linear. It may be *holistic*. To see how a holistic theory of knowledge (and justification) works, consider a question that evokes a justification. John wonders how I know, as I sit reading, that the wind is blowing. I say that the leaves are rustling. He then asks how I know that Sally is not just shaking down apples. I reply that the apple trees are too far away. He now wonders whether I can distinguish rustling leaves from the sound of a quiet car on the pebbled driveway. I reply that what I hear is too much like a whisper to be the crunchy sound of pebbles. In giving this justification I apparently go only one step along the inferential line: just to my belief that the leaves are rustling. For my belief that there is a wind *is* based on this belief about the leaves. After that, I do not even mention anything that this belief, in turn, is based on; rather, I defend my beliefs as appropriate, in terms of an entire pattern of beliefs I hold. And I may cite many different parts of the pattern. For instance, I might have said that a shaken tree sounds different from a windblown one. On the coherentist view then, beliefs representing knowledge do not lie at one end of a grounded chain; they fit a coherent pattern, and their justification emerges from their fitting that pattern in an appropriate way.

Consider a different sort of example. A gift is delivered to you with its card apparently missing. The only people you can think of who send you gifts at this time of year live in Washington and virtually never leave there, but this is from Omaha. That origin does not cohere well with your hypothesis that it was sent by your Washington benefactors, the Smiths. Then you open it and discover that it is frozen steak. You realize that this can be ordered from anywhere. But it is not the sort of gift you would expect from the Smiths. A moment later you recall that you recently sent them cheese. You suppose that they probably are sending something in response. Suddenly you remember that they once asked if you had ever tried frozen gourmet steaks, and when you said you hadn't they replied that they would have to serve you some one of these days. You might now be justified in believing that they sent the package. When you at last find their card at the bottom of the box, then (normally) you would *know* that they sent the package. The crucial things to notice here are how, initially, a kind of *incoherence* prevents justification of your first hypothesis (that the box came from the Smiths) and how, as relevant pieces of the pattern developed, you became justified and (presumably) came to know that the Smiths sent it. Arriving at a justified belief, on this view, is more like answering a question in the light of a whole battery of relevant information than like deducing a theorem by successive inferential steps from a set of axioms.

It is important to see how, using examples like those just given, holistic coherentism can respond to the regress argument. It need *not* embrace the possibility of an epistemic circle (though its proponents need not reject that either). Instead, it can deny that there are only the four kinds of possible epistemic chains I specified. There is a fifth: that the chain terminates with belief that is *psychologically direct* and *epistemically indirect* (or, if we are talking of coherentism about justification, *justificationally indirect*). Hence, the last link is, as belief, direct, yet, as knowledge, *in*direct, not in the usual sense that it is inferential but in the broad sense that the belief constitutes knowledge only by virtue of receiving support from other knowledge or belief. Thus, my belief that there is a rustling sound is psychologically direct because it is simply grounded, causally, in my hearing and is not inferentially based on any other belief; yet my *knowledge* that there is such a sound is not epistemically direct. It is epistemically, but not inferentially, based on the coherence of my belief that there is a rustling with my other beliefs, presumably including many that represent knowledge themselves. It is thus knowledge *through,* but not by inference from, other knowledge—or at least through justified beliefs—and hence epistemically indirect. Hence, it is misleading to call the *knowledge* direct at all. Granted, the belief element *in* my knowledge is non-inferentially grounded in perception and is in that sense direct; but the belief constitutes knowledge only by virtue of coherence with my other beliefs.

One could insist that if a non-inferential, thus psychologically direct, belief constitutes knowledge, it *must* be direct knowledge. But the coherentist would reply that in that case there will be two kinds of direct knowledge: the kind the foundationalist posits, which derives from grounding in a basic experiential or rational source, and the kind the coherentist posits, which derives from coherence with other beliefs and not from being based on those sources. This is surely a plausible response.

Is the holistic coherentist trying to have it both ways? Not necessarily. Holistic coherentism can grant that a variant of the regress argument holds for belief, since the only kind of belief chain that it is psychologically realistic to attribute to us is the kind terminating in direct (non-inferential) belief. But even on the assumption that knowledge is constituted by (certain kinds of) beliefs, it does not follow that direct belief which is knowledge is also direct *knowledge*. Thus, the coherentist is granting a kind of *psychological foundationalism*, which says (in part) that if we have any beliefs at all, we have some direct ones, yet denying epistemological foundationalism, which requires that there be knowledge which is epistemically (and normally also psychologically) direct, if there is any knowledge at all. Holistic coherentism may grant experience and reason the status of psychological foundations of our entire structure of beliefs. But it gives them no place, independently of coherence, in generating justification or knowledge.

THE NATURE OF COHERENCE

If holistic coherentism is interpreted as I have described it, it avoids some of the major problems for linear coherentism. But there remain serious difficulties for it. I want to discuss two of them in this section. First, what *is* coherence? Second, what reason is there to think that coherence *alone* counts towards the justification of a belief, or towards its truth, as it must in some way if it is to give us a good account of knowledge?

It turns out to be very difficult to explain what coherence is. It is not mere consistency, though *in*consistency is the clearest case of incoherence. Coherence is sometimes connected with explanation. Certainly, if the Smiths' sending the package explains why the card bears their names, then my belief of the first proposition coheres with my belief of the second (other things being equal). Probability is also relevant to coherence. If the probability of the proposition that they sent the steaks is raised in the light of the proposition that I sent them cheese, this at least counts in favor of my belief of the first cohering with my belief of the second. But how are we to understand the notions of explanation and of probability? Let us consider these questions.

Does one proposition (genuinely) explain another so long as, if the first is (or is assumed to be) true, then it is clear why the second is true? Apparently not; for if that were so, then the proposition that a benevolent genie delivered the box explains why it arrived. In any event, if that proposition did explain why the box arrived, would I be justified in believing it because my believing it coheres with my believing that I know not what other source the box might have come from? Surely not. Even if we can say what notion of explanation is relevant, it will remain very difficult to specify when an explanatory relation generates enough coherence to create justification. For one thing, consider cases in which a proposition, say that Jill hurt Jack's feelings, would, if true, very adequately explain something we believe, such as that Jack is upset. Believing Jill did this might cohere well with his being upset, but that would not, by itself, justify our believing it.

Similar points hold for probability. Not just any proposition I believe which raises the probability of my hypothesis that the gift is from the Smiths will strengthen my justification for believing that it is. Consider, for example, the proposition that the Smiths send such gifts to all their friends. Suppose I have no justification for believing this, say because I have accepted it only on the basis of testimony I should see to be unreliable (and would see to be unreliable if I thought carefully about it). Then, while the proposition raises the probability of my hypothesis and (let us assume) coheres with what I already believe, I am not entitled to believe it, and my believing it will not add to my justification for believing that the Smiths sent the box. It might be replied that this belief about the Smiths' habits does not cohere well with *other* things I believe, such as that people do not generally behave like that. But suppose I knew almost nothing about the Smiths' or other people's habits of gift-giving, and I happened, without grounds, to believe the Smiths to be both generous and rich. Then there might be a significant degree of coherence between my belief that the Smiths send gifts to all their friends and my other beliefs; yet my forming the belief that they give gifts to all their friends still would not strengthen my justification for my hypothesis.

These examples bring us to the second problem. So far as we do understand coherence, what reason is there to think that by itself it generates any justification or truth at all? Whatever coherence among beliefs is, it is an *internal* relation, in the sense that it is a matter of how one's beliefs are related *to one another* and not to anything outside one's system of beliefs, such as one's perceptual experience. Now why could there not be many, many equally coherent systems of beliefs that are mutually incompatible, so that no two of them can be true? This is part of what might be called the *isolation problem*: the problem of explaining why coherent systems of beliefs are not readily isolated from truth, and thus do not contain knowledge, which implies truth.

Consider a schizophrenic who thinks he is Napoléon. If he has a completely consistent story with enough detail, his belief system may be superbly coherent. Yet obviously there are coherent belief systems that conflict with his, such as those of his psychiatrists. If coherence alone generates justification, however, we must say that each system is equally well justified—assuming their belief systems are *as* coherent as his. We need not attribute knowledge to any of the systems, since any of them might contain falsehood. But is it plausible to say that a system of beliefs is highly justified when there is no limit to the number of radically different yet equally justified belief systems—even on the part of other people with experience of or pertaining to many of the same things the beliefs are about—that are incompatible with it in this thoroughgoing way? The question is especially striking when we realize that two equally coherent systems, even on the part of the same person at different times, might differ not just on one point but on *every* point: each belief in one might be opposed by an incompatible belief in the other.

One would think, moreover, that a well-justified belief may be reasonably considered *true*. But if the degree of justification of a belief is entirely a matter of its support by considerations of coherence, no degree of justification by itself can carry any greater presumption of truth than is created by the same degree of support from coherence on the part of a belief of the contradictory proposition. Thus, if "Napoléon" has a sufficiently coherent set of beliefs yielding justification of his belief that he won the Battle of Waterloo, this belief may be as well justified as his psychiatrists' belief that he did not. But if this is how justification is conceived, is there any reason to suppose that a belief justified solely by considerations of coherence is true? And if Napoléon's and the psychiatrists' belief systems are equally coherent, how can we justify our apparently quite reasonable tendency to regard their belief systems as more likely to represent truths, and on that count more likely to contain knowledge, than his? Granted, their belief that he did not win the Battle coheres with our beliefs; but why should our own beliefs be privileged over equally coherent conflicting sets? And why should agreement even with nearly everyone's beliefs, say about Napoléon's being dead, be a factor, unless we are assuming that some element other than coherence, such as perception or memory, confers justification independently? If coherence alone confers justification, it is not clear how perception or memory or introspection contribute to it. Moreover, even what seems the highest degree of justification, such as we might have for simple introspective beliefs and beliefs of self-evident truths, provides us with no presumption of truth or knowledge.

COHERENCE, REASON, AND EXPERIENCE

This brings us to a third major problem for coherentism: how can it explain the role of experience and reason as sources of justification and knowledge? Certainly experience and reason *seem* to be basic sources of justification and knowledge. Coherentists themselves commonly *use* beliefs from these sources to illustrate coherent bodies of belief that are good candidates for knowledge. How can holistic coherentism explain the role of these sources in relation to justification and knowledge? Why is it that when I have a vivid experience of the kind characteristic of seeing a blue spruce, I am apparently justified, simply by that experience, in believing that there *is* a blue spruce before me? And why do I seem so very strongly justified, simply on the basis of my rational grasp of the proposition that if some dogs are pets then some pets are dogs, in believing this? One thing a coherentist might say here is that in fact many of our beliefs are *causally* and non-inferentially based on perception or on the use of reason; and given these similarities of origin, it is to be expected that they often cohere with one another. Hence, while we do not, and do not need to, infer propositions like those just cited from any others that might provide justifying evidence for them, they *do* cohere with many other things we believe, and that coherence justifies them.

This response is more plausible for perceptual belief than for belief of simple logical truths, at least if coherence is construed as more than consistency and as related to explanation, probability, and justification. For notice that the proposition that if some dogs are pets then some pets are dogs apparently need not explain, render probable, or justify anything else I believe, nor is it obvious that anything else I believe need explain, render probable, or justify it. Yet my belief of this proposition is justified to about as high a degree as any belief I have. On the other hand, the proposition that there is a blue spruce before me *does* cohere with other things I believe: that there is a conifer there, that I am in my backyard, and so forth; and there appear to be some explanatory and probability relations among them. For instance, that there is a blue spruce before me adds to the probability that I am in my backyard; and that I am in that yard partly explains why I see a blue spruce there.

A coherentist might respond to the difference just indicated by qualifying the view, applying it only to beliefs of empirical, rather than a priori, propositions. This move could be defended on the assumption that propositions known a priori are necessary and hence are not appropriately said to be made probable by other propositions, nor to be explained by them in the same way empirical propositions are explained. It might be argued that while we can explain the *basis* of a necessary truth and thereby show *that* it holds, still, since it cannot fail to hold, there is no explaining *why* it, *as opposed to something else*, holds. This is plausible but inconclusive reasoning. We may just as reasonably say that we can sometimes explain why a necessary truth holds and in doing so explain why a contrasting proposition is false. Imagine that someone mistakenly takes a certain geometrical proposition to be a theorem and cannot see why a closely similar, true principle is a theorem. If we now prove the correct one step by step, with accompanying examples, we might explain why it, as opposed to the other proposition, is true.

So far as explanation is central to coherence, then, coherentism apparently owes us an account of knowledge of at least some necessary truths. But suppose that it can account for knowledge of *some* necessary truths. There remain others, such as simple self-evident ones, for which we cannot find anything plausibly said to explain why they hold, nor any other way of accounting for knowledge of them as grounded in coherence. Consider how one might explain why, if it is true that Jane Austen wrote *Persuasion*, then it is not false that she did. If someone did not see this, it would probably not help to point out that no proposition is both true and false. For if one needs to have the truth of an instance of this general truth explained, one presumably cannot understand the general truth either. But suppose this is not so, and that one's grasp of the general truth is somehow the basis of one's seeing the particular truth that instantiates it; then the same point would apply to the general truth: there would apparently be nothing plausibly said to explain why *it* is true.

It might now be objected that the general truth that no proposition is both true and false, and the instances of it, are *mutually explanatory*: its truth explains why they hold, and their truth explains why it holds; and this is the chief basis of their coherence with one another. But is it really possible for one proposition to explain another *and* the other to explain it? If what explains why the grass is wet is that there is dew on it, then the same proposition—that there is dew on it—is not explained by the proposition that the grass is wet (instead, condensation explains that). Reflection on other examples also suggests that two propositions cannot explain each other, and there are apparently no general arguments that show this to be possible. Perhaps it is somehow possible; but until such an argument is given, we should conclude that even if an explanatory relation between propositions is sufficient for a belief of one to cohere with a belief of the other, coherentism does not in general provide a good account of knowledge of self-evident truths.

If coherentism applies only to empirical beliefs, however, it is not a general theory of justification or knowledge and leaves us in need of a different account of a priori justification (and knowledge). In any case, it would be premature to conclude that coherentism does account for empirical justification. Let us return to the perceptual case.

It might seem that we could decisively refute the coherence theory of justification by noting that one might have only a single belief, say that there is a blue spruce before one, and that this lone belief might still be justified. For then there would be a justified belief that coheres with no other beliefs one has. But could one have just a single belief? Could one, for instance, believe that there is a blue spruce before one, yet not believe, say, that it has branches? It is not clear that one could; and foundationalism does not assume this possibility, though the theory may easily be wrongly criticized for implying it. Foundationalism is in fact consistent with *one* kind of coherentism, namely, a *coherence theory of concepts* according to which a person acquires concepts, say of colors and shapes, only in relation to one another and must acquire an entire set of related concepts in order to acquire any concept.

We must directly ask, then, whether one's justification for believing that there is a blue spruce *derives* from the coherence of the belief with others. Let us first grant an important point. Suppose this belief turns out to be *in*coherent with a second belief, such as that one is standing where one seems to see the tree yet *feels* nothing before one and can walk right across the spot. Then the first belief may *cease* to be justified. But this only shows that its justification is *defeasible*—liable to being outweighed (overridden) or undermined—should sufficiently serious incoherence *arise*, not that it is derivative from coherence in the first place. In this case the justification of one's visually grounded belief is outweighed: one's better justified beliefs, including the conviction that a tree must be touchable, make it more reasonable for one to believe that there is *not* a tree there. Two important questions arise here. First, could incoherence outweigh justification of a belief in the first place if we were not *independently* justified in believing that a proposition incoherent with certain other ones is, or probably is, false? Second, aren't the relevant others precisely the kind for which, directly or inferentially, we have some degree of justification through the basic experiential and rational sources? Foundationalists are likely to answer the first negatively and the second affirmatively.

There is also a second case, in which one's justification is simply undermined: one ceases to be justified in believing the proposition in question, though one does not become justified in believing it false. Suppose I cease to see the tree if I move twenty feet to my left. This could justify my believing that I might be hallucinating. This belief does not cohere with, and undermines the justification of, my visual belief that the tree is there, though it does not by itself justify my believing that there is *no* tree there. Again, however, I am apparently justified, independently of coherence, in believing that my seeing the tree there is incoherent with my merely hallucinating it there. It seems, then, that coherence has the role it does in justification only because *some* beliefs are justified independently of it.

Examples like these show that it is essential to distinguish *negative epistemic dependence*—which is simply a form of defeasibility—from *positive epistemic dependence*—the kind beliefs bear to the sources from which they *derive* any justification they have or, if they represent knowledge, their status as knowledge. The defeasibility of a belief's justification by incoherence does not imply that, as coherentists must hold, this justification positively depends on coherence. If my well is my source of water, I (positively) depend on it. The possibility that people could poison it does not make their non-malevolence part of my source of water, or imply a (positive) dependence on them, such as I have on the rainfall. Moreover, it is the rainfall that explains both my having the water and its level. So it is with perceptual experience as a source of justification. Foundationalists need not claim that justification does not negatively depend on anything else, for as we have seen they need not claim that justification must be indefeasible. But negative dependence does not imply positive dependence. Justification can be defeasible by incoherence, and thus outweighed or undermined should incoherence arise, without owing its existence to coherence in the first place.

COHERENCE AND SECOND-ORDER JUSTIFICATION

There is something further we should grant to the coherentist, and in assessing it we can learn more about both coherentism and justification. *If* one should set out to *show* that one's belief is justified, one *would* have to cite propositions that cohere with the one in question, say the proposition that there is a blue spruce before me. In some cases, these are not even propositions one already believes. Often, in defending the original belief, one forms new beliefs, such as the belief one acquires, in moving one's head, that one can vividly see the changes in perspective that go with seeing a physical object. More important, *these* beliefs are especially appropriate to the *process of justifying* one's belief; and the result of that process is *showing* that the original belief is justified, together with one's forming the second-order belief that the belief is justified. Thus, coherence is important in showing that a belief is justified and is in *that* sense an element in (the process of) justification.

The moment we reflect on this point, however, we may wonder why the beliefs appropriate to showing that a belief is justified have to be involved in its *being* justified in the first place. There is no good reason to think they need be. Indeed, why should one's simply having a justified belief imply even that one is (situationally) justified *in* holding beliefs appropriate to showing that it is justified? It would seem that just as one can be virtuous even if one does not know how to defend one's character against attack, one can have a justified belief even if, in response to someone who doubts that one has it, one could not show that one does.

Justifying a second-order belief—a belief about a belief, such as a perceptual one, which is not about any other belief—is a sophisticated process. The process is particularly sophisticated if the second-order belief concerns a special property like the justification of the original belief. Simply being justified in a belief about the color of an object is a much simpler matter. But confusion is easy here. Consider the question of how a simple perceptual belief "is justified." The very phrase is ambiguous. For all it tells us, the question could be 'By what process, say of reasoning, has the belief been (or might it be) justified?' or, on the other hand, 'In virtue of what is the belief justified?' These are two very different questions. But much of our talk about justification makes it easy to run them together. A justified belief could be one that *has* justification or one that *has been* justified; and request for someone's justification could be a request for a list of justifying factors or for a recounting of the process by which the person justified the belief.

Does coherentism have any plausible argument, not grounded in the mistakes just pointed out, for the (positive) dependence of perceptual justification on coherence? I do not see that it does, though given how hard it is to discern what specifically coherence *is*, we cannot be confident that no direct argument is forthcoming. Granted, one could point to the oddity of saying things like, 'I am justified in believing that there is a blue spruce before me, but I cannot justify the belief'. One might think this is odd because, if I have a justified belief, I can surely give a justification for it by appeal to beliefs that cohere with it. But look closely. Typically, in asserting something, I suggest that I *can* justify it in some way or other (particularly if the belief I express is not grounded in a basic source); yet here I deny that very suggestion. It is apparently my *asserting* that my belief is justified, rather than its being so, that gives the appearance that I must here be able to give a justification of the belief.

To be sure, when I say that there is a blue spruce before me, I can give a justification: for instance, that I see it. But I need not *believe* that I see it, *before* the question of justification arises. That question leads me to focus on my circumstances, in which I first had a belief solely about the *tree*. I did also have a *disposition*, based on my visual experience, to form the belief that *I see* the tree, and this is largely why, in the course of justifying that belief, I then *form* the further belief that I *do* see it. But a *disposition to believe* something does not imply a *dispositional belief* of it: here I tend to form the belief that I see the tree if, as I view it, the question whether I see it arises; yet I need not have subliminally believed this already. The justification I offer, then, is not by appeal to coherence with other beliefs I already had—such as that I saw the tree—but by reference to a basic source, perceptual experience. It is thus precisely the kind of justification which foundationalists are likely to consider appropriate for a non-inferential belief. Indeed, one consideration favoring foundationalism about both justification and knowledge, at least as an account of our epistemic practices in everyday life, including much scientific practice, is that typically we cease offering justification or defending a knowledge claim precisely when we reach a basic source.

Suppose, however, that I would be dumbfounded if asked, in clear daylight, what justifies me in believing there is a blue spruce before me. Would it follow that I am not justified? No, for I might be simply unable to marshal my quite ample justificatory resources; and coherentism offers us no good argument to show that being justified requires being able to show that one is, any more than having good character entails being able to show that one has it.

There is one further point to be made here. If coherentism regards justification as deriving from coherence alone, then it accords *no* justificatory weight to experiential or rational grounding except insofar as they contribute to coherence. Our reflections about examples cast doubt on this view. But consider another implication of coherentism: if I want to have the best justified body of beliefs possible—which is surely a rational goal—then I am free to consider adopting (or somehow causing myself to form) an entirely new system of beliefs even if it contains few of the experiential and a priori beliefs I now have and perhaps eventually contains none of them at all. We are apparently incapable of changing our belief systems in this way, but suppose that we could do so by properly setting a neurological machine to instill an optimally coherent set and remove the rest. Would that be rational from the point of view of maximizing the justification of one's beliefs? I do not believe that it would, particularly if, in seeking justification, we aim, as we normally do, at discovering or retaining *truths*.

A coherentist might reply that if we are talking not only about justification but also about *knowledge*, then we must give some special role to beliefs grounded in experience and reason, for if we ignore these sources we cannot expect our justified beliefs to be true, hence cannot expect them to constitute knowledge. Now, however, we face what seems an artificial separation between what justifies a belief and what is plausibly taken to count towards its truth. If, because it implies truth, knowledge must in some way reflect experience or reason, should not justification, which seems in some way to count toward truth, also reflect them? Is it really reasonable to suppose that what justifies a belief may in no way count towards its truth? It is not, nor have coherentists generally thought that it is (though some have held a coherence theory of truth of a kind to be discussed in Chapter 7). Often, what motivates asking for a justification of a belief is doubt that it is true; and if so, then the view that what justifies a belief has no tendency whatever to show that it is true seems plainly mistaken. Moreover, if we can know a priori, as I believe may be possible, that perceptual and rational grounding of beliefs count in some way toward their truth, why may we not know equally well that they count toward justifying beliefs, as they surely appear to?

MODEST FOUNDATIONALISM

There is far more to say about both foundationalism and coherentism. But if what has emerged here is on the right track, then the problems confronting coherentism are worse than those confronting foundationalism. The most serious problems for foundationalism are widely taken to be the difficulties of specifying source conditions for justification and knowledge and, secondly, of accounting, on the basis of those sources, for all that we seem to know. The first of these problems is addressed in Part One, which describes the basic sources and illustrates how they generate direct—though not indefeasible—knowledge, and direct (though again not generally indefeasible) justification. The second problem is treated in Chapter 5, which indicates many ways in which, even without actual inferences, knowledge and justification can be transmitted from beliefs which are justified, or represent knowledge, by virtue of being grounded in the basic sources, to other beliefs. Both problems are difficult, and they have not been completely solved here. But enough has been said to make clear along what lines they may be dealt with in a foundationalist framework.

Still another problem for foundationalism is the difficulty of accounting for the place of coherence in justification. But this is not a crippling difficulty for the kind of foundationalism I have been describing, which need not restrict the role of coherence any more than is required by the regress argument. Indeed, while (pure) coherentism grants nothing to foundationalism beyond perhaps its underlying psychological picture of how our belief systems are structured, foundationalism can account for some of the insights of coherentism, for instance the point that a coherence theory of the acquisition of concepts is plausible.

More positively, foundationalism can acknowledge a significant role for coherence in relation to justification and can thereby answer one traditional coherentist objection. I have in mind a kind of *modest foundationalism*: a foundationalist view of knowledge or justification which (a) takes the justification of foundational beliefs to be at least typically defeasible, (b) is not *deductivist*, that is, does not demand that principles governing the inferential transmission of knowledge or justification be deductive, and (c) allows a significant role for coherence by requiring, not that inferentially justified beliefs derive *all* their justification from foundational ones, but only that they derive enough of it from the latter so that they would remain justified if any other justification they have were eliminated. (A slightly different formulation may be required, if, for the sorts of reasons to be given in Chapter 7, knowledge does not entail justification, but the formulation given will serve here.) Some versions are more modest than others, but the most plausible ones give coherence at least two roles.

The first role modest foundationalism may give to coherence, or at least to incoherence, is negative: *in*coherence may defeat justification or knowledge, even of a directly justified (foundational) belief, as where my justification for believing I may be hallucinating prevents me from knowing, or remaining justified in believing, that the spruce is before me. (If this is not ultimately a role for coherence itself, it *is* a role crucial for explaining points stressed by coherentism.) Second, modest foundationalism can employ a principle commonly emphasized by coherentists, though foundationalists need not grant that the truth of the principle is based on coherence. This is an *independence principle*: that the larger the number of independent mutually coherent factors one believes to support the truth of a proposition, the better one's justification for believing it (other things being equal). This principle can explain, for instance, why my justification for believing that the box of steaks is from the Smiths increases as I acquire new beliefs each of which supports that conclusion. Similar principles consistent with foundationalism can accommodate other cases in which coherence enhances justification, say those in which a proposition's explaining, and thereby cohering with, something one justifiably believes tends to confer some degree of justification on that proposition.

Modest foundationalism contrasts with *strong foundationalism*, which, in one form, is deductivist, takes foundational beliefs as indefeasibly justified, and allows coherence only a minimal role. To meet these conditions, strong foundationalists may reduce the basic sources of justification to reason and some form of introspection. Moreover, since they are committed to the indefeasibility of foundational justification, they would not grant that incoherence can defeat the justification of foundational beliefs. They would also concede to coherentism, and hence to any independence principle they recognize, only a minimal positive role, say by insisting that if a belief is supported by two or more independent cohering sources, its justification is increased only additively, that is, only by bringing together the justification transmitted separately from each relevant basic source.

By contrast, what modest foundationalism denies regarding coherence is only that it is a basic source of justification. Coherence by itself is not sufficient for justification. Thus, the independence principle does not apply to sources that have *no* justification; at most, it allows coherence to raise the level of justification originally drawn from other sources to a level *higher* than it would be if those sources were not mutually coherent. Similarly, if inference is a basic source of coherence (as some coherentists seem to have believed), it is not a basic source of justification. It may enhance justification, as where one strengthens one's justification for believing someone's testimony by inferring the same point from someone else's. But inference *alone* does not generate justification: I might infer any number of propositions from several I already believe merely through wishful thinking; yet even if I thereby arrive at a highly coherent set of beliefs, I have not thereby increased my justification for believing any of them.

If modest foundationalism is correct, however, it still tells us only what sort of structure a body of knowledge or of justified belief has. It says that if one has any knowledge or justified belief, then one has some direct knowledge or directly justified belief, and any other knowledge or justified belief one has is traceable to those foundations. A belief direct and foundational at one time may be indirect and non-foundational at another; it may gain or lose justification; and some foundational beliefs may even be false or cease to be justified at all. By leaving this much open, modest foundationalism avoids a narrow account of what it takes to have knowledge and justification and allows many routes to their acquisition. For similar reasons, it avoids *dogmatism*, in the sense of an attitude of smug certainty concerning claims that are not self-evident. For it allows alternative kinds of foundational beliefs for different people and under different circumstances; and, by acknowledging the fallibility of the experiential sources and of many inferences from the beliefs they generate, it also explains why it is so difficult to know that one has knowledge or justified belief, and hence important to be open to the possibility of mistakes. Foundationalism *is* committed to unmoved movers; it is not committed to unmovable movers. It leaves open, moreover, just what knowledge is, and even whether there actually is any. These questions must still be faced.

The Nature and Scope of Knowledge and Justification

CHAPTER 7

The Analysis of Knowledge

Knowledge arises in experience. It emerges from reflection. It develops through inference. It acquires a structure. The same holds for justified belief. But what exactly is knowledge? If it arises and develops in the way I have described, then knowing is at least believing. But clearly it is much more. A false belief is not knowledge. A belief based on a lucky guess is not knowledge either, even if it is true. Can something be added to the notion of true belief to yield an analysis of what knowledge is, that is, to provide a kind of account of what constitutes knowledge? Plato (*c*.427–347 B.C.) addressed a question significantly like this. He formulated, but in the end did not endorse, an account of knowledge which has sometimes been loosely interpreted as taking knowledge to be justified true belief (the most important passages are probably those in his *Theaetetus*, 201c–210b). If we substitute, as most interpreters of Plato would—minimally—have us do, one or another term for 'belief', say 'conviction', 'certainty', or 'understanding', then the account may be nearer to what Plato held and closer to some of the historically influential conceptions of knowledge. In any case, the notion of belief, as we have seen, is wide, subtle, and powerful; and one or another form of the justified true belief account prevailed during much of this century until the 1960s. What can be said for it?

KNOWLEDGE AND JUSTIFIED TRUE BELIEF

What is not true is not known. When we claim we know something and later discover that it is false, we sometimes say things like 'Well, I certainly believed it'; but we do not seriously maintain that we nonetheless knew it. If we said so, others would likely conclude that we do not really believe that it is false, or perhaps that we are using 'knew', as people occasionally do, to mean 'felt great confidence', as in 'I just knew I'd win—I still can't really believe I lost'.

These points suggest that knowledge is at least true belief. Admittedly, people who feel certain of something, for instance that a friend is angry, may say that they don't believe it, but *know* it. This is best understood, however, to mean that they do not *merely* believe it, but know it. Similarly, it may be misleading to say 'I believe he's angry' where I think I know it—unless I intend, for instance, to indicate caution or perhaps polite disagreement with someone I think mistaken. But it is often misleading to say less than one is fully entitled to say; and my saying that I believe he is angry may be misleading precisely because I am expressing only *part* of what I am entitled to express, namely that I know he is. For I am thereby suggesting that I do not know, or perhaps doubt, that he is. If this point is what explains why my statement is misleading, that confirms that knowing implies believing.

Does knowing something also imply *justifiably* believing it? If it does, that would explain why a true belief based on a lucky guess is not knowledge. If, from a distance, I see Jim walk hurriedly down the hall and simply guess that he is angry, I am not justified in believing that he is angry. If my belief turns out to be true, it still does not constitute knowledge. That seems explainable by its lack of justification. Now suppose I go into his office and see him briskly shuffling papers and angrily mumbling curses. At this point I might come to know that he is angry; and my acquiring knowledge that he is can be explained by my having acquired evidence which justifies my belief that he is.

Still, *could* a true belief that is not justified constitute knowledge? Suppose I simply see Jim briskly shuffling papers as I pass his office, but do not hear any curses. A bit later, I see him walk hurriedly down the hall. Given that I know his fiery temperament, I might have just enough evidence so that I do not *un*justifiably believe he is angry, even though I am not quite justified in believing this. Might I now have a kind of low-grade knowledge that he is angry? I do not think so. But the case does show this much: that as our evidence for something we truly believe mounts up in a way that brings us closer to justification, we also tend to get closer to knowledge. These and similar points support the view that justified belief is an element in knowledge. This view is highly plausible, and for the time being let's assume it.

We are, then, on the way toward an analysis of knowledge. For it looks as if we have three necessary conditions. Specifically, it seems that knowledge is at least *justified true belief*: that one knows something only if one believes it, it is true, and one's belief of it is justified. But a correct, illuminating analysis, one that provides a good account of the nature of what is being analyzed, must also provide sufficient conditions. Now it might be true that I know something *only* if I justifiably and truly believe it, yet false that *if* I justifiably and truly believe something, I know it. And this apparently is false. Suppose that when I first visit the Smiths I have no idea that they have a photographic collection which includes very realistic, life-size pictures of themselves. When I approach the door to their living room I see, just twelve feet before me, and constituting all I can see through the doorway, a life-size picture of Jane, standing facing me and smiling like the good hostess she is, with the background looking just like the living room's rear wall. I say 'hello' before I get close enough to realize that I see only a photograph of her. I discover that the picture is so lifelike that this happens to everyone who knows Jane and enters unaware of the photograph. I might thus be quite justified, for a moment, in my belief that Jane is opposite me. As it happens, however, Jane is standing opposite me—in the next room, right behind the wall on which the picture is hung. My belief that she is opposite me is thus true, as well as justified. But I do not know that she is opposite me. (If I had believed that she is *directly* opposite me, in the sense that there is no obstacle between us, my belief would have been false; but I would not normally have believed that here, where I have no reason even to imagine obstacles.)

This example shows that if we analyze knowledge as justified true belief, we include too much: our analysis is too broad. What can be done to improve it? If we think we are on the right track, we can add something to restrict the kind or degree of justification involved. We might also suspect that justification is not so important after all, but only correlated with something that is important, and seek an account in which justification is not central to understanding knowledge. There are many approaches of both kinds. I want to consider two of each, starting with the "justificationist" accounts.

SOME JUSTIFICATIONIST ACCOUNTS OF KNOWLEDGE

In the photographic case, something seems wrong with the kind of justification I have. We might call it *defeated*. This is not to say that it is eliminated, but rather (in part) that it is prevented from playing what would be its normal role in such a case, namely, rendering a true belief knowledge. Perhaps, then, knowledge might be analyzed as *undefeated justified true belief*.

But how is defeat to be characterized? One natural view is that the justification of a belief is defeated provided the belief depends on a falsehood. It might depend on one in either or both of the following ways. First, it might depend on a falsehood in the sense that it would not be justified except on the basis of one's being (situationally) justified *in believing* a falsehood about the subject in question (say, Jane). This is a kind of justificational dependence (dependence for justification) which I'll call *presuppositional dependence*. In the photographic case, one falsehood on which my belief that Jane is opposite me depends presuppositionally is that I am seeing her directly. The point is not that in order to know she is opposite me I have to believe this false proposition; but its truth seems somehow presupposed by the visually grounded belief being knowledge. After all, it seems to be because this proposition is false that I do not know Jane is opposite me. The second case is *psychological dependence*: a belief might psychologically depend on a falsehood in the sense that one would not hold it unless one *did* believe it on the basis of a falsehood. My belief about Jane would psychologically depend on falsehood if, say, I knew about the photographs, yet trusted my vision and believed that Jane is opposite me on the basis of concluding that I am viewing her directly.

But the appeal to a false presupposition, or even to other kinds of dependence on falsehood, may not always do what is needed. Recall the sweepstakes with a million coupons. You might have a justified true belief that you will lose, but you do not know that you will. What falsehood defeats your justification here? You are not making any mistake. It might seem that your belief that you will lose depends on the false proposition that the outcome of a chance process can be known beforehand by merely calculating odds. But does your belief depend on this? You might reject this and still believe you will lose, whereas I could not reject the false presupposition that I see Jane directly and still believe (justifiably, at least) that she is in front of me. In fact, you might still quite justifiably believe you will lose. So we cannot plausibly say that either your belief or its justification depends on the falsehood about foreknowledge of chance outcomes. Points like these do not show that nothing can save the undefeated justified true belief analysis. But it is at least not easy to make the analysis work, and I want to consider others.

The sweepstakes example suggests that knowledge requires one's having *conclusively justified true belief*: belief justified in such a way that what justifies it guarantees its truth. For it is plausible to claim that if the evidence guarantees that you will lose, say because it includes knowledge of the sweepstakes being fixed in favor of someone else, then you *would* know you will lose. Different theories offer different accounts of such a guarantee, as will be apparent when we discuss skepticism in Chapter 9. The sweepstakes example tends to support the view that knowledge is conclusively justified belief. After all, we can have as many coupons as we like and you would still not know yours will lose. Thus, no matter how *probable* it is that you will lose, your justification is not sufficient for knowledge.

Another reason to think that knowledge requires conclusive justification is that knowing is closely associated with certainty. When I wonder if I know, I sometimes ask myself how I can be certain. I also sometimes wonder if what I believe *is* certain. Particularly in the latter case, I am not talking mainly about *psychological certainty*, which is, roughly speaking, confidence of the truth of what one believes. Even 'How can I be certain?' does not concern only psychological certainty; it means something like 'How may I justifiably be (psychologically) certain?' And if I say that *it* is not certain that your coupon will lose, I am talking about *propositional certainty*, roughly, the certainty a proposition has when there are extremely strong grounds for it, grounds that guarantee its truth (I leave open how readily *available* the grounds must be, if readily available at all). Given these points, one might hold that knowledge is conclusively justified true belief, meaning that (1) the believer may justifiably be certain of the true proposition in question and (2) this proposition is so well grounded as to be propositionally certain. Call knowledge constituted by such belief *epistemic certainty*.

This analysis seems too narrow. It would, for instance, apparently rule out most knowledge based on testimony. If Jane tells me that she wants to meet with me to discuss something, and I know her well and have no good reason to doubt her word, may I not know that she wants to meet with me? Yet I do not have conclusive justification. Unlikely though it is, error is barely possible for me; she could act out of character and deceive me. Moreover, it is doubtful that, at the time, it is propositionally certain that she wants to meet with me (but the notion of propositional certainty is vague, and it is often difficult to tell whether it applies). Thus, my knowledge here is apparently not knowledge of something that is certain. Indeed, we speak sometimes of knowing something *for certain*, implying a contrast with simply knowing. Someone probing my grounds for thinking Tom mistaken about Jane might ask if I know for certain, not from doubt whether *I* know, but to find out if the *proposition* is certain, perhaps because much hangs on it, as in a criminal trial. The existence of such cases suggests that what is not known for certain still *can* be known.

Perhaps what can be known at all can always be known for certain, as I might come to know for certain, provided I do enough checking into her motivation, that Jane wants to meet with me. But even if what is knowable *is* knowable for certain, it is doubtful (as examples to be given will also suggest) that everything that is known *is* certain.

A further question is whether what one knows must at least be the sort of thing that *can* be certain. Our example suggests that it need not be: I might know that Jane wanted to meet with me even if she has just died and the additional evidence on the basis of which this can be certain is unavailable. Perhaps, however, this point shows only that I cannot *make certain* that she wants to meet with me. There might still *be* a basis for this proposition which renders it (propositionally) certain. I will leave open the question whether what is known is the sort of thing that can be certain, since knowledge, not certainty, is my main concern here. But it will help, in that connection, to consider how an understanding of the notion of making certain may bear on the view that knowledge requires conclusive justification.

If we can make certain of something we already know, then apparently conclusive justification is *not* required for knowledge. Suppose I lock the back door and, as I get in my car, have a clear recollection of doing so. Still, if someone asks me if I am absolutely sure I did, I may truly believe I know I did, yet still check to make certain I did. Now where we need to make certain of something we know, it would appear that it need not be either certain *or* conclusively justified: getting conclusive justification seems the main point of making certain. It might be replied that here 'make certain' means not 'make it certain' but, roughly, 'make sure it *is* certain', and that if I really knew it, it was certain in the first place. But suppose I do not make certain, because it begins to hail and I must leave. It does not follow that I do not know the door is locked; and, on later finding that it was, I would be correct in saying that I was right all along to think I knew. Moreover, this apparently does not imply that it was certain all along, and I at least had good reason at the time to think it was not certain. Thus, the possibility of making certain of what we already know suggests that knowing a proposition does not entail its being certain. Moreover, if we can know something, yet make certain it is so, then apparently we can know it without being conclusively justified in believing it.

Notice that similar points apply to what we know from memory. Even on topics with respect to which our memory is highly reliable, the justification of our memory beliefs is generally not conclusive. Even if I can recite a stanza from memory, my justification for believing I have it right need not be conclusive. Yet I may well know that I have it right, and confirm that I do when I look it up to make certain, and find that it reads just as I thought.

SOME NATURALISTIC ACCOUNTS OF KNOWLEDGE

Perhaps we should consider a quite different approach. Must we appeal to the notion of justification to understand knowledge? Suppose we think of knowing as *registering truth*, somewhat as a thermometer registers temperature. Knowledge, so conceived, results from the successful functioning of our epistemic equipment, which consists of fine perceptual, memorial, introspective, and rational instruments.

This view goes well with the idea that we are biological creatures with sense receptors that gather information and mental capacities that manipulate it. Indeed, perhaps we can analyze knowledge *naturalistically*, that is, in the way the natural sciences understand things: not by appeal to value-laden notions like that of justification, but (largely) in terms of physical, chemical, biological, and psychological properties, together with causal relations among these. I want to consider two naturalistic approaches. The first emphasizes the role of causation in producing our knowledge, as in the case of perceptual beliefs caused by the perceived object. The second stresses the reliability of the processes, such as seeing, through which knowledge arises.

On the causal theory, knowledge is *suitably caused true belief*, where suitable (causal) production of a belief is its production in relation to the fact, object, event, or other thing in virtue of which the belief is true. The idea, very roughly, is that a belief is knowledge because it is caused in a way that guarantees its *truth*. Thus, I know that there is a blue spruce before me because the tree itself plays a major part, through my vision, in causing me to believe there is. I know that Jane wants to meet with me because her wanting to do so plays a major part in causing her to say she does, and thereby in causing me to believe that she does. I know that the stanza has four lines because its having them is a major causal factor, operating through my memory, in my believing that it does.

The causal view can even accommodate knowledge of the future. I know that I am going to continue thinking about the nature of knowledge for a long time. That truth (about the future) does not cause me to believe this; but that truth is causally connected with my belief, and in a way that suggests why the belief may be expected to be true. For what causally explains *both* why it is true *and* why I believe it, is the same element: my intending to continue thinking about knowledge. Here my belief is knowledge, but not by virtue of being produced by the thing it is *about*—my future thinking—for that has not occurred. Hence my belief is not knowledge by virtue of what it is about being the way the belief represents it, as in the case of the tree's being before me causing me to believe that it *is* before me. Still, my belief that I will continue thinking about knowledge *is* caused by something—my intention to continue thinking about it—of a kind that makes it at least likely that I will be as the belief represents me.

There are, however, serious troubles for the causal theory. One problem is how to apply it to a priori knowledge. How might the truth that if one tree is taller than another, then the second is shorter than the first be causally connected with my believing this truth? This truth is not perceptually known, nor is its status dependent on any particular object in the world, as is the case with the (empirical) knowledge to which the causal theory best applies. It appears that the only way a truth can be causally connected with a belief so as to render it knowledge is through a connection with something in the world that *does* at least partly cause (or is at least partly an effect of) the belief. The truth that there is a blue spruce before me is about an object that produces visual impressions in me. But the a priori knowledge just cited does not depend on trees in that way. It does not even depend on there ever being any trees. It seems to be based simply on a grasp of the concepts involved. My having this grasp does not appear to imply causally interacting with those concepts (supposing it is even possible to interact causally with concepts).

There is another serious problem concerning the causal account, this time in relation to empirical beliefs. Consider a case in which something causes me to have a true belief, yet that belief is not knowledge. Suppose Tom tells me that Jim is angry, and as a result I believe this. My belief might be justified and true. But imagine that Tom is in general highly unreliable, and sometimes lies, in what he says about Jim, although I have no reason whatever to believe this about Tom. The mere fact of Tom's unreliability prevents me from knowing through his testimony that Jim is angry. Even if *Tom* knows Jim is angry, and knows it because he observes Jim acting angrily, his knowledge is not transmitted to me. For he might well have said this even if Jim had merely acted, say, hurriedly, and was not angry. The causal connections seem to be what they usually are in testimony cases, yet I do not know. Jim's anger causes Tom to believe him angry; Tom's belief (partly) causes his telling me Jim is angry; his telling me this causes me to believe it. But, though I have a justified true belief that Jim is angry, I do not know it. For while Tom has it right this time, he is in general unreliable regarding Jim.

The testimony example brings out something very revealing. It suggests that the reason I do not know on the basis of Tom's testimony is that he is not *reliable*. By contrast, perception normally does seem reliable; at least we may justifiably count on the beliefs it typically produces to be true, and presumably perception is also reliable in the sense that the vast majority of beliefs it produces *are* true. Where there is a photograph that we are unaware of, however, our perception through it is typically not reliable. Cases of that sort suggest that we might plausibly analyze knowledge as *reliably produced true belief.* Even a priori knowledge might perhaps be accommodated on this view. For it is at least normally produced by grasping concepts and their relations, or by permissible inference on the basis of beliefs grounded in such a grasp; and these processes of producing belief seem reliable. In both the empirical and a priori cases, then, when we know, we have reliably *registered* the truth.

To see how this approach works, recall Tom's testimony about Jim. Suppose that Tom is only very occasionally mistaken about Jim. Then might I acquire knowledge on the basis of Tom's testimony? A crucial question is *how* reliable a belief-producing process, such as testimony, must be in order to yield knowledge. The theory gives us no precise way to answer this. It can be defended, however, by noting that the concept of knowledge is itself not precise. This means that there will be times when, no matter how much information we have, we cannot be sure whether someone knows or not, just as, because the term 'bald' is vague, we cannot always be sure whether it applies, no matter how much information we have (including the number of hairs on the person's head). It might be added that *as* the reliability of Jim's testimony goes up, so does our inclination to say that I know on the basis of it. This seems to confirm the reliability theory.

PROBLEMS FOR RELIABILITY THEORIES

The reliability theory apparently does receive support from the kind of correlation illustrated here: the tendency to count my true belief about Jim as knowledge apparently varies with the tendency to regard the belief's testimonial basis as reliable. But perhaps our underlying thought in so speaking about the belief is that the more reliable Tom is, the better is my justification for believing what he says. If so, then the reliability theory might give the right results here because it draws on the role of *justification* as a constituent in knowledge. To be sure, I need not *believe* anything specific about Tom's reliability in order to acquire justified beliefs from his testimony. But it might be argued that I do presuppose that he is sufficiently reliable to justify my accepting his testimony, and that it is this presupposition whose falsity defeats my justification for believing his testimony in the first place. Thus, even if the reliability account is correct, its success may be due to its tacit dependence on the justificationist concepts it seeks to abandon.

There is a different kind of problem that must also be faced by the reliability theory. This difficulty is deeper than the question of how reliable a process has to be in order to ground knowledge. It concerns how to specify what is reliable in the first place. It really will not do to say simply that the reliable processes we are talking about are mainly those by which the experiential and rational sources of knowledge produce belief. Consider vision. Its reliability varies so much with conditions of observation that it would be wrong to say without qualification that it is a reliable belief-producing process. It might seem that we may say that it is reliable in producing beliefs in good light with the object of vision near enough relative to the visual powers of the perceiver. But this will not do either. It does not rule out external interferences like deceptive photographs, such as the one of Jane. It also fails to rule out internal interferences like hallucinogenic drugs. These interferences might produce false beliefs about objects which one clearly sees and concerning which one also has many true beliefs, as where, because of brain damage, one hallucinates a dark blight on a blue tree which one otherwise sees plainly as it is.

There are, moreover, so many possible factors that affect reliability that it is not clear that we can list them all without using blanket terms such as 'too far away' as applied to the object, and 'insufficiently attentive' or 'not acute enough' as applied to the perceiver. These terms are not only quite vague; the more important point is that they seem to come to something like 'too far to be reliably (or justifiably) judged', 'too inattentive to form reliable (or justified) beliefs', and 'not acute enough for reliable (or justified) judgment of the features of the object'. If so, their interpretation may well depend on our already having a good philosophical understanding of reliability (or justification), and they are thus unlikely to help us much in clarifying reliability.

Even if we can devise a vocabulary that overcomes these problems, another, related difficulty may persist. Belief-production might be reliable described in one way and unreliable described in another. Hence, even if we are able to specify what, in general, a reliable belief-producing process is, we need a way of deciding what reliable-process description to use in order to understand a particular case. Recall my seeing Jane in the photograph and thereby believing that she is opposite me. Suppose we say—what seems correct—that my belief arises from a process of seeing someone in a photograph that accurately shows the person's features and general location. Then my belief presumably should be knowledge. For the picture shows her to be where she is: opposite me. Suppose, on the other hand, we say something else that is true: that the process is one of seeing a person in a picture which gives the false impression that the person is *directly* in front of one. Then my belief arising from the process is not reliably produced—since often in such cases the person is *not* opposite one at all—and the belief should thus not be knowledge. The trouble is that *both* descriptions apply to the production of my belief. Using one description, the theory says I know; using the other, it says I do not.

How can the theory enable us to choose between the two correct reliable-process descriptions, or justify our choosing whatever kind of description it accepts? Call this the *description problem*. If we *first* have to decide whether I know that Jane is in front of me and then frame a description, the theory gives us quite limited help in understanding knowledge. For the theory itself can be put to work only insofar as we already understand knowledge quite well, at least well enough to be in a position to tell systematically, in a vast range of cases of true belief, whether or not the belief constitutes knowledge. But the deeper point is that if we seek to clarify knowledge (or justification) by appeal to reliable belief-producing processes, we need a way of explaining what those processes are without appealing, in our explanation, to the concept of knowledge (or justification). A belief that is knowledge should be such because it is reliably produced true belief; a reliable belief-producing process should not be characterized as the kind that yields, say, perceptual knowledge. Similarly, if we have to find the right reliable-process description in terms of what I am *justified* in presupposing, say that I have direct visual access to what is before me, then the theory works only insofar as it can exploit some justificationist principles. In that case, it would be more accurately described as a reliabilistic justification theory.

The sweepstakes example also challenges reliability theories of knowledge, as it does justificationist theories, and it, too, illustrates the description problem. Granted, we *can* characterize the process producing my belief that I will lose as one in which chance is crucial, and thus claim that the process is not reliable. But since I hold just one out of a million coupons, we might also truly describe it as a process that yields true beliefs virtually 100 percent of the time (and we can get as high a percentage as we like by increasing the number of coupons). Under this description, the process sounds very reliable indeed; yet it does not produce knowledge. If something like the former description is what the theory would have us use, why is that?

There could well be a way around these problems. For instance, one might point out that in the photographic case my belief about Jane's location does not causally *depend* on where she is, since I would believe she is before me even if she were not behind the picture. But this is only the beginning of a solution. For suppose I see her in a mirror, again without knowing that I am not seeing her directly, perhaps because I do not realize that there are trick mirrors at the yard party I am attending. Imagine that she happens to be opposite me, behind the mirror in which I see her, and is reflected into it by other mirrors I do not see (and have no reason to think are there). Here my belief about where she is *would* depend on where she is, since her movements would be reflected in the mirror in which I see her; yet I would not know that she is opposite me. Similarly, my belief that I will lose the sweepstakes depends on my beliefs about, and in that way may indirectly depend on, the mechanisms that actually result in my losing; but still the belief is not knowledge. The dependence is of course not of the required *kind*. But now we have another description problem: how to describe the right kind of dependency. If there is a way to solve these and related problems, it is not obvious what it is. It appears, then, that reliability theories face serious difficulties, as do the other theories we have considered.

One conclusion that might be drawn here is that knowledge is simply un-analyzable. But that certainly should not be inferred from the difficulties I have brought out. They may be resolvable; and I have of course not discussed all the promising lines of analysis of knowledge there are. One might also conclude that the concept of knowledge is simply so vague that we should not hope for an account any more precise than, say, the view that knowledge is *appropriately justified true belief* or, if one prefers a naturalistic account, *suitably produced true belief*. But that conclusion would be premature, particularly so far as it favors a justificationist account of knowledge. Indeed, it is time to consider some very special cases that raise the question whether justification is even strictly necessary for knowledge.

KNOWLEDGE AND JUSTIFICATION

Imagine a man who foretells the results of horse races. He always gets them right, even though he never inspects the horses or their records. He has no idea why he believes what he does about the results; and after the races he does not even check his accuracy. It is not clear *how* such a thing is possible; but it clearly *is* possible. There could be a way, for instance, in which both his belief that a horse will win and its actually winning are common effects of the same causes, so that his getting the right answers is not lucky accident, but prophetic in a way, or perhaps sixth-sensory. Now it *appears* that he knows who will win the races. But he surely does not have justified beliefs. He *would* have them if he kept track of his record and noted how well his forecasts turn out. But he has no idea that he is getting the results right.

One might protest that he has a kind of foresight which generates directly justified beliefs somewhat in the way perception does. But is there any reason to say this, other than to preserve the view that knowledge implies justified belief? There is no candidate for a sense organ; and while we assume that there is some causal process by which he receives the crucial information, we have no idea what it is and cannot plausibly regard it as conferring justification.

Here is another case that argues for the same point. In some of the literature of psychology we read of the *idiot savant*. Such people are considered mentally deficient, yet have some extraordinary abilities. Some can apparently just reel off the answers to arithmetical problems that normally require calculation in writing. Let us assume that they regularly get them right, yet can give no account of how they do so: it is not, for instance, by rapidly doing in their head what we would laboriously do in our heads if our memories enabled us to solve the problem mentally. It is not known how they do it. Now consider the first time one of these people reels off the answer to a multiplication problem involving two three-digit numbers. There is no time to realize that one has a built-in ability or to note a series of successes. But the person believes the answer and might also know it. For the belief is a manifestation of an arithmetic ability that is stable and reliable. Again, one can say that there is a mathematical sense that yields directly justified beliefs. But this seems to be an ad hoc move, designed only to save the view which the example counters: the view that knowing entails justifiably believing.

If we all turned out to have this mathematical ability under certain conditions, then we might *come* to believe that there is an arithmetic sense which generates such directly justified beliefs. Perhaps that shows that our concept of justification might evolve; but it does not show that the arithmetic beliefs in question are justified. If, however, these beliefs and those of the horse race predictor are knowledge, they are special cases. We might call them *natural knowledge*, since they seem rooted in the nature of their possessors and do not depend on their having learned anything (beyond acquiring the concepts required to hold the beliefs in question) or on their using either their senses or, so far as we can tell, their powers of reason. But even if natural knowledge is rare, its possibility would show that justified belief is not *necessarily* a constituent in knowledge.

If there can be natural knowledge, that possibility may show something important about both knowledge and justification. What inclines us to grant that the idiot savant knows the answer is chiefly the regularity of correct results and apparent stability of the mechanism yielding them. The accuracy of the results cannot, we suppose, be accidental; it must be rooted in some inner arithmetic process which regularly yields the right results. On being presented with the problem, the person registers the truth. By contrast, there is no mental process of arithmetic calculation of which the person is *aware*, nor anything else in which to *ground* justification, as one can ground it in visual impressions even when one is (unknowingly) having a vivid hallucination. This contrast suggests that there may be a major difference between knowledge and justification that explains why the former seems possible without the latter.

INTERNALISM AND EXTERNALISM

Could it be that justification and knowledge are grounded in quite different ways? Perhaps justification is grounded in what is *internal* to the mind of, and thus introspectively accessible to, the subject—a view we might call *internalism about justification*—whereas knowledge is grounded, at least in part, in what is *external*, and hence not introspectively accessible, to the subject—a view we might call *externalism about knowledge*. These forms of internalism and externalism are compatible, whereas parallel internalist and externalist views cannot both hold for justification alone or for knowledge alone. Internalist views differ regarding how readily the justifiers are accessible to introspection, and externalist views differ in the kind of non-introspective grasp they take to be possible regarding the grounds of knowledge.

Many points underlie the contrast between internalism and externalism. My concern will be chiefly with what seem the most plausible internalist and externalist views: internalism about justification and externalism about knowledge. To simplify matters, let us consider these views only in reference to grounds of justification and knowledge, not as applied to *how*, or *how strongly*, those sources justify. Thus, the imagined internalist about justification holds only that the grounds of one's justified beliefs are internal, for instance sensory states of the kind present in perception; it is not required that how or how strongly those grounds justify beliefs based on them (say, by guaranteeing their truth) be an internal matter and so, in principle, accessible to introspection. Similarly, the imagined externalist holds that what grounds knowledge—reliable production of true belief—is not wholly internal, and so not wholly accessible to introspection, even if part of the ground, say sensory experience, is. It is of course natural to hold (as reliabilists tend to) that *how* such belief production grounds knowledge is less likely to be accessible to introspection than *what* grounds it.

If these internalist and externalist views, about justification and knowledge respectively, are roughly correct, then the main point of contrast between knowledge and justification is this. Apart from self-knowledge, whose object is in some sense mental and thus in some way internal, what one knows is known on the basis of one's meeting conditions that are not introspectively accessible, as states or processes in one's consciousness are. By contrast, what one justifiably believes or is simply justified in believing, *is* determined by mental states and processes to which one has introspective access: one's visual experiences, for instance, or one's memory impressions, or one's reasoning processes, all of which are paradigms of the sorts of things about which we can have much introspective knowledge.

It is significant that for the externalist about knowledge, even introspective knowledge is based partly on what is not accessible to introspection, namely on the appropriate kind of dependence between the thing known, say one's imaging, and one's beliefs about it that constitute one's self-knowledge. Roughly, because one's imaging process reliably produces one's believing that one is imaging, one knows one is; but we have no internal access (and ordinarily none at all) to the relevant connections. What is crucial for knowledge, on the externalist view, is that the beliefs which constitute it register truth, and this depends on factors that are not internal in the crucial way: they are not accessible to introspection.

On the other hand, what is crucial for internalism about justification is that justified beliefs be those that one is in some sense entitled to hold, given the sensory impressions, rational intuitions, and other internal materials introspectively accessible to one. In very broad terms, the strongest contrast may be this. The internalist regarding justification tends to conceive justification, in accordance with certain justificational standards, as a matter of having a *right to believe*; the externalist about knowledge tends to conceive knowledge, in accordance with certain epistemic standards, as a matter of *being right*. The first view becomes *internalism about knowledge* if one adds the requirement that the belief be true and one strengthens the standards of justification. The second view becomes *externalism about justification* if one subtracts the requirement that the belief be true and weakens the epistemic standards, such as the required degree of reliability.

The idea that knowledge is externally grounded and justification internally grounded would help to explain why reliability theories are, in the ways I have indicated, as plausible as they are for knowledge, yet much less plausible for justification. It is true that the sources of justification of belief seem generally to be sources of true belief. But must they be? Could not my apparently normal visual experience in hallucinating a blue spruce where there is none justify me in believing there is one quite as strongly as an ordinary seeing of it? Surely it could. Moreover, though I would not know that there is a blue spruce before me, the internalist would hold that my justification for believing there is could be quite as good as it would be if I did know it.

It is true that if I justifiably believe I may be hallucinating, then I am unlikely to be justified in believing there is a blue spruce there. But my beliefs, including beliefs about possible hallucinations, are themselves internal; we thus have one internal factor affecting the way another bears on justification, not an external factor preventing the generation of justification by a basic source of it. Moreover, notice how the clear cases of highly reliable belief production illustrated by the predictor and the lightning calculator do *not* appear to generate justification, though they do appear to generate knowledge. Furthermore, no matter how reliable my perceptual processes are, say in giving me impressions of birds flying by, and thereby true beliefs that they are flying by, if I confidently and reflectively believe, and especially if I also justifiably believe, that my vision is *un*reliable, then it is doubtful that I am justified in believing that birds are flying by. The more confident and reflective my belief that my vision is unreliable, the less the justification, if any, of my belief that birds are flying by.

If knowledge and justification do contrast in the suggested way, why is justification important to knowledge at all, as it certainly seems to be? Part of the answer may be that first, the sources of justified belief—experience and reason—are generally sources of knowledge, and second, virtually the only knowledge we can conceive of for beings like ourselves is apparently grounded, at least indirectly, in those sources. If these points are correct, then we can at least understand how knowledge typically arises if we think of it as justified belief; and if we think of it as appropriately justified true belief, then, conceiving knowledge under that description, we can at least pick out the vast majority of its instances.

JUSTIFICATION AND TRUTH

There may be a further, perhaps deeper, point implicit in what has been said about justification and knowledge. Justification by its very nature has some kind of connection with *truth*. One can see this by noting that there is something fundamentally wrong with supposing that a belief's being justified has nothing whatever to do with its truth. This is perhaps most readily seen with a priori justification. In the paradigm cases, as with beliefs of self-evident propositions and very simple proofs of theorems of logic, it is arguable that one's having a priori justification *entails* the truth of the beliefs so justified. These cases are unlike perceptual ones in that if a belief claimed to be so justified turns out to be false, there is at least normally a defect in the purported justification, say a careless error in the proof. But justification of empirical beliefs also seems connected with truth. If, for instance, we discovered that the sense of smell almost never yielded beliefs that corresponded to the facts (thus to truth) as determined by other sources of belief, we would have good reason to cease to regard olfactory impressions as a source of direct justification, or at least to consider it a far weaker source.

These points about the relation of justification to truth suggest that even if it is an internal matter whether a belief is justified, the standards we use for determining justification are responsive to our considered judgments about which internal sources tend to produce true beliefs. The way we conceive justification, then, makes it well suited to help us understand knowledge, in at least this way: when a belief is justified, it has the sort of property which, by its very nature as apparently grounding the belief in the real world, we *take* to count toward the truth of the belief, hence (other things being equal) towards its being knowledge. Justified true belief need not be knowledge, and knowledge apparently need not be justified belief. But normally knowledge arises from the same sources as justification: normally, the internal states and processes that entitle us to believe also connect our beliefs with the external facts in virtue of which our beliefs are true.

This way of speaking of truth suggests that (except in the case of propositions about oneself) it too is external. That is indeed the view I am taking. I am thinking of true propositions along the lines of a version of *the correspondence theory of truth*, whose central thesis is that true propositions "correspond" with reality. It is usually added that they are true *in virtue of* that correspondence. Thus, the proposition that there is a blue spruce before me is true provided that in reality there *is* a blue spruce before me; and it might also be said that it is true in virtue of there really being such a tree before me. An apparently equivalent expression of the first, modest formulation would be this: to say that the proposition is true is to say that it represents reality. This, in turn, is usually taken to mean that it is, or at least expresses, a *fact*. How else could we even think of truth, one might wonder? What else could it mean to say that a proposition is true than that things (or the facts) really are as the proposition has it?

There are alternatives to the correspondence view. The most widely known is perhaps *the coherence theory of truth*. Though it takes many forms, its central idea, expressed very broadly, is that a true proposition is one that coheres appropriately with certain other propositions. (The theory may also be expressed in terms of what it is for *beliefs* to be true, but that formulation invites confusion of the coherence theory of truth with the coherence theory of knowledge, which is a quite different thing.) I cannot discuss truth in detail here, but let me indicate how a coherence theory of truth might go if justification is its central concept. The theory might say that a true proposition is one which is fully justified by virtue of coherence with every other relevant justified proposition, where a justified proposition is, minimally, one that at least someone is (or anyway might be) justified in believing.

There are difficulties in selecting the justified propositions relevant to the truth of another proposition which is true in virtue of coherence with them. A plausible example of how truth can be based on coherence might be a proposition I am perceptually justified in believing, say that there is a spruce before me, which coheres with what I justifiably believe on the basis of memory, introspection, inference, and so on, as well as with what I or others *would* be justified in believing in these ways. This proposition would be true in virtue of coherence with others, such as that I seem to remember a spruce there. But the propositions for which I now have justification are not the only ones that matter. If they were, then if I visually hallucinated a spruce systematically enough, say with accompanying tactual hallucinations and supporting memory impressions, it would be true that there is one before me. By making the set of relevant propositions indefinitely large, the theory seeks to prevent such embarrassing results. Thus, if I am hallucinating, there is surely some proposition I could come to be justified in believing, say that the "tree" will not burn, which is not coherent with the proposition that there is a spruce there.

There is also a negative motivation for the coherence theory of truth. When we try to understand what correspondence means, we seem thrown back on some kind of coherence. To say that the proposition that the tree is blue corresponds with reality seems to come to little more than saying that in testing this proposition, say by examining the tree in good light, one will always get (or will at least in the main get) confirming results, that is, discover propositions that cohere well with the original one. This kind of point has even led some thinkers to go further and hold a *pragmatic theory of truth*, on which true propositions are simply those that "work," in the sense that believing them, acting on them, and otherwise confirming them, leads (at least in the long run) to positive results, such as spectrographic confirmation of the tree's color.

Correspondence theorists have replied that points made by proponents of coherence (and pragmatic) theories of truth confuse the *criteria* of truth, roughly, the standards for determining whether a proposition is true, with what truth *is*. In support of this, they often argue that a false proposition *could* cohere with all propositions that are ever justified, including those discovered in attempted confirmation of it. We might, after all, be permanently unlucky in testing it, so that we never discover its falsity; or a malevolent demon might always prevent us from discovering our mistake. These points parallel some made against phenomenalism, which may (though it need not) be held by a proponent of a coherence theory of truth. A malevolent demon, for instance, might similarly prevent one from discovering that a stable, recurring set of sense-data which coheres with one's other sense-data represents hallucination rather than a concrete object. If it is possible for coherence to be systematically misleading in this way, then neither coherence with justified propositions nor any other kind of pure coherence can be what truth *is*.

I cannot pursue this issue, but it should be plain that it is crucial to assessing the coherence theory of truth. I want to add only that despite the similarities between the coherence theory of truth and the coherence theory of justification, neither theory entails the other. The analysis of knowledge, moreover, can be discussed within either framework for conceiving truth. But particularly if one favors a reliability theory of knowledge, the correspondence view of truth seems more appropriate. This is in part because the notion of reliable production is not readily analyzed along coherentist lines, especially if the notion of justification is central in that of truth as the coherence theory of truth conceives truth. For then an apparently value-laden notion would be required for understanding reliability, which is conceived in part as a property belonging to processes that produce *true* beliefs.

Is there no analysis of knowledge that we may tentatively accept as correct and illuminating? There certainly may be; the ones I have discussed are only a representative sample of the available theories, and even they can be refined in response to problems of the kind I have raised. But I am not aware of any straightforward analysis of knowledge which is *both* illuminating and clearly correct.

We may, however, be able to formulate a sound *conception* of knowledge which helps in seeking a full-dress account. We might say that knowledge is *true belief based in the right way on the right kind of ground*. This conception leaves a great deal open, but what we have seen in this chapter and earlier ones indicates many ways in which one might develop it into a detailed account. It may, but need not, turn out that the right kind of basis is in part causal. It may, but need not, turn out that the right kind of ground always justifies the belief. And it may, but need not, turn out that ultimately epistemic chains terminate in justification, or in some other kind of ground of knowledge, that is direct in the way foundationalism maintains it is. No matter how these questions are resolved, the conception indicates where a great deal of the work in understanding knowledge must be done. We need an account of how knowledge is based on that in virtue of which it is knowledge, for instance perception, introspection, and reason; and this will require an account of inferential transmission as well as non-inferential grounding. We need an understanding of whether the appropriate bases of knowledge must produce it through generating justified belief, or may yield knowledge independently of justification. We must also have a general understanding of what it is for a belief constituting knowledge to be true. And we need an account of whether the ultimate grounding of knowledge is some kind of coherence among one's beliefs or, as I think more likely, anchoring in experiential and rational foundations.

The Scope of Knowledge

In perceiving the world around me I constantly acquire knowledge: of colors and shapes, objects and events, people and their doings. I also acquire knowledge as I look into my own consciousness. By thinking about things I already know and by drawing inferences from that, I extend some of my knowledge. And through memory, I retain much of my knowledge. Justification is acquired, extended, and retained in much the same way. That point holds even if knowledge does not entail justified belief. But how far does our knowledge extend? I have explored how knowledge is transmitted, but not how far. I now want to consider three important domains to which it is widely thought to extend: the scientific, the moral, and the religious. I shall do this briefly; I simply want to see how the framework laid out so far might help in understanding knowledge in relation to a few important aspects of science, ethics, and religion. My focus will be more on knowledge than on justification. But much of what comes to light regarding knowledge will apply to justification, and some of it may hold in other domains, such as that of art or history or literature.

SCIENTIFIC KNOWLEDGE

If I knew nothing through perception, I would have no scientific knowledge. And however much scientific knowledge one can acquire by instruction from someone else, the *discoveries* which that knowledge represents must be made partly on the basis of perceptual experience: if not through that person's laboratory work or observations of nature, then by someone on whose perceptions the discoveries depend, directly or indirectly. But how does scientific discovery fit into the framework I have developed? The simple picture which readily comes to mind is that one makes observations, inductively generalizes from them, and comes to know the truth of a generalization, by virtue of inductive transmission of knowledge from one's premises to one's conclusion. Imagine Galileo rolling balls down his famous inclined plane. He measures their acceleration, collects the individual items of knowledge he thereby acquires, arrays them as premises, and generalizes (in a special way) to his formula that gives the rate of acceleration for such balls in general. What does a case like this show?

First, the example rightly suggests that scientists tend to be interested in the nature and the behavior of *kinds* of things, such as accelerating objects, and that what is typically considered scientific knowledge is of *generalizations*: for instance, propositions about all freely falling bodies, not any particular one. Knowledge of particulars is needed to obtain such general knowledge, but the former may be simply ordinary perceptual knowledge. Granted, knowledge which is of a particular thing, but *derived* from a scientific generalization, say knowledge that a parachutist will reach the ground at a specific time, is scientific in the sense that it is scientifically *based*. Still, it is not the sort of knowledge typically regarded as scientific, nor the kind scientists directly seek in trying to understand nature.

The second point suggested by the example is that scientific knowledge is inductively, not deductively, grounded. For instance, the generalization Galileo discovered does not *follow* from the premises he formulated in expressing his data, say that ball 1 accelerated at a certain rate, that ball 2 accelerated at that rate, and so on. The generalization is strongly *confirmed* by such premises, but not entailed by them. For this reason, such premises, regardless of how well they *justify* it, do not *prove* it. The same holds for premises of other scientific reasoning that yields, from knowledge of data, knowledge of a generalization. Thus, it is best to avoid calling the reasoning that establishes a scientific generalization "scientific proof," as some people do. It is not even deductively valid, much less the kind of reasoning illustrated by a geometrical proof of a theorem from axioms.

A third aspect of the example, however, may mislead. The example portrays Galileo simply observing and then generalizing, yet says nothing about *why* he is observing. But he made his observations for a reason. This is to be expected; scientific knowledge typically does not arise simply from haphazard observations. Normally there is a *question*, such as whether falling objects speed up, that leads to observing a particular kind of thing. Moreover, normally there is a tentative answer to such a question, a *hypothesis*, which both guides observation *and* sets the epistemic goal of the observations or the experiments that lead to scientific discovery. For instance, one might hypothesize that the balls speed up 100 percent in a given time interval and thus observe their speed at each such interval to see whether it doubles, quadruples, and so on. One's goal in this is to show that the hypothesis is true and thereby come to know it, or, if it is not true, to find a hypothesis that does account for the behavior of the balls.

The central point here is that scientific knowledge does not automatically arise as we observe our surroundings. Normally, we must first raise questions about the world; they direct our inquiry. Only in the light of such questions are we in a good position to formulate hypotheses. These, in turn, are the raw material of scientific knowledge. Some are rejected, some are confirmed, and some that are confirmed become knowledge. Scientific knowledge does not develop, then, simply by inferential extension of what we already know. Normally, it emerges only after we use some *imagination*, both in formulating questions and in framing hypotheses to answer them. This is one place where scientific *invention* occurs. It is not only machines and devices that are invented but also hypotheses and theories.

The essential place of imagination in the development of scientific knowledge is also illustrated by discoveries that result not from coming to know a generalization, but from apparent *refutations* of a proposition thought to be already known. The planet Neptune was discovered because the observed orbit of Uranus (then the farthest known planet) was not as expected according to the laws of planetary motion, the principles astronomers use in describing the motions and paths of the planets. Partly in order to avoid having to revise well confirmed laws, it was hypothesized that the deviation of Uranus from its expected orbit might be explained by the gravitational effect of another, more distant planet. The observations made to test this hypothesis revealed Neptune. Once again, through imagination, a hypothesis is formulated; and through testing it, a discovery is made and new knowledge acquired. And again, the basis of the new knowledge is inductive, though unlike Galileo's knowledge about freely falling bodies, it is not a result of generalization. The pattern here is a successful case of *inference to the best explanation*. One imaginatively hypothesizes that a gravitational influence by another planet best explains the deviation, tentatively infers that there is such a planet, tests the hypothesis, and, through positive results of the test, comes to know that the hypothesis is true.

These examples do not imply that deduction has no substantial role in the development of scientific knowledge. Far from it. Once we have a hypothesis, we typically need deduction to determine how to test it. For instance, one needs deductive mathematical reasoning to predict where to look for an as yet undiscovered planet, given a certain deviation in the orbit of Uranus. Moreover, from very general laws, such as Newton's laws of motion, one may deduce less general laws, for instance the laws of planetary motion and Galileo's law of acceleration. (Actually, the best that one may be able to do is deduce generalizations which these laws only approximate; for instance, Galileo's law does not take account of slight changes in acceleration due to minute increases in gravitational attraction as the falling object nears the earth. But this deduction still helps to explain why we should get approximately the results we do in testing or applying that law.)

Deductions of these kinds help to *unify* scientific knowledge. For example, they enable us to exhibit all the laws of motion—for planets, for falling bodies, for projectiles, and so on—as instances of the general laws of motion. Even the behavior of gases, conceived as collections of molecular particles, can be explained by appeal to the general laws of motion. Their pressure in a container of air, for instance, is explainable in terms of how hard the particles hit its walls; this pressure, in turn, is connected with their temperature viewed as explainable by their average speed of movement. Thus, the laws of motion provide an understanding of what determines both pressure and temperature. They also give us, by appropriate deductive inferences, a subsidiary law (Boyle's Law) correlating temperature with pressure at a constant volume.

Can we, then, have scientific proof after all, where we validly deduce a special law of, say, motion, from more general ones? No; for while we might prove the special law *relative to* the more general ones, our knowledge of the more general laws is ultimately inductive: it is based on inference to the best explanation or on generalization from observed data or, more likely, on a combination of these procedures. If our scientific premises are not proved, and if indeed they stand to be revised as new discoveries are made—which is a common fate of generalizations in science—then what we know only through deduction from them is not proved either.

So far, I have sketched some of the ways in which scientific knowledge develops and have criticized certain stereotypes of science. It is not, for instance, a domain in which hypotheses are proved conclusively, nor are they typically discovered by simply generalizing from observations we happen to collect. These points, however, imply nothing about whether scientific generalizations are *true*, or can be known.

If a common fate of generalizations in science is their eventual revision, one might now wonder whether we should not also reject the idea that there is scientific *knowledge* at all. Even the incomparable Sir Isaac Newton, as he was called, turned out to be mistaken on some important points; and even if discovering this took centuries, is there good reason to believe that any other scientific generalizations are, strictly speaking, true, in the sense that they describe the world both correctly and timelessly, and apply to its past, present, and future? If some are true, that may not be typical. Very commonly, what we call scientific knowledge is regarded by scientists as needing refinement and as possibly mistaken. Quite properly, their attitude is fallibilistic. But if they accept *fallibilism* regarding scientific beliefs—the view that these beliefs may be mistaken—they also tend to hold a kind of *objectivism*: the position that there is an objective method for ascertaining whether beliefs about the world are true, that is (roughly speaking), a method which can be used by any competent investigator and tends to yield the same results when properly applied by different competent investigators to the same problem. Scientific method is widely taken by scientists and philosophers alike to be a paradigm of an objective method.

Since we cannot know what is not true, one might conclude that we should really not speak of scientific knowledge at all, but only of relatively well-confirmed scientific hypotheses. This is a defensible position. I prefer, however, to account for the apparent facts in a way that allows us to maintain that there is scientific knowledge. One possibility is that in speaking of scientific knowledge we are often speaking a bit loosely of what might be called *approximate knowledge*: well-grounded belief which, apart from minor inaccuracies, is true. Newton's laws have not, after all, been found to be completely inaccurate. In building bridges, as opposed to dealing with astronomical distances or elementary particles, they seem to be an adequate guide, and their being only approximately true need cause no trouble. One can insist that what is not precisely true is simply not known. But we could also say that what is approximately true may be an object of approximate knowledge, and that beliefs of such propositions are both fallible and typically held with an openness to their revision in the light of new discoveries. I prefer the latter way of speaking.

There is, however, a second way to account for the apparent falsity of certain scientific generalizations. It seems that often their formulations are not properly taken to be absolutely precise, and that, rightly interpreted, they are true so far as they go. Consider the general law that metals are conductors of electricity. Perhaps this should be interpreted with the understanding that certain abnormal (or for practical purposes impossible) conditions do not obtain. If metals should fail to conduct electricity at absolute zero, would this show the generalization false or simply that its appropriate *scope of application* is limited? The latter view seems more plausible. I am not denying that scientific generalizations *can* be shown to be simply false. My point is that in some cases, instead of saying that scientific generalizations are not really true, it is preferable to speak either of approximate knowledge of a precisely formulated, but only approximately true, generalization or, as in this case, of *unqualified knowledge of an imprecisely formulated truth*. The difference is roughly that between approximate knowledge and knowledge of an approximation. In practice, however, there is no easy way to decide which, if either, of these cases one is confronted with.

If we consider science in historical perspective and do not idealize it, then, it turns out that there is no unqualified answer to the question whether what is called scientific knowledge is knowledge as I have been conceiving it. If we assume that there are some scientific propositions which are strictly true—and I see no reason to believe there are none—then we apparently have no good ground for thinking that they *cannot* be known (or at least justifiably believed). But the history of science indicates much change and extensive, apparently ceaseless correction of previously accepted hypotheses. For all the progress it exhibits, it also gives us cause to wonder whether even at this advanced stage in scientific development we grasp *many* scientific truths about the world that future investigation will never show to be inaccurate. I am inclined to say that we nevertheless do have much scientific knowledge, though it is perhaps all only approximate knowledge, or knowledge of approximations. But even if we have a great deal of scientific knowledge, if much of it is approximate or is knowledge of approximations, we are quite some distance from the picture one might have of scientific knowledge as a set of beliefs of precisely formulated and strictly true generalizations, arrived at by inductive transmission of knowledge from its basic sources in experience and reason. Those sources remain basic, and scientific method provides an objective way of building on them. But there is no straightforward transmission, nor, when transmission occurs, any clearly final destination toward which it proceeds.

MORAL KNOWLEDGE

The possibility of moral knowledge raises rather different sorts of questions from those just explored. Moreover, whereas there is a widespread tendency to take for granted that there is much scientific knowledge, there is also a widespread inclination to take moral judgments to represent at best cultural assumptions with no claim to genuine truth. Consider the judgment that cruelty to children is wrong. We *accept* this, but do we know it? Suppose someone denies it or simply asks us to justify it. It does not appear that we can establish it scientifically. It is apparently not a scientific judgment in the first place. Furthermore, it is not in any obvious way a judgment grounded in perception, nor is it clearly grounded in reason, at least in the way the a priori truths I have discussed apparently are. Many people find it natural to consider this judgment to be grounded in our culture and to be accepted simply as part of the social fabric that holds our lives together.

There are two main variants of the view that moral judgments are somehow grounded in our culture. One—*a form of relativism*—says roughly that such judgments are *true relative to* our culture, but not unqualifiedly true, as judgments of fact, such as that a blue spruce is before me, may be. The other—*the attitudinal view*—says roughly that such judgments are not literally true at all; rather, they are expressions of moral attitudes—normally, attitudes rooted in the culture of the person judging—not assertions of a proposition. On this view, to say that cruelty to children is wrong is like uttering 'Cruelty to children!' in a tone expressing revulsion and adding, 'I hereby take a negative attitude towards it'. An attitude may be reasonable or unreasonable and may be defended with reference to what *is* true or false; but attitudes are not themselves true or false.

On both views, there is no moral knowledge, since there either are no moral propositions at all (the negative claim of the attitudinal view), or at least none that are true unqualifiedly, as propositions expressing empirical or necessary truths are (the negative claim of the relativist view in question). The attitudinal view is thus committed to *non-cognitivism*, which is roughly the claim that there are no moral propositions to be known, or otherwise "cognized." The relativist position in question need not make this claim; but, as will be evident in some examples, it is not clear precisely how propositions *can* be true in a way other than the way empirical and necessary truths are.

The attitudinal interpretation of moral judgments is on the surface the more radical view. If it is true, then there simply are no moral truths, and there are no moral falsehoods either. There are no moral propositions to be known, or to be justifiably or even mistakenly believed in the first place. What makes this view plausible? Suppose one is very impressed with the basic sources of knowledge as our only routes to knowledge, and one notes that apparently *no* propositions known on the basis of sense experience seem to entail the truth of any moral judgment. For instance, that cruelty to children causes them pain does not *entail* that it is wrong. Needed surgery, after all, may cause them pain yet not be wrong. When we judge something to be wrong we apparently go beyond the evidence of the senses, and indeed beyond scientific evidence. For example, suppose that (as is surely possible) we know scientifically that in fact cruelty to children commonly breeds brutality in its victims. Unless we already know or are justified in believing that breeding brutality is wrong, this fact does not justify us in believing that cruelty to children is wrong. It thus seems that we cannot know that cruelty to children is wrong just on the basis of the fact that it causes brutality; this fact would (deductively) ground that knowledge for us only if we *already* knew that brutality is wrong. Now suppose we also assume that nothing known a priori entails that cruelty to children is wrong: no logical truth surely, and not even a proposition like the truth that nothing is red and green all over. These points serve as premises for the negative conclusion that there is no moral knowledge. For if knowledge is grounded in the basic sources and moral judgments are not, then moral judgments do not constitute knowledge.

There is also a positive thesis held by the attitudinal theory: that even though moral judgments do not express propositions, they *do* express significant attitudes. A main reason for saying that they express attitudes is that we are not *neutral* in making moral judgments; we are (normally) pro or con. Moreover, normally we at least indirectly *commend or condemn* when we make a positive or negative moral judgment. Suppose we take these points together with the premises for the negative conclusion that there are no moral propositions, which itself implies that there is no moral knowledge. It is now plausible to conclude that the *point* of a moral judgment is not to assert an unknowable proposition, but to express a positive or negative attitude and thereby to influence human conduct, if only by endorsing or condemning one or another kind of behavior. This position does not imply that in moral matters "anything goes"; for it is still possible to hold an unreasonable attitude, say one based on misinformation and prejudice. The view can thus allow that there are even moral mistakes. But mistakes that are specifically moral are mistakes in attitude, not about what is true.

The relativistic view that moral judgments are culturally grounded endorses the first argument just set out, based on the premise that those judgments are not rooted in the basic sources of knowledge, but not the second, attitudinal argument. On this relativist view, while moral judgments are not rooted in those basic sources, they are learned as we absorb (or react against) our culture, and they may thus share with judgments that do represent knowledge a wide social acceptability. Still, we are at best entitled to assert them *within* our society (or one that morally agrees with it), and they are at best *true for* one or another society. They are not unqualifiedly true, hence not genuinely known. If they express propositions, those propositions are assertible in our culture, but not unqualifiedly true.

Consider first the part of each position not shared with the other one. Is there an alternative explanation of the attitudinal aspect of moral judgments? Might they be true or false and still have, for instance, the commendatory or condemnatory force they do? Consider the utterance, 'The curtains are on fire!' Sincerely uttered by any normal person, this would commonly express alarm and be meant to evoke action. But it is clearly factual and can be unqualifiedly true. Moreover, it seems to be *because* of its factual content that it expresses the kind of alarm it does. Perhaps certain statements of those facts that are significantly and obviously linked to human concerns are no more attitudinally neutral than are typical moral judgments. For this reason (among others), one might resist the idea that either the distinctive or the main function of moral judgments is to express attitudes, as opposed to asserting propositions.

Similarly, one might explain the fact that moral judgments are, in some cases, culturally tinged and differ from one culture to another, by arguing that the *beliefs* they express may be learned through absorbing a culture, even if what *justifies* those beliefs or renders them knowledge does not depend on a particular culture, for example on its customs or prejudices. Clearly, the origin of a belief need not be what justifies it. Thus, we might learn a moral principle through something characteristic of our culture (such as our moral education), even though what justifies it is not grounded only in our culture.

Suppose that our moral beliefs do arise from our education and culture. There is good reason to say that at least many of our scientific beliefs do too. If we need not thereby regard the relevant scientific beliefs as culturally relative, why should we so regard moral beliefs? Both kinds of judgments, moreover, are "true for" the social groups that hold them, at least *in the sense that* the people in question *believe* them. But anything we believe is in that sense true for us. If this is how moral judgments are "relative to" those who make them, their "relativity" is shared with simple self-evident truths, such as that if the spruce is taller than the birch, then the birch is not taller than the spruce. There may be important moral principles true for one society and not another, in the sense that in one of the societies, but not the other, people generally believe them. But, as the analogy to scientific disagreement indicates, that would show nothing about whether moral principles or judgments can be known or justifiably believed.

We are now getting to the heart of the issue. For it will be objected that we can use experience and reason to test scientific beliefs, but not to test moral judgments. We are back to the argument which the relativist and attitudinal views share: that since experience and reason do not ground moral judgments, those judgments cannot express knowledge. This argument must be squarely met.

The first thing to be stressed is that, from the premise that moral judgments are not *deducible* from facts, it simply does not follow that they are not *justifiable* by appeal to facts. That this conclusion does not follow seems evident from our discussion of scientific knowledge which—assuming there is some—illustrates that knowledge can arise through inductive transmission from evidential premises. Scientific generalizations, for example, are inductively known on the basis of the facts (such as observational data) which we use to confirm them. If there can be scientific knowledge on this basis, then there *can* be knowledge based on inductive grounds, grounds that do not entail the proposition we know on the basis of them. Thus, there might be inductively grounded moral knowledge even if no moral knowledge is deductively grounded.

The obvious reply to this argument is that moral generalizations are not even inductively supported by the facts. But is that true? We certainly appeal to facts to justify moral judgments. I might justify my judgment that I must meet with Jane by citing the simple fact that I promised to. Someone might then ask why I should keep my promises in the first place. I could perhaps explain why I believe this. But suppose that I cannot justify it by appeal to anything more fundamental. This would not show that I do not know or justifiably believe it. At some point or other in defending a *factual* judgment I may be equally incapable of giving a further justification. It would not follow that the judgment I am defending does not express knowledge or justified belief.

The issue before us should be explicitly considered in the light of what we saw concerning the structure of knowledge. A foundationalist may say that (with some special exceptions) the principle that one should keep one's promises, or at least some more general principle, such as that people should be treated with respect, is simply obvious and needs no defense. Foundationalists might argue that such a response is legitimate when we get to certain stages in a process of justification because some beliefs are foundational in a way that entitles us to hold them without doing so on the basis of prior premises. If that were not true, then we could not be justified in holding anything. A coherentist may be willing to go on arguing, perhaps pointing out that if we do not keep our promises life will be unbearable, and then defending each thesis attacked with respect to one or more others. The objector may not be pacified by this approach either. But neither approach can simply be rejected out of hand. To be warranted in rejecting either approach, one must have a plausible alternative conception of knowledge and justification. What would it be? That is far from evident, as we shall soon see in exploring skepticism.

These responses on behalf of the possibility of moral knowledge do not go as far as one might like. They rest on limited analogies and on simply showing that the case against moral knowledge is inconclusive. But there are two very important direct responses we should consider. One, defended perhaps most powerfully by Kant and later Kantians, construes knowledge of moral principles as a priori. The other, defended perhaps most powerfully by Mill and later utilitarians, represents moral principles as empirical. In either case, moral knowledge—and moral justification—are grounded in the basic experiential and rational sources I have been discussing. Let us briefly consider these responses.

To understand the first, broadly Kantian, response, consider a qualified version of our sample principle. Let us say that flogging infants for pleasure is wrong. There is some plausibility in saying that we know this. It seems correct on reflection, and it is at least difficult to conceive exceptions. Perhaps flogging an infant for pleasure might be *excusable*. Terrorists might electrically manipulate my brain so that I change in personality and am somehow brought to flog an infant for pleasure, but even then I would be doing something wrong, though doing it excusably.

Consider another example, a modest version of something more powerful: we ought to treat people equally in matters of life and death unless they differ in some relevant way (and not merely in being different people). This is a kind of principle of *consistency*. It says that such prima facie inconsistent treatment is wrong and that differential treatment in these mortal matters must be justified by a difference. It does not specify what kind of difference is relevant, for example that skin color is irrelevant. Specifying relevant differences is a further step. But the principle is still a moral one, and it implies the important requirement that a *reason* be given to justify the indicated differences in treatment. Particularly since it is a consistency principle, there is some reason to believe that if it is true, it is knowable a priori, though defending this idea would be a major task.

The second response, which is utilitarian, is very different. It says that (1) our moral judgments are knowable on the basis of factual knowledge of how our acting in accordance with them would contribute to something that is *intrinsically good*, that is, good in itself, independently of what it leads to. Mill maintained that (2) only pleasure and freedom from pain are good in themselves. He believed that if these two premises can themselves be known (as he thought they could be), they justify holding, as one's fundamental moral principle, something like this: that precisely those acts are right which contribute at least as much to pleasure (and freedom from pain) in the world as any alternative available to the agent in question. Since, on his view, we can determine what acts those are, that is, what acts have the most *utility*, by a combination of common sense and scientific procedures, moral judgments are knowable in the same way as common sense and scientific statements.

The question that now arises is how we know that pleasure or anything else is intrinsically good. Mill argued that we can know this by determining what people by nature actually desire for its own sake. But the utilitarian approach is by no means committed to that view (which many commentators on Mill find implausible). For instance, it might be argued instead that what is intrinsically good is what people want or would want for its own sake *provided* their wants are adequately rational, say held in the light of reflection that is logically and scientifically rational, vivid, and appropriately focused on the nature of the thing wanted.

The Kantian and utilitarian responses to challenges to moral knowledge are nicely parallel to Kant's and Mill's views of the truths of reason. On Kant's rationalistic view (only part of which has been introduced), moral principles must be (synthetic) a priori. On Mill's empiricist view (only part of which I have stated), moral principles must be empirical. There is a further epistemologically interesting contrast between these two views. On Kant's approach (or at least on some approaches of the same rationalistic kind), there can be *direct* moral knowledge. For at least one moral principle is so basic that knowledge of it need not be inferentially grounded in knowledge of any other propositions. On the utilitarian approach, there cannot be *direct* moral knowledge—except where such knowledge is only *memorially direct*, that is, direct as preserved in memory, but *originally* indirect and now direct just by virtue of one's forgetting one's evidential grounds for it, as one forgets the steps in proving a theorem and remembers only the theorem. On Mill's view, knowledge that, say, keeping one's promises is obligatory would ultimately depend on someone's knowing a good deal about the effects of promise-keeping on happiness. One could know the principle through parental teaching given in the course of one's moral education, and one could establish it for oneself by studying human behavior and then retain one's knowledge of it after forgetting one's grounds. But no one could know it directly unless *someone* knew it inferentially, through evidence.

This difference between Kant and Mill is no accident: for Mill's utilitarianism, moral properties, such as being obligatory, are unlike sensory properties in not being *directly experienced*. As an empiricistic, and thus experienced-based, moral theory, it must treat knowledge of moral truths as *ultimately* indirect (unless, as has occasionally been done, it posits moral experience as a source of knowledge that grounds knowledge rather in the way perception does). Thus, even if, by memory, I have some direct moral knowledge, no moral knowledge is *basic*, in the sense that it *need* not at any time be grounded in another kind of knowledge. If I know that cruelty to children is wrong, it is by virtue of my (or someone's) knowing that it does not contribute optimally to happiness in the world. For a broadly Kantian view, on the other hand, we can rationally grasp this principle, and apparently we can sometimes even *directly* grasp a moral principle, for instance that arbitrarily unequal treatment of persons in matters of life and death is wrong. We can thus have moral knowledge which is direct and basic. But even if Kant is best interpreted as construing the most general moral knowledge as depending on non-moral premises, he took all moral knowledge to be deductively derivable from (and only from) a priori premises and thus itself a priori (at least on the assumption that the derivations are short enough not to render one's knowledge of their conclusions dependent on memory).

Should Kantian or utilitarian views convince us that there is moral knowledge? From what I have said about them, it is not obvious that they should. But, when carefully developed, they are each plausible, and both may be held with the attitude of objectivistic fallibilism that is also appropriate to scientific beliefs. Both views certainly seem to warrant the conclusion that there *can* be moral knowledge, despite the sorts of relativistic and attitudinal arguments I raised to indicate why some thinkers deny its possibility. There are, of course, other issues that should be explored in deciding whether moral principles or judgments can be known, or even justifiably believed. There may, for instance, be sources of knowledge, such as a special moral faculty analogous to perception, which are not in the end rooted in experience or reason as conceived in Part One. But I see no reason to believe there are. Indeed, if we have a special moral faculty, it presumably *is* a kind of rational capacity whose insights are rational ones. Whatever the problems that remain, perhaps enough has been said to connect those problems with the epistemological framework I have developed. Certainly, locating moral judgments in that framework is at least a good way to approach the question whether they can constitute knowledge.

RELIGIOUS KNOWLEDGE

The case of possible religious knowledge is different in many ways from that of possible moral knowledge, but it can still be clarified in the light of some of the concepts and principles I have introduced. Again, I want to be quite brief and to start with the negative view that religious propositions are simply beyond the scope of our knowledge. I have in mind, of course, propositions about God, such as that God exists, brought order out of chaos, and loves us: propositions that do not merely have a religious subject matter but also imply that there *is* a God (or some other spiritual reality worthy of a central place in a religion).

Why would it be thought that no religious propositions are known? The most common ground for holding this view is very much like the most common reason for holding that there is no moral knowledge, namely, that religious propositions, such as that God exists, cannot be known either a priori or on the basis of experience, say by inferring God's existence from the premise that God's designing the universe is the best explanation of the order we find in it.

Both aspects of this negative claim have been discussed by philosophers and theologians at great length, and there are well-known arguments for the existence of God meant to provide knowledge that God exists. Some of these make use only of a priori premises; others use only empirical propositions as premises. For instance, the ontological argument, in one form, proceeds from the a priori premises that God is supremely perfect (has all perfections in the highest degree), and that existence is a perfection, to the conclusion that God exists. By contrast, the argument from first cause (in one form) uses the empirical premise that there is motion, together with the general premise that there cannot be an infinite chain of causes of motion, and concludes that God, as an unmoved first mover, exists.

There is a vast literature about these and all the other historically important arguments for the existence of God. I am not concerned here with arguments for God's existence. All I want to say about those arguments is that nothing in the framework I have developed implies either that there can or that there cannot be cogent arguments for God's existence. For instance, nothing said about the basic sources of knowledge or about its transmission implies that those sources could not lead to knowledge of a spiritual reality. The same point applies to transmission of justification, and both points hold within either a foundationalist or a coherentist epistemology. Moreover, I believe that nothing in the *concept* of a spiritual reality, or of God in particular, makes knowledge (or justified belief) that God exists impossible to establish by argument within the epistemological framework of this book.

But what about the possibility—far less often discussed than arguments for God's existence—of *direct* (non-inferential) knowledge of God? Does the framework rule out that possibility? General epistemological considerations have sometimes been thought to do so, but they do not. Indeed, if there can be what I have called natural knowledge, as in the case of direct knowledge of arithmetical results ordinarily knowable only through lengthy calculation, then there is some reason to think that knowledge can be built-in in such a way that there could be direct knowledge of God, though to be sure there may be less mystery about how a calculational mechanism could be built into the brain than about how knowledge of an external, spiritual reality could be. Still, if it is even *possible* that there is an omnipotent God, that God could create such direct knowledge. If there can be such knowledge, then one form of what is called *evidentialism* is mistaken, namely, *evidentialism about knowledge*, the view that knowledge of God is impossible except on the basis of adequate evidence. (A more modest form of evidentialism holding only that there *is* no actual direct knowledge of God, would be unaffected by the possible existence of an omnipotent God.)

How might evidentialism apply to justification? Recall the prima facie cases of direct knowledge of something that is ordinarily knowable only through evidence or inference, such as the results of multiplying two three-digit numbers. If there is direct knowledge here, it need not be a case of justified belief. So we cannot use such examples to refute *evidentialism about justification*: the view that justified beliefs about God are impossible except on the basis of evidence.

Could one be directly justified in believing such religious propositions as that God exists? Would this require one's having a sixth sense, or some kind of mystical faculty? And even if there should be such a thing, would it generate justification directly, or only through one's discovering adequately strong *correlations* with what is believed through reason and ordinary experience, for instance through one's religious views enabling one to predict publicly observable events? In the latter case, the mystical faculty would not be a basic source of justification; before it could justify the beliefs it produces, it would have to earn its justificational credentials through a sufficient proportion of those beliefs receiving confirmation from other sources, such as perception and introspection.

There is, however, a way to combat evidentialism, and argue for the possibility of direct justification of certain religious beliefs, without assuming that there are any sources of justification beyond reason and normal experience. In particular, this approach need not posit either mystical apprehensions, such as overpowering, ineffable otherworldly experiences, or special divine revelations, whether in those experiences or in the presence of apparently miraculous changes in the external world. I call the position I have in mind *experientialism*, since it grounds the justification of some very important religious beliefs in experience rather than evidential beliefs or direct rational apprehension. Religious people sometimes say that, in perfectly ordinary life, God speaks to them, they are aware of God in the beauty of nature, and they can feel God's presence. Descriptions of these sorts might be considered metaphorical. But if God is, as many think, properly conceived as a (divine) person, these avowals might have a literal meaning.

It is natural to object that all one directly hears in such experiences is a special kind of voice (presumably in one's mind's ear), that all one directly sees is the natural beauty which one *takes* to manifest God, and that one simply feels a spiritual tone in one's experience. From these moves it is easy to conclude that one is at best indirectly justified in believing one is experiencing God. After all, one believes it inferentially; for instance, on the basis of one's belief that the voice one hears is God's, one might believe that the beauty one sees is a manifestation of divine creation, and so forth. But compare perception. Suppose it is argued that one is only indirectly justified in believing there is a blue spruce before one, since one believes it on the basis of believing that there is a blue color, a conical shape, and so on. Must we accept this? I think not. I do not normally even *have* these beliefs when I believe there is a blue spruce before me, even if I do see it *by* seeing its color and shape.

The matter is far more complicated than this, however. It may be argued that since God is both infinite and non-physical, one *cannot* be acquainted with God through experience. But this argument will not do. Even if a stream were infinitely long, I could still see it by seeing part of it. Seeing an infinite thing is not seeing its infinity. On the other hand, if seeing the stream is not seeing its infinity, then how can seeing it be a basis for knowing that the stream *is* infinite?

Similarly, if God is experienced, how can the experience reveal that it is God who is experienced? The problem is not that God is non-physical; for it appears that the non-physical can be quite readily experienced directly. Thus, even if in fact my introspective experience is really of something physical, say a brain process, it presumably *need* not be of something physical; and even if it must be (because of some necessary connection that might hold between the mental and the physical), it is not experience of, say, my thoughts *as* physical. The problem, then, is not that there cannot be experience, even quite unmystical experience, of God. It is (in part) that if experiencing, say, God's speaking to one, is possible, it is not clear how one could know (or justifiably believe) that it *is* God speaking. How would one know that one was not having a merely internal experience, such as talking to oneself in a voice one thinks is God's, or even hallucinating a divine voice?

Here it is important to recall the perceptual analogy. Why would it be less likely that my experience of looking toward the blue spruce is hallucinatory? It is true that there is a difference: we can, with all the other senses, verify that we see a spruce, whereas God seems perceptually accessible at most to sight and hearing—presumably indirectly, since God is seen *in* appropriate things and heard through hearing voices that are not literally God's (at least if a being's voice must be physically grounded in a physical embodiment, though even in that case, some theologians might argue that God's voice *was* physically embodied in Christ). But the force of this difference can be exaggerated. Surely it is not true that sense experience can be trusted only when verification by all the other senses is possible. If that were so, we could not justifiably believe we see a beam of light that is perceptually accessible to *only* our vision.

There are many other relevant questions. *Do* people ever really believe directly that, say, God is speaking to them, or is such a belief based—though not self-consciously—on believing that the voice in question has certain characteristics, where one takes these to indicate God's speaking? How is the possibility of corroboration by other people—what we might call *social justification*—relevant? Does it, for instance, matter crucially, for experiential justification for believing in God, that not just any normal person can be expected to see God in the beauty of nature, whereas any normal person *can* be expected to see my blue spruce? Or is this contrast blunted by the marked differences in perceptual acuity we find between clearly normal people, particularly in complicated matters such as aesthetic perception in music and painting, where what is directly heard or seen nevertheless cannot be seen or heard without both practice and sensitivity? And can God be seen in, rather than so to speak inferred from, nature? After all, assuming that nature is God's work, it is still not partly constitutive of God, at least not in the *way* that the color and shape by which I see the spruce presumably are in part constitutive of the tree. Or is nature, as some views apparently have it, partly constitutive of God after all? But if so, then directly perceiving God may be in a way too easy, or at least quite easy to do without directly perceiving the divinity in what one sees. One could not see a beautiful landscape without seeing God, though one could see it without seeing it *as* manifesting God.

The dimensions of these questions quickly widen, and despite the many points that have come to light we are left in no position to say whether there can be directly justified religious beliefs. It has so often been taken to be obvious that there cannot be, however, that it is important to see why it is really not obvious. It is at best very difficult to establish absolute restrictions on what sorts of beliefs can be directly justified. This holds even if the only way beliefs *can* be directly justified is by virtue of their grounding in the basic sources of justification.

A parallel point holds for absolute restrictions on what we can justifiably believe (or know) on the basis of one or more arguments. It is particularly difficult to determine what can be justifiably believed (or known) through a combination of plausible but individually inconclusive arguments for the same conclusion. As both coherentists and modest foundationalists are at pains to show, there are times when a belief is justified not by grounding in one or more conclusive arguments, but by its support from—which implies some degree of coherence with—many sets of independent premises none of which, alone, would suffice to justify it.

Furthermore, it is often hard in practice to distinguish, even in our own case, between beliefs that are grounded directly on one of the basic sources, and beliefs that are grounded in those sources through other beliefs of which we may not even be aware, or through inferences we do not realize we are making from propositions which we are aware we believe. This means that what we take to be direct belief may really be based on at least one other belief and may depend for its justification on the evidence or grounds which some other belief expresses. If there cannot be directly justified religious beliefs of the kind we have been discussing, however, it might still be true that there can be direct knowledge of such propositions; and for some religious people, even knowledge without justification might be considered very precious in this case. It would, perhaps, be one kind of faith.

The question how far our knowledge and justification extend beyond our belief grounded directly in experience or reason turns out to be complicated. We have at least found warrant for rejecting the stereotypic view that whereas there obviously exists scientific knowledge as an upshot of proof, it is at best doubtful that there is any moral knowledge, or even can be religious knowledge. It seems a mistake to talk of scientific proof at all if that means (deductive) proof of scientific hypotheses or theories from observational or other scientific evidence. Moreover, scientific knowledge apparently does not often represent uncontroversial beliefs of precise generalizations, but is typically either approximate knowledge, often recognized to need refinement, or knowledge of approximations, formulated with the appropriate restrictions left unspecified. There is good reason to think that we also have, and certainly have not been shown not to have, moral knowledge. And there is apparently no decisive reason to deny the possibility of religious knowledge. There are, of course, important skeptical arguments we have not considered, arguments that attempt to undermine all these positive conclusions and many views about the scope of knowledge and justification. It is time to examine some of those arguments.

CHAPTER 9

Skepticism

I think that we all know many things. I know many facts about my immediate surroundings, much about myself, something about the past, and a little about the future. I believe that we also have some approximate scientific knowledge, that we know some general moral truths, and that we may possibly know some religious truths. But there are reasons to doubt all of this. There are reasons to think that at best we know very little, perhaps just self-evident necessary truths, such as that if no vixens are males then no males are vixens, and a few propositions about our present consciousness, such as that I am now thinking about the scope of human knowledge.

THE POSSIBILITY OF PERVASIVE ERROR

As I consider these matters, I look back at the blue spruce. It occurs to me that I see it vividly. I certainly cannot help believing that it is there. But an inescapable belief need not be knowledge, nor even justified. Suppose I am hallucinating. Then I would not know (through vision, at least) that the tree is there. I find it impossible to believe that I am hallucinating. But I might find that impossible even if I were, provided the hallucination was as vivid and steady as my present visual experience. I wonder, then, whether I really *know* that I am not hallucinating. If I do not know this, then even if I am in fact not hallucinating, can I *know* that there is a blue spruce before me? Similarly, if I do not know that I am not simply having a vivid dream in which it seems to me that there is a blue spruce before me, can I know there is one there?

Remembering that one can justifiably believe something even if one does not know it, I think that at least I may justifiably believe that there is a blue spruce before me, even if I do not know that I am not hallucinating one (or merely "seeing" one in a dream). Moreover, if I justifiably believe this, how much does it matter whether I know it? It matters whether the belief is *true*. But the likelihood that it is true, so far as I can discern that likelihood, depends on how probable the presence of the tree is, given the sensory experience on which my belief is based; and in my attentiveness and caution as an observer, I have contributed all I can to that probability. If I still do not have knowledge, that is an external matter. My belief remains justified and is as likely to be true as I can make it by any steps in my power, such as observing carefully. Internally, in my own consciousness, I am being perfectly reasonable in continuing to believe that there is a blue spruce there. So far as justification is concerned, I am beyond reproach.

These points about justification are plausible, but they give false comfort. Doubtless, I may have a justified true belief that is not knowledge even if I am hallucinating; yet it is now not merely possible that I am hallucinating, I am also quite *aware* that I could be. Given this awareness, am I *still* justified in believing that there is a blue spruce there? Should I not regard this belief as unjustified, suspend judgment on whether the spruce is there, and merely hope that it is? I want to believe that it is there if it truly is, for *I want to believe as many significant truths as I can*. But I do not want to believe that it is there if it is not, for *I want to avoid believing falsehoods*. These two desires are important to me, and they represent ideals that run deep in my thinking. But the two ideals pull against each other: the former inclines me to believe readily, since I may otherwise miss believing a truth; the latter inclines me toward suspending judgment, lest I fall into error by believing a falsehood. How can one balance these ideals with each other? So far in this book, I have spoken more about how we fulfill the former than about how we might fulfill the latter. Clearly, the easiest way to fulfill the desire to avoid believing falsehoods would be to suspend judgment on every proposition one entertains, or at least all those which, unlike self-evident truths, do not utterly compel assent by virtue of their luminous certainty.

These reflections about possible error through hallucination, about the apparent vulnerability of justification in the face of such possibilities, and about the ideal of avoiding error suggest why philosophers have been so concerned with *skepticism*: which, in very broad terms, is the view that there is little if any knowledge. Skepticism may also concern justification, and typically skeptics do not take our justified beliefs to be of a significantly larger number than our beliefs constituting knowledge. How far-reaching might a plausible skepticism be, and how is skepticism to be assessed? I want to pursue these questions in that order and at some length.

It may seem that skepticism offends so blatantly against common sense that it should be dismissed as preposterous. But it will soon be evident that skepticism is a serious, perhaps even irrefutable, challenge to common sense. Moreover, even if skepticism turns out, as phenomenalism apparently does, to be quite unreasonable, we learn a great deal about knowledge and justification from studying it. A serious exploration of skepticism, whether or not we finally accept some form of it, tends to help us avoid dogmatism about our own personal views and a self-satisfied assurance that our collective outlook as rational observers of the world embodies knowledge of the sorts of things we think it does: facts about ourselves, our surroundings, and the ways of nature.

Much skepticism, whether about knowledge or about justification, is restricted to a given kind of subject, for instance to propositions about the world outside oneself, or about the past, or about the future. Skeptical views also differ in the status of the knowledge, and in the degree of the justification, they concern. A strong skepticism regarding propositions about the past, for instance, might hold that there is no knowledge, nor even partially justified belief, about the past; a weaker skepticism might hold that while there are beliefs about the past justified to some degree, there is neither certain knowledge of the past nor any beliefs about it that are *sufficiently* justified to make it more reasonable to hold them than to suspend judgment on them.

Still another difference concerns the order of a skeptical position. The usual skepticism is *first order*, in the sense that it concerns the sorts of beliefs we have discussed as typical of those grounded in experience or reason, and not beliefs *about* such beliefs, say beliefs that ordinary perceptual beliefs often do constitute knowledge. But it is natural for a first-order skeptic also to maintain *second-order skepticism*, holding, for instance, that there is no second-order knowledge to the effect that there is (first-order) knowledge. I do not intend to discuss skepticism in detail in each of these forms; but implicitly all of them will be considered in what follows, and if we want to make a serious assessment of them it is important to note their differences.

SKEPTICISM GENERALIZED

The skeptical challenges I have brought forward can be directed against *all* our beliefs about the external world, all our memory beliefs, all our beliefs about the future, and indeed all our beliefs about any subject provided they depend on our memory for their justification or for their status as knowledge. For memory is at least as fallible as vision. Plainly, if any of the senses can deceive through hallucination, then beliefs grounded in the senses may be justificationally or epistemically *undermined* in the same way my belief that there is a blue spruce before me may be undermined by a realization that I might have been hallucinating. That is, quite apart from whether perceptual beliefs are true, skeptics tend to claim that either the possibility of such hallucinations prevents them from being justified or, even if they remain justified, it precludes their constituting knowledge. Suppose, for instance, that I might be having an auditory hallucination of bird songs. Then my present experience of (apparently) hearing them may not justify my believing that there are birds nearby and is not a sufficient basis for my knowing there are, even if it is true that there are. Similarly, there is a counterpart of hallucination for memory beliefs: *memorial hallucination*, we might call it. I may have the memorial impression that when I was four I saw my parents kissing under the mistletoe, but this could be just a romantic fantasy masquerading as a memory.

Beliefs about the future are rather different from memory beliefs, in that they are not grounded in experiential states we think of as in some way causally deriving from the object about which we have knowledge. But even if there is no counterpart of memorial hallucination, there are equally undermining possibilities. For instance, a confident belief, grounded in remembering my long-standing intention to talk with Jane, that I will talk with her may be a product of wishful thinking. Perhaps it could be an anticipatory delusion. Even my belief that I will live to discuss skepticism could be mistaken for many sorts of reasons, including dangers to me of which I am now unaware.

Now consider my general a priori and scientific "knowledge," say of arithmetic truths and scientific laws. Since it is possible to misremember propositions, or to seem to remember them when one does not, or to have a kind of memorial hallucination that gives rise to a completely groundless belief, it would seem that our only secure beliefs are of general propositions that we can know directly without *ever* having needed any evidence. This apparently leaves none of our general scientific beliefs, and only our a priori knowledge of self-evident propositions, epistemically unscathed.

Even if we leave problems about perceptual and memory beliefs aside, there is a difficulty for the commonsense view that justification or knowledge grounded in a basic source can be transmitted inductively. The classical statement of this *problem of induction* comes from Hume (see, for instance, Section IV of his *Inquiry Concerning Human Understanding*). Hume pointed out (in different terms) that one cannot know a priori that if the premises of a specific piece of inductive reasoning are true, then its conclusion is also true. Thus, no matter how good the inductive reasoning is, it is always (deductively) invalid. Consider the inductive reasoning from the premise that the sun always has arisen each twenty-four hours to the conclusion that it will rise tomorrow. Of all such reasoning, which Hume calls reasoning "concerning matter of fact and existence," he says, "That there are no demonstrative [roughly, valid and conclusive] arguments in the case seems evident, since it implies no contradiction that the course of nature may change and that an object, seemingly like those which we have experienced, may be attended with different or contrary effects." Hence, even if I do know that the sun has arisen every day since time immemorial, and on that basis I believe that it will rise tomorrow, I *could* be mistaken in believing this, and I must question whether I have any justification for believing it.

More generally, Hume's arguments lead us to ask whether, if our premises could be true, yet our conclusion false, we have any *reason* at all, on the basis of the premises, for believing the conclusion. And how can we ever *know* the conclusion on the basis of such premises? Indeed, how can we even be minimally justified in believing the conclusion on the basis of such premises? The problem of induction, as most often understood, is largely the difficulty of adequately answering these questions.

It will not do to argue that I am justified in believing my conclusion on the basis of inductive support for it, since past experience has shown that reasoning like this, which has had true premises, has also had true conclusions. For this way of defending an inductively based conclusion simply gives a kind of inductive reasoning to support the view that certain kinds of inductive arguments justify one in believing their conclusions. It just inductively generalizes about inductive arguments themselves, using as a guide past experience in finding that by and large their conclusions turned out true when their premises were true. That begs the question against Hume: it simply assumes part of what he contends is false, namely, that inductive inference constitutes reasoning that can ground knowledge of its conclusion or can at least justify, in the sense of providing good reason for, its conclusion.

The point that Hume so powerfully defended is by no means restricted to beliefs about the future, though such beliefs are so prominent in his work that sometimes the problem of induction is narrowly conceived as that of how we can show that we have any reason to believe the future will be like the past. Recall my observing Jim briskly shuffling papers and angrily mumbling curses. I cannot help believing, on this basis, that he is angry. But even if I know my premises (through perception), it does not *follow* that he is angry. He could be pretending. This case is alarmingly representative. Everything I believe about what is occurring in the inner lives of others seems to rest on grounds that are inductive in this way: what I observe—above all, their behavior—does not entail anything about their minds. So if I cannot have knowledge of another person's inner life here, I apparently can never have it.

Worse still, if I cannot know anything about the inner lives of others, can I even know that there *are* others, as opposed to mere bodies controlled externally or by hidden machinery, rather than directed through beliefs and intentions of the kind that animate me? There is, then, a *problem of other minds.* Can we know, or even justifiably believe, that there are any? The problem is compounded when we realize that we cannot directly verify, as we introspectively can in our own case, what is occurring in someone else's consciousness. Thus, all I can do to check on my inductively grounded beliefs about the inner lives of others is get further inductive evidence, for instance by observing whether they behave as they should if I am right in thinking them to be, say, angry. I cannot, as in my own case, introspectively focus on the events in their consciousness. How can I know anything about the mental and emotional life of others if I am in principle debarred from decisively verifying my beliefs about the contents and events of their consciousness? Even if I am sometimes right, I can never tell when.

It is only a short step from here to a *problem of the body.* If, as a skeptic might well hold, my apparent knowledge of my own body is inductively grounded, being based on perceptions and bodily sensations somewhat as beliefs about external objects are, then can I know, or even justifiably believe, that I have a body? Could I not be steadily hallucinating even my own flesh? Again, it might be argued that thought necessarily requires an embodied thinker. But that point would only imply that I have *some* kind of body, not that I can know anything about it. The point is also far from self-evident and is indeed denied by philosophers in the powerful tradition of Descartes. In any case, even if it is true, the only embodiment necessary might be a brain. Hence, on the skeptical view imagined, the most one could know is that one is embodied in some way, say in a brain. Whether that brain is itself embodied, or ever interacts with anything else, would be beyond one's knowledge.

THE EGOCENTRIC PREDICAMENT

In this way, skepticism can drive us into an *egocentric predicament*: all we can (empirically) know about the world, perhaps all we can justifiably believe about it as well, concerns our own present experience. For all I know, I am a lone conscious ego vividly hallucinating a physical world that has no external reality. Most skeptics have tended to push no further, or at least not to express very much doubt about our capacity to know propositions about what is currently going on in our minds and at least those a priori propositions that are self-evident. But skeptics can push further, and Descartes, in the first of his *Meditations*, seriously entertained the possibility that there was nothing of which he could (justifiably) be certain. Recall introspectively grounded beliefs, such as that I am thinking about introspection. It seems *possible* that this belief is mistaken. If that is possible, how can I *know* that I am thinking about introspection? If I know, I cannot be wrong. But here error is possible. Perhaps I do not even have knowledge of my own conscious states.

To make this sort of argument work with beliefs of self-evident propositions we must, I think, strain. Descartes raised the question whether it is possible that God, being omnipotent, could have brought it about that even propositions of the sort I am calling self-evident might be false. Let us pursue this question. Could there be an omnipotent being who brings it about that while some dogs are pets, no pets are dogs? I see no reason to think so. As St. Thomas Aquinas (c. 1224–1274) and many other philosophers have brought out, omnipotence is simply not the power to "do" things that are absolutely impossible (see, for example his *Summa Theologica*, Ia, question 25, a.3). If one accepts this point, one might argue that there *is* no act of bringing it about that while some dogs are pets, no pets are dogs. To speak of this as an act is to misuse the vocabulary of action. Hence, the impossibility that an omnipotent being can bring it about, or more broadly, can create something at once red and green all over, does not imply that there is any deed which that being cannot perform.

Granted, this reasoning is controversial; and I do not think it settles the matter. However, the reasoning is sufficiently plausible to warrant leaving aside skepticism concerning beliefs of self-evident necessary propositions, particularly since these propositions seem not only incapable of falsehood, but also incapable of even being unjustifiably believed, at least when carefully and comprehendingly considered. Leaving such skepticism aside takes little from the skeptic in any case. If these are the only propositions we can know, then we can know nothing about our world, not even anything about our innermost consciousness. We are at best in an egocentric predicament.

FALLIBILITY

In appraising skepticism, I will formulate some of the principles that underlie it in what seem its most plausible forms. If they can be shown to be unreasonable, then the skeptical threat to the commonsense view that we have a great deal of knowledge and justification can at least be blunted. In formulating and assessing these principles, it is well to distinguish skeptical threats to the generation of knowledge (or justification) from skeptical threats to its transmission. It is natural to start with questions about its generation. If no knowledge is generated, there is none to be transmitted.

Is there really any reason to doubt that, normally, introspectively grounded beliefs constitute knowledge? It *may* be true that such beliefs *could* be mistaken, but what is a skeptic entitled to make of this? The skeptical argument which comes to mind here is based on what I will call *the infallibility formulation*: that if you know, you can't be wrong. If we simply add the premise that you can be wrong in holding a given introspective belief, say that you are thinking about skepticism, it would seem to follow that such beliefs do not represent knowledge. This kind of *argument from fallibility*, as we might call it, can be applied to just about every sort of proposition we tend to think we know.

If, however, we look closely, we find that the infallibility formulation is multiply ambiguous. There are at least three quite different things the words in that formulation might mean, and hence really three different infallibility principles.

The claim, "If you know, you can't be wrong," might have the meaning of (1) it must be the case that if you know that something is true, then it *is* true (you cannot know something false). Call (1) the *verity principle*, since it says simply that knowledge must be of *truths*.

The claim might, on the other hand, have the meaning of (2) if you know that something is true, then *it* must be true, that is, the proposition you know is necessarily true (you can know only necessary truths). Call (2) the *necessity principle*, since it says simply that knowledge must be of necessary truths.

The claim might also have the meaning of (3) if you know that something is true, then your *belief* of it must be true, in the sense that your believing it entails its truth (only beliefs that cannot be false constitute knowledge). Call (3) the *infallibility principle proper*, since it says that only infallible beliefs constitute knowledge. Unlike (2), (3) allows for knowledge of *contingent* (non-necessary) truths, such as that I exist. This *proposition* can be false, but my *belief* of it is infallible and cannot be false. If I now believe that I exist, it follows that I do exist.

We can now assess the skeptical reasoning that employs the infallibility formulation in one or another interpretation. I will be quite brief in discussing the first two; the third is most controversial and most important for skepticism.

The verity principle, (1), is plainly true: one cannot know something that is false. But if this is all the infallibility formulation comes to, it provides no reason to conclude that I do not know that I am thinking. Granted, it must be true that *if* I know I am thinking, then I am. But that tells us nothing about whether I do know I am. On the other hand, the necessity principle, (2), seems quite mistaken. Surely I know some propositions that are not necessary, such as that I exist (it is not a necessary truth that I exist, as it is that vixens are female). Even the skeptic would grant that I cannot falsely believe this, since my believing it entails that I exist. It may indeed be impossible for me even to be unjustified in believing it when I comprehendingly consider it. The same holds, of course, for you in relation to your belief that you exist.

Even if the necessity principle were true, however, it is so very far from self-evident that a skeptic could not reasonably *use* it, without adequate argument, against the view that introspective beliefs normally constitute knowledge. For clearly they are not beliefs of necessary truths, nor do defenders of common sense take them to be; hence, using the principle against common sense, without arguing for it, would be just to *assume* that such beliefs are not knowledge. That would *beg the question* against the commonsense view. Suppose, for instance, that a skeptic says that if you know, you can't be wrong, where this means (2), then notes that introspective beliefs (which are of propositions that are not necessary) can be false, and concludes that such beliefs do not constitute knowledge. This would not be presenting a good reason to believe the conclusion, but just asserting, disguisedly, that the commonsense view is mistaken.

The infallibility principle proper, (3), in effect says that only infallible beliefs can be knowledge. Now *some* beliefs of empirical propositions *are* infallible, for instance my belief that I now exist, and my more specific belief that I have a belief. I *cannot* falsely believe these propositions. Their infallibility shows that despite appearances, (3) is *not* equivalent to (2). But why should we accept (3)? What reason can the skeptic give for it? Not that if you know, you cannot be wrong; for when we look closely, we find that when plausibly interpreted, as meaning (1), that is no help to the skeptic, and when interpreted as (2) or (3) it just asserts the skeptical position against common sense.

What makes it seem that the infallibility formulation gives the skeptic an argument against common sense is the way skepticism can *trade on* the ambiguity of that formulation: one finds the argument from fallibility attractive because its main premise, conceived as equivalent to (1), is so plausible; yet the argument succeeds against common sense only if (2) or (3) are legitimate premises, and it is doubtful that the skeptic has any cogent argument for them.

UNCERTAINTY

Like fallibility, uncertainty has seemed to many skeptics to leave us with little, if any, knowledge. Recall the possibility that I am hallucinating a blue spruce before me when there is none there. Can I tell for certain whether or not I am hallucinating a spruce where there is none? And if I cannot tell for certain, do I know I am not? The skeptic may argue that I do not know that I am not hallucinating, surely I do not know that there is a spruce there. At least two important principles are suggested here.

One principle suggested by reflection on these questions about possible error is *the certainty principle*: if one cannot tell for certain whether something is so, then one does not know it is so. This principle is plausible in part because 'How can you tell?' and 'How can you be certain?' are, typically, appropriate challenges to a claim to know something. Moreover, 'I know, but I am not certain' sounds self-defeating, in a way that might encourage a skeptic to consider it contradictory.

Another principle suggested by our questions about the possibility of hallucination is *the backup principle*: if one believes something, say that there is a tree before one, which is inconsistent with a further proposition—such as that one is merely hallucinating a tree where none exists—then one's belief is knowledge only if it is backed up by one's knowing, or at least being in a *position* to know, that the further (undermining) proposition is false. This principle is plausible in part because one is in a sense responsible for the implications of what one claims to know. If, for instance, I claim to know that there is a blue spruce before me, and that proposition implies that the tree is not a green spruce cleverly painted to look like a blue one, it would seem that I had better be justified in believing that it is not such a green one, which, in turn, implies that I must be justified in rejecting this strange possibility. Thus, if I know that there is a blue spruce before me, I must be prepared to back that up by justifiably rejecting exactly the sorts of possibilities the skeptic reminds us are, in abundance, always there. But must I be? Let us consider the certainty and backup principles in turn.

In Chapter 7 I argued that knowing does not imply knowing for certain. That suggests that the kind of certainty in question, epistemic certainty, is not required for knowledge, and that having such certainty may be something quite different from simply knowing. Still, from the point that knowing need not be knowing for certain, it does not follow that one can know without being *able* to tell for certain. Thus, the skeptic may still maintain that the certainty principle undermines the commonsense view that we have perceptual knowledge.

Let us first ask what it is to tell for certain. A skeptic may mean by this acquiring knowledge, in the form of an infallible belief, of a proposition that entails the truth of what one can tell is so. Thus, to tell (for certain) that one is not hallucinating one might, like Descartes, prove that there is a God of such goodness and power that—since it would be evil for God to allow it—one *could* not be mistaken in such a vivid and steadfast perception as one now has of a blue spruce. But to require that a belief can be knowledge only if it can be, in this or a similar way, conclusively shown to be true would again beg the question against the view that a belief can constitute knowledge without being infallible. Thus, if skeptics have no good argument for the principle of infallibility proper, they should not assume that principle in defending the view that we can know only what we can tell for certain in this strong sense.

Perhaps, on the other hand, telling for certain is simply a matter of ascertaining the truth in question by some means that justifies one in *being* (psychologically) certain of what one can tell. If so, perhaps we normally *can* tell for certain that we are not hallucinating, for instance by seeing whether the senses of touch and smell confirm our visual impression. The confirming experiences do not *entail* that there is a blue spruce before me. But we still have no good argument that certainty (or knowledge) may arise only from entailing grounds (another controversial view, shortly to be discussed). Thus, this point does not establish that confirming experiences cannot enable us to tell for certain that we are not hallucinating.

Moreover, suppose that we interpret telling for certain in the modest way just suggested, and that we *can* tell for certain in *this* sense that what we know is true. In that case perhaps there *is* a weak sense in which beliefs constituting knowledge *are* infallible. They need not be such that it is absolutely impossible that they be false, as in the case of my belief that I exist. There need only be something about our grounds for them in virtue of which they (empirically) cannot be false. In this case, however, it will be arguable that many of our beliefs grounded in experience, such as my belief that there is a blue spruce before me, cannot be mistaken. There surely might be causal laws which guarantee that if one is situated before a tree in good light, as I am, and has visual experiences like mine caused by the tree as mine are, then one *sees* it, and hence cannot falsely believe that it is there. The skeptic gives us no good argument to show that there are no such laws.

The backup principle fares no better than the infallibility principle proper. For one thing, it rests on the assumption, which defenders of common sense stoutly reject, that in order to know that something is true, one must have grounds that entail its truth. To see this, consider the proposition that it is *false* that there is a blue spruce before me. This is inconsistent with what I believe, namely, that there *is* one before me. Hence, the backup principle requires that I at least be in a position to know that this is false. Now the falsity of this negative proposition entails that there *is* a blue spruce before me; for if it is false *that* it is false that there is one, then it is true that there is one. Thus, if I do know that this negative proposition is false, then I *have* (and know) an entailing ground for the truth of what I originally believed—that there is a blue spruce before me.

Consider also the proposition that what I take to be a blue spruce is really a green one so cleverly dyed blue that I cannot tell (perceptually) that it is really green. Must I be in a position to know that this is false in order to know that there is a blue spruce before me? The very description of the case suggests that I cannot know, at least by using the senses unaided by experimentation or specialized knowledge, that the tree is not a cleverly dyed green spruce. But why must I be able to tell this at all? Is there any *reason* to think that the tree might actually be dyed? Must I, in order to know, not only have a well-grounded true belief but also the further capacity to know, for every possible explanation of how my belief *could* be false, that this explanation is incorrect? I do not see that I must.

One might object that in order to know a proposition I must be in a position to know whatever follows from it (or at least obviously follows from it), since, if something *does* follow, I could infer it by valid steps from what I initially know, and thereby come to know it. This is an important objection. But in discussing the transmission of knowledge, we considered cases that apparently show the objection to be mistaken. I can know the sum of a column of figures even if I cannot, without further checking, know something which follows from it: that if my wife (a better arithmetician) says this is not the sum, then she is wrong. Neither knowledge nor justification is automatically transmitted across valid deductive inference. Nor are they necessarily transmissible from propositions we believe to those they entail, even when the entailment is, as in our example, quite obvious.

Even supposing that knowledge and justification are always transmitted across valid deductive inference, it may be plausibly argued that I do have enough justification to warrant rejecting the hypothesis that the spruce is really green and cleverly painted to look blue. It is not just that it appears to me that it is blue; I also have no reason to think there is anything abnormal in the situation, and some reason to think that, in cases like this, large, nearby familiar kinds of things *are* as they appear to me in such vivid and careful observation. There are other factors one might cite, indeed, too many to discuss here. My point is simply this. Since the skeptic has not provided good reasons for the principles I have already rejected (or comparably strong principles), even if knowledge and justification are always transmitted across valid inference, there *may* be good reason to say that skeptical hypotheses, such as that the spruce is cleverly painted green, may be justifiably rejected.

I grant that in order to *show* the skeptic that my original belief is knowledge, in the face of the *suggestion* that one of those explanations of its falsity holds, I may have to know that, and why, this explanation does not hold. But why must I have this capacity in the *absence* of the suggestion, as the principle would require? Surely I need not. I can know that if some dogs are pets then some pets are dogs, even if I cannot show this—perhaps simply because I can think of nothing more obvious to use as a reasonable premise from which to show it. And if my wife raises no question of whether my answer is correct, I can know the answer even if I cannot show—without obtaining further grounds for this answer—that if she says it is wrong, then she is wrong.

In the context of thinking about skepticism, it is easy to forget that knowing something does not require being able to show that one knows it. For we are likely to be trying to defend, against a skeptical onslaught, the commonsense view that there is much knowledge, and we easily think of defending this view as requiring us to *show* that there is knowledge. A *negative defense of common sense*, however, one that shows that skeptical arguments do not justify the skeptic's conclusion, does not require that second-order task. It requires only showing that skepticism provides no good argument against common sense. And I do not see that skepticism does provide one. Why, for instance, should the skeptic's merely suggesting a possible explanation of how there could be no blue spruce before me, without giving any reason for thinking the explanation is correct, require me to know, or be in a position to know, that it *is* not correct? On balance, then, I reject the backup principle.

DEDUCIBILITY AND EPISTEMIC TRANSMISSION

When we come to the problem of induction, it seems clear that one assumption the skeptic is making is that if we believe something on the basis of one or more premises, then we can know it on the basis of those premises only if it follows from them, in the sense that they entail it. Call this the *entailment principle*. It says in effect that knowledge can be transmitted only deductively.

But why should we accept this? Not simply because inductive reasoning is "invalid"; for that term may be held to be improperly applied to it: inductive reasoning is strong or weak, probable or otherwise, but does not even "aim" at validity. Even if it may be properly said to be (deductively) invalid, however, that may be considered an uncontroversial technical point about its logical classification. So conceived, the point does not imply either that knowledge of the premises of inductive reasoning cannot ground knowledge of its conclusions, or that justified beliefs of those premises cannot ground justified beliefs of their conclusions.

One might, on the other hand, accept the entailment principle and argue that when properly spelled out inductive reasoning can be replaced by valid deductive reasoning. For instance, suppose we add, as an overarching premise in inductive reasoning, the plausible principle that nature is uniform. From this principle, *together with* the premise that the sun always has risen each day it apparently does follow that it will rise tomorrow. But what entitles us to the premise that nature is uniform? Hume would reply that it is not knowable a priori, and that to say that we know it through experience—which would require our depending on inductive reasoning—would beg the question against him. (For on Hume's view, if the principle is grounded in premises that only inductively support it, it is not known.) I believe that this Humean response is correct. The problem of induction must be approached differently.

What perhaps above all makes the entailment principle plausible is the thought that if our premises could be *true* and yet our conclusion *might be false*, then we cannot *know* (or even justifiably believe) the conclusion on the basis of those premises. At first, this thought may sound like just another formulation of the entailment principle. It is not; it is different and considerably stronger, and that is partly why it seems to support the entailment principle. The 'might' in question is epistemic; it is like a physician's in 'Those stomach pains might mean cancer'. This suggests not only that for all we know they do mean cancer but also that there is reason for at least some degree of suspicion that there is cancer and perhaps some need to rule it out. It is not merely a statement of a bare *logical possibility* of cancer—a statement that cancer is possible without contradiction—based, say, on no one's being absolutely immune to it. If that statement represents all we know about the case, we are not entitled to say that the pains might mean cancer. Similarly, it is not a logical impossibility that the Golden Gate Bridge levitate far above the waters; but we would be quite unjustified in saying that it *might*.

This distinction between *epistemic possibility*—what is expressed by the epistemic 'might' just illustrated—and mere logical possibility bears importantly on the problem of induction. It is true that *if*, no matter how good inductive reasoning is, its premises could be true and yet its conclusion might, in the epistemic sense, be false, perhaps we cannot know the conclusion on the basis of them. But is this generally the case with inductive reasoning? I cannot see that it is.

Moreover, suppose it could be true that, relative to its premises, the conclusion of inductive reasoning might, in the epistemic sense, be false, what reason is there to think that this really is true? Skeptics cannot justifiably argue for this claim as they sometimes do, maintaining, simply on the ground that the premises do not entail the conclusion, that the conclusion *might* be false. Arguing in this way is rather like saying, of just any stomachache a child gets after eating too much Halloween candy, that it might mean cancer. It is barely possible that, relative to all we know or are justified in believing about the child, it means cancer. But from that bare possibility we may not *automatically* conclude that cancer *is* epistemically possible—roughly, that relative to all we know or are justified in believing, we are unjustified in *dis*believing that the stomachache might mean cancer. Nor does this bare possibility rule out our knowing, on inductive grounds, that overeating is the cause.

There are other reasons for the attractiveness of the entailment principle, at least from a skeptical point of view. If one embraces the infallibility principle, one is in fact *committed* to the entailment principle. For suppose that, from known—and hence on this view infallibly believed—premises, one inductively derives a belief which is not itself infallible, as (empirical) beliefs which are inferentially grounded normally are not. Since inductive transmission allows inference of a false conclusion from true premises, the belief one derives *could*, as far as sheer logic goes, be false despite the truth of its inductive premises *and* one's infallibly believing them. But then, being fallible, the belief of the conclusion would not be knowledge. Thus, knowledge can be inferentially transmitted only by deductive inference. *Only valid deduction inferentially preserves infallibility.*

If one thinks of knowledge as entailing absolute certainty, one might again be drawn to the entailment principle. For even if a fallible belief can be absolutely certain, a belief that is only inductively based on it will presumably be at least a bit less certain and thus not absolutely certain, since its truth is implied by that of the original belief only with some (perhaps high) degree of probability, rather than with absolute certainty. To see this, suppose that the premise belief only minimally meets the standard for absolute certainty. Then a belief inductively grounded on it can fall below that standard and thereby fail to be knowledge. Hence, again the skeptic will argue that only deduction is sufficient to transmit knowledge. But we have already seen reason to doubt both the infallibility principle and the view that a belief constitutes knowledge only if it is absolutely certain. Indeed, I do not see that skeptics give us good reason to believe either these principles or the entailment principle. It does not follow that the principles are, as they appear to be, false; but if there is no good reason to believe them, even skeptics would approve of our refusing to accept them. Absolute certainty is a high, and in some ways beautiful, ideal; but it is neither adequate to the concept of knowledge nor appropriate to the human condition.

EPISTEMIC AUTHORITY AND COGENT GROUNDS

There is one further principle I want to consider, one rather different from those examined so far and apparently more modest. It derives in part from the idea that if you know something, you have a certain *authority* regarding it, an authority presumably due to your being in a position to grasp the truth which you know. This authority is in part what accounts for the possibility of knowledge through testimony: if you know something, you have an authority about it such that normally I can come to know it, as well as to believe it justifiably, from your testimony. Indeed, if you tell someone that you know something, you put yourself on the line; it is as if you gave your firmest assurance—an epistemic promise, as it were—that it is true, and if it turns out to be false your position is somewhat like that of a person who has broken a promise.

A stronger, but closely associated view is that if you know that a proposition is true, then you must be able to say something on behalf of it. After all, the question how one knows is always intelligible, at least for beliefs that are not of self-evident truths or propositions about one's current consciousness; and if one really does know, one should be able to give more than a dogmatic answer, such as 'I just see that it is true'. The associated principle might be expressed as follows.

With the possible exception of beliefs of self-evident propositions and propositions about one's current consciousness, one knows that something is so only if one has grounds for it from which one can in principle argue cogently for it on the basis of those grounds. Call this *the cogency principle*.

Since the cogency principle requires only that one *can* argue cogently for what one knows, temporary inability to mount an argument would not prevent one's knowing. Even little children might have knowledge, for perhaps if they could just express their grounds they could provide cogent arguments. And since self-evident propositions and propositions about one's current consciousness are excepted and may be objects of directly justified belief, there is a stopping place in epistemic chains and no regress need result when one produces a series of arguments to support a claim. What is known must simply be either traceable to those secure foundations or otherwise defensible by appeal to adequate grounds.

If the cogency principle is combined with the entailment principle, it will immediately preclude anyone's having knowledge on inductive grounds; for the entailment principle implies that inductive grounds are never cogent. But it need not be combined with the entailment principle. If it is not, it can allow for inductive reasoning of certain kinds to be cogent and thereby to transmit knowledge. Granted, even a moderate skeptic is likely to accept only a restricted kind of induction, a kind whose premises make its conclusion at least close to certain. The point, however, is that the cogency principle is separable from the entailment principle.

Even if the cogency principle is not combined with the entailment principle, however, the cogency principle can be very hostile to the commonsense view that we can know the sorts of things I have been suggesting we can know, at least if this view is understood in a foundationalist framework. For this principle strikes at some of the *sources* of knowledge as they are plausibly understood, and it threatens to undermine our claim to knowledge of the past, the future, and the external world. It is true that *some* of our beliefs that constitute direct knowledge (and are directly justified) *can* be supported by apparently more secure premises. For instance, my belief that I see a blue spruce before me can be supported by premises about how things appear to me, which concern only my present consciousness. After all, that this is so seems to be the best explanation of why my visual field contains a blue spruce. But a proponent of the cogency principle would certainly tend to deny that my memory can be trusted as a source of direct justification, in part because memory seems far more subject to error than perception. Moreover, I might be unable to provide good inductive reasoning to support its reliability even in cases where it is very vivid, if only because such an argument would require depending on my memory for my justification in believing its premises, say premises about how often my past memory beliefs have been confirmed. Yet even if I could give no cogent argument to justify my memorial beliefs, it does not follow that they are not justified.

Must we accept even this apparently modest skeptical principle? I do not see why. Certainly one can have a kind of authority without being able to defend it by premises or exhibit it in argumentation. Consider, for instance, someone who can always tell "identical" twins apart, but cannot say how. Moreover, saying 'I see it' *need* not be a dogmatic answer to 'How do you know?' It may simply specify one's grounds. It says *how* one knows; it need not (though it may) show *that* one does, particularly if this requires more than exhibiting an appropriate source of the challenged belief. Saying that I see it would be dogmatic if intended to show conclusively, say to prove, that I know. And perhaps it is precisely because the skeptic's 'How do you know?' is meant as a challenge to be shown conclusively that one knows, and not as a request for a source, that 'I see it' seems dogmatic in the context of discussing skepticism.

If the issue is whether we can show that we have knowledge, the point that an appeal to visual experience does not conclusively establish visual knowledge is an important concession. But the issue here is whether the skeptic succeeds in showing that we do not have visual knowledge. In that context, the point is not a concession. Once again, we can see how skepticism can gain credibility because skeptics make it *sound* as if their case against the existence of one or another kind of knowledge succeeds if we cannot *show* that there is such knowledge. In fact, we need not be able to show that there is; and the skeptic must give us good reason not to believe that there is.

| REFUTATION AND REBUTTAL

Have I, then, *refuted* skepticism, even in the few forms considered here? I have not tried to. That would require showing that skepticism is wrong, which would entail showing that there *is* knowledge (and justified belief). What I have tried to do is to *rebut* skepticism in certain plausible forms, to show that the arguments for those skeptical views do not establish that we do not have knowledge (and justified belief). Now suppose I have succeeded. Where do we stand? May we believe that we have knowledge, or may we only suspend judgment both on this and on skeptical claims that we do not?

I have already argued, by implication, that one *can* know something without knowing that one knows it. For instance, in arguing that much of our knowledge is not self-conscious, I indicated how I can know that there is a blue spruce before me without even believing that I know this; I do not even form such self-conscious beliefs in most everyday situations. Moreover, toddlers who do not even understand what knowledge is—and so are not in a position to believe they *know* anything—can apparently know such simple things as that Mama is before them. Note, too, that even if I did know that I know the spruce is there, I surely would not possess—if it is even possible for me to possess—the infinite series of beliefs required by the view that knowing entails knowing that one knows: the series that continues with my knowing that I know that I know; knowing that I know, that I know that I know, and so forth. Given these and related points, it would be a mistake to think, as some skeptics might like us to, that if we do not know that we have knowledge, then we do not; and this, in turn, opens up the possibility that we might be justified in believing that we have knowledge even if we are properly unwilling to claim that we know we do.

Let us now be more positive. If foundationalism is correct, then if one can know anything, one can know at least some things directly. Moreover, some of the sorts of things a plausible foundationalism says we know directly—for instance, self-evident truths and some propositions about our present consciousness—are the kinds of things which, simply on the basis of reflection on the examples involved, it is plausible to think we know. Perhaps, of course, this reflection, even if it does not involve arguing from premises, *shows* that we have knowledge. In any case, I think that we are justified in believing that we have some knowledge even if we cannot show that we do, and I am aware of no good argument against the view that we have some knowledge.

Might there be a way, however, to give a cogent *positive defense of common sense*: to show that we have knowledge, even of the external world? And could we establish this second-order thesis even to the satisfaction of some skeptics? To be sure, there is no satisfying a *radical skeptic*, one who denies that there can be *any* knowledge or justified belief (including justification of that very claim, which the skeptic simply asserts as a challenge). For nothing one presents as a reason for asserting something will be counted as justifying it. But could anything be said that might be plausible to a *moderate skeptic*: one who holds, say, that although transmission of justification and knowledge must be deductive, we may justifiably believe, and perhaps know, at least self-evident propositions and propositions about our present consciousness? Even if the answer is negative, perhaps one can show that there is knowledge, or at least justified belief, whether any skeptics would find one's argument plausible or not.

PROSPECTS FOR A POSITIVE DEFENSE OF COMMON SENSE

How might an argument for a positive defense of common sense go? Let's consider justified belief first, since showing that certain of our beliefs are justified does not require showing that the beliefs in question are true.

One might view the issue this way: if we are to show that there are justified beliefs, then one result of our argument will itself be justification, specifically justification for the second-order belief that there are justified beliefs. For to show something by argument is at least to produce justification for believing it.

If we are to provide such second-order justification, we apparently need at least two things: a general premise expressing a sufficient condition for justification, and one or more specific premises saying that a particular belief meets that condition. For instance, the general premise might be that (1) a belief to the effect that one is now in an occurrent mental state, such as thinking, is justified, at least if *attentive*, that is, based on careful attention to the matter in question; and the particular premise might be that (2) I attentively believe I am now in such a state, namely thinking. If I am justified in believing these premises, I would surely be justified in deductively inferring from them, and thereby in believing on the basis of them, what they self-evidently entail: that (3) my belief that I am thinking is justified. (At least, I am inferentially justified in believing this if I can hold all three propositions before my mind in a way that avoids dependence on memory of my premises; and this seems possible for me.)

But how am I now justified in believing premises (1) and (2), if I am? My believing the general principle, (1), is arguably justified directly by reflection, and so my belief of it might itself be directly justified. This is not to deny that it could be justified by prior premises; the point is only that it is arguably justified by reflection not dependent on one's appealing to such premises. As for the particular premise, (2), I might be non-inferentially justified in holding it by virtue of a principle similar to the general one, but applying to beliefs, a principle to the effect that if, on careful introspection, one believes that one attentively believes something, then one is justified in believing one does (presumably directly justified, if one has introspected carefully). Now *if* my belief of my general premise is justified, and *if* I may justifiably hold the particular premise, then surely I may justifiably conclude that my belief that I am thinking is justified. I may justifiably conclude this even if my justification in believing my premises is not direct, as I am tentatively assuming it is. Moreover, if my beliefs of (1) to (3) are true, they may also constitute knowledge.

Supposing this line of argument against the skeptic is sound, have I shown anything? If showing something is producing a good argument for it from true premises that one is justified in believing, perhaps I have. But even if I have shown my conclusion, which seems especially likely if I am directly justified in believing my premises, I might not be justified in saying or even believing that I *have* shown it. For justification for saying or believing that would ordinarily require *third*-order beliefs, such as the belief that my second-order belief that I believe I am thinking is justified and true (since this second-order belief has been supported by good argument). Still, even if I do not know that I have shown that my belief that I am thinking is justified, I may yet *have* shown this; and if I have, then I may well know the proposition that I have shown: that my belief that I am thinking is justified.

Given the plausibility of the premises just used to try to show that I have a justified belief, I am inclined to believe that it can be shown that there are some justified beliefs. But even if the line of argument I have used is successful, will it extend to any beliefs about the external world?

What would be our general principle for, say, visual perceptual beliefs? Might we say that (a) if one believes, on the basis of a vivid and steady visual experience in which one has the impression of something blue before one, that there *is* something blue before one, then one is justified in so believing? Perhaps we may say this, particularly since the justification in question is admittedly defeasible. (It could, for instance, be undermined by my knowing that I have frequently been hallucinating blues lately.) If this premise may be believed with direct justification, and we may also believe (possibly with direct justification) that (b) I have a belief (that there is something blue before me) grounded in the way the premise—principle (a)—requires, then I may, as before, justifiably conclude that (c) I justifiably believe there is something blue before me. Even if principle (a) is too strong and provides the basis for only prima facie justification, I might conclude that my perceptual belief is *prima facie justified*—roughly, justified in the absence of defeating factors. This would be a significant conclusion, even if—as seems possible—I could not, by reflection alone, rule out those underminers.

Again, the reasoning bears on skepticism about knowledge. If the premise beliefs, (a) and (b), are true, they may constitute knowledge. I may, then, not only be showing that I have a justified belief about the external world but also may, as a result of my reasoning, know that I do. I do not, however, automatically know that I *am* showing this. Suppose I do not know, but only hope, that I am showing it. Then, even if I do know that I have a justified belief about the external world, I may not be justified in holding the third-order belief that I have (second-order) knowledge that I have this (first-order) justified belief, the belief that there is something blue before me. I have as yet no principle that would justify me in concluding that I know I have a justified first-order belief: a principle stating conditions that generate *second*-order knowledge or second-order justified belief. It seems, however, that the *sort* of justification I apparently have for all the relevant beliefs, including the belief that I have a justified belief about the external world, is the kind such that when the belief in question is true, it constitutes knowledge. Thus, through reasoning using premises like (a) and (b) I may well know that I have justified beliefs about the external world. Certainly I have reason to think that the skeptic does not know, or justifiably believe, that I lack justified beliefs about the external world.

One assumption of this strategy against skepticism deserves emphasis: the assumption that the crucial principles of justification are a priori, and believing them is justified by reflection (directly, or at least on the basis of self-evident steps from directly justified beliefs of a priori premises). Suppose the principles to be empirical. Then our justification for believing them would presumably be broadly inductive. A skeptic would find it easy to deny that, on an inductive basis, we can justifiably believe them. There would also be a circularity problem. For justifying them by inductive reasoning would seem to *presuppose* using just such principles, principles that say, for instance, under what conditions inductive inference can transmit justification or knowledge.

Are the kinds of principles of justification I have been using a priori? That is certainly arguable; but it is also controversial. On a reliability theory of justification, for instance, a belief is justified by virtue of being grounded in reliable belief-producing processes such as perception; and it is apparently not an a priori matter what processes are reliable, that is, actually produce a suitably large proportion of true beliefs. Thus, in order to know what principles account for justification, one must *know* what processes tend to generate true beliefs. One could determine that only through considerable experience. Hence, the circularity problem just mentioned would beset the attempt to justify these principles if they are empirical. On the other hand, I argued above that reliability theories are less plausible for justification than for knowledge, and I believe that it is more reasonable, though by no means obviously correct, to suppose that at least some principles about the conditions for justification are a priori. I would include various principles expressing ways in which—as described by Chapters 1 through 4—justification is produced by its basic sources.

Where, then, does all this leave us with respect to our appraisal of skepticism? To begin with, there are forms of skepticism I have not mentioned, and I have also not discussed every plausible argument for the skeptical principles I have addressed: chiefly the infallibility, certainty, backup, entailment, and cogency principles. But these principles are in some important ways representative of those on which skepticism rests. I have offered reasons to reject them, and on that basis I have maintained that skepticism, at least insofar as it depends on these and similar principles, can be rebutted. It can be shown to be rationally resistible. We are warranted in refusing to accept it. If it is not false, it is at least unjustified. It is not clear, however, that anything said above *refutes* the kinds of skepticism we have considered. For refuting those views entails showing them to be false, and it is not altogether clear what that requires.

Positively, I have suggested that on one plausible notion of showing something, namely, deductively and justifiably deducing it from true premises which one justifiably believes and are good grounds for it, we can show that there are some justified beliefs, probably even some justified beliefs about the external world (possibly including some about the inner lives of others). But I am less inclined to say that we can—by this strategy—show that there is knowledge, particularly knowledge of the external world. I have argued, however, that we *can* know that there is both justified belief and knowledge about the external world even if we cannot show that there is. Skeptics certainly do not seem to have shown that we do not know this. I believe that we do know it, and that we also know that we know some a priori propositions. Perhaps this may be thought to be an article of epistemological faith. I do not think it is; but the difficulty of determining whether it is partly an article of faith, or can be established by cogent argument, or is more than the former yet less than the latter, is some testimony to the depth and complexity of skeptical problems.

Conclusion

Once again, I look at the blue spruce tree. A haze has obscured it; but as the afternoon sun streams down on it, it comes into clear view. Its shape and its shades of color are plainly in my sight. The birds are still singing. The arm of my chair is hard and smooth. I still remember planting the tree twice. I recall the sapling in burlap, and the recollection is so vivid that as the scene fills my consciousness, I become almost unaware of what I see on the hillside before me.

I cannot help having these experiences of color and shape and sound unless I deaden my senses to the world; and I cannot help forming beliefs as I perceive the world or look into my consciousness. I can walk away and change the external sources of my belief. But I cannot resist those sources. If my senses are open to them, I perceive them; if I perceive them, I tend to form beliefs about them: about their colors and shapes, their sounds and scents and textures. These beliefs seem to arise directly from my perceptions, not by a process of inference from anything else I believe. I realize that they are fallible, and I understand the profound inclination toward skepticism which one experiences as one reflects on the significance of that fallibility. Still, I find no reason to think these everyday beliefs doubtful, and I am convinced that for the most part they are justified and constitute knowledge.

When I look within my own consciousness, I also find beliefs arising in the same natural, seemingly irresistible way, though I have far more control over the scenes and events that I experience only inwardly. I can dismiss my image of the sapling and call up an image of the friends who gave it. But I cannot help believing that the image of the sapling is of something with a bluish cast. The inner world, like the outer world, produces certain beliefs directly and irresistibly. And these beliefs tend to be both justified and to constitute knowledge.

I can also turn my attention to abstract matters, even while my senses bombard me with impressions. Looking at the hawthorn and the birch in an uphill line from the spruce, I realize that I cannot see whether the spruce is taller than the birch. But I can see that it is taller than the hawthorn and that the hawthorn is taller than the birch. Clearly, then, the spruce is taller than the birch. Reason makes it obvious that if the spruce is taller than the hawthorn and the hawthorn taller than the birch, then the spruce is taller than the birch. This belief is as natural, and would be at least as difficult to resist, as my belief that there is something blue before me when I squarely see the spruce. Clearly, this a priori belief is also justified, and it constitutes knowledge.

On the basis of my beliefs that the spruce is taller than the hawthorn and that the hawthorn is taller than the birch, together with my belief that if those things are so then the spruce is taller than the birch, I infer that the spruce is indeed taller than the birch. I began with non-inferential beliefs grounded directly in basic sources of knowledge: perception and reason. By a simple, spontaneous deductive inference, I extended both my knowledge and my justification. And when I heard rapid knocking, believed it to sound like that of a woodpecker, and inferred that there was a woodpecker nearby, I extended my knowledge by inductive inference. Knowledge and justification can grow indefinitely in these ways.

Our beliefs are countless and varied. A vast proportion of them are stored in memory, though beliefs do not normally originate there. Memory preserves, but does not by itself normally produce, belief. It also preserves, but does not create, knowledge. Once I come to know through perception and memory that the spruce is taller than the birch, I may know this from memory even when I have forgotten my evidence for it. If I cease to know it, because the birch has somehow outgrown the spruce, my memorially preserved belief, though now mistaken and hence not knowledge, may still be justified. Memory *is* a basic source of justification. It can be the only present source of justification for many beliefs stored therein, beliefs whose original grounds are long forgotten. It can also produce justification of certain new beliefs which, in a suitable way, seem to represent what I remember, even if I later discover that despite their apparent authenticity they arose from wishful thinking.

Our justification for believing what is, so far as we can tell, grounded in memory, is defeasible, but significantly strong. If it lacked a certain minimal strength, we would not be warranted in trusting our memories without external evidence of their reliability; and it is doubtful that we could get enough such evidence if we could not trust our memory directly in at least some cases. To test my memory of the texture of the spruce by going closer to it, for instance, I must *retain* the belief whose truth I am trying to confirm. If memory were not a basic source of justification, we could never have a large enough store of justified beliefs to yield premises adequate for significant deductive and inductive extension of our justification. The scope of our justified belief would be drastically narrowed. At least a great deal, and perhaps all, of our knowledge of the past, the future, and general empirical propositions would also be undermined.

A picture has emerged. We are in almost constant interaction with the world, external and internal. We are regularly bombarded by sensation, often immersed in the stream of our consciousness, and sometimes occupied with reflection on abstract matters. Beliefs are a natural product of these engagements. They arise in perception, introspection, and reflection; they are preserved in memory; they are multiplied by inference. Many are grounded in the basic sources, or preserved, as non-inferential beliefs, in memory; many others are inferentially grounded in these direct beliefs. This picture has foundational beliefs anchored in the bedrock of experience and reason, and a superstructure of vast complexity erected from it by the building blocks of inference. The theory associated with this picture of our beliefs in relation to the world is psychological foundationalism. The picture is natural; and there is much to be said for the theory.

Another natural picture, similar to the first, emerges. The theory associated with it is epistemological foundationalism. I know that the spruce is taller than the birch. I know this on the basis of knowing that the spruce is taller than the hawthorn and the hawthorn taller than the birch, together with the proposition that if this is so, then the spruce is taller than the birch. And I know that proposition directly, through rationally comprehending it, and know the other premises by sight. I do not readily see how to go any further; and even if I can go on, it is not clear how I could have knowledge at all if there were not some point or other at which my belief is connected with the reality in virtue of which it is true: the tree with its woody skeleton and prickly fur; the unchanging abstract relations grasped by reason. Metaphorically, this picture portrays both knowledge and justification as grounded in looking and thereby in seeing. Perception looks outward, and through it we see the physical world. Memory looks backward, and through it we see the past, at least some of our own past. Introspection looks inward, and through it we see the stream of our own consciousness. And reason looks beyond experience of the world of space and time, and through it we see relations of concepts.

The foundational pictures, both in epistemology and in psychology, have their appeal; yet one can imagine going further in the process of justification than they suggest we should. It may be natural to think that, at any given time, a chain of justification or knowledge will be anchored in the bedrock of experience or reason, just as its constituent beliefs apparently are. But coherentism challenges this. Its proponents may grant that a foundational picture fits our psychological makeup. But their view of the structure of our knowledge and justified belief is different. They see this structure as like a vast fabric of interlocking fibers. Some of these may be connected to experience, but those are not privileged in generating knowledge or justification. True beliefs constitute knowledge when they are suitably woven into the whole fabric, which in turn must hold together in a systematic way. Justification is also a matter of how beliefs are connected with the rest of the fabric. A belief that is a largely isolated strand, for instance not inferentially based on any other or even significantly connected with any other in subject matter, would not be justified.

This and other coherentist pictures also have profound appeal, particularly in understanding the process of justification, in which we do attempt to show a belief justified by connecting it with others that support it and thereby cohere with it. But the process of justification should not dominate our understanding what it is for a belief to *be* justified. Moreover, when it comes to knowledge, which entails truth, the coherence picture is less plausible. For indefinitely many fabrics can have internally coherent patterns; and coherentism—unless alloyed with foundationalist elements—does not require that any of the strands be anchored to the world, whether in perception or introspection or in any other way. Why, then, should we expect a coherent set of beliefs to contain truths that represent the world, and thereby to embody knowledge?

Indeed, if a belief's being justified in some way counts towards its truth, then why should coherence *alone* be the basis of justification given that coherence by itself implies nothing about truth? Furthermore, self-evident propositions, such as that if no vixens are males, then no males are vixens, seem such that we need only understand them to be able to know or justifiably believe them. How does our knowledge or justification here depend on coherence at all? There may be compelling answers to these questions. There are certainly plausible attempts to provide such answers. But I am not aware of any clear success in doing so.

Whether the structure of my knowledge is foundational or not, I may know that there is rapid knocking nearby. Coherentists and foundationalists alike agree that I know this only if it is true, and they tend to agree that at least this sort of knowledge requires justified belief. But what is knowledge? My knowing that there is rapid knocking may seem to be simply my justifiably and truly believing this. But it is not. I could just happen to be hallucinating such a knocking while my ears, quite unbeknownst to me, are temporarily blocked. I could then have a justified true belief which is not knowledge. The suggested account of knowledge as justified true belief is, then, too broad. It also seems too narrow. For there might be knowledge without justification, as with someone who, by virtue of a stable capacity, unerringly computes difficult arithmetic results, but is unaware of the success and is not (at first) justified in believing the answers.

We can strengthen our requirements on justification to deal with the true belief based on hallucination, and we can weaken them to deal with the lightning calculator. But it is not evident that this strategy will yield a correct and illuminating account of knowledge. We can abandon the concept of justification as a central element in understanding knowledge and try to account for knowledge by appeal to the notion of reliably produced true belief. But it is not clear that this approach will fully succeed either, and it certainly leaves us with the problem of explaining why justification at least has the close connection it does have to knowledge. Moreover, justification is epistemologically important in its own right, and reliability theories seem less likely to succeed in accounting for justification than for knowledge. This is at least in part because the grounds of justification seem internal in a way the grounds of knowledge, or at least some of them, do not. We may say at least this, however: that knowledge is true belief based in the right way on the right kind of ground. Justification or reliability or both may be essential to filling out this idea; and while it is not clear just how it is to be filled out, many of the important elements can be gathered from what we have seen concerning the sources, development, structure, and analysis of knowledge.

However we analyze what knowledge is, there remains the question of how much of it, if any, we have. It is sometimes thought that we have a great deal, including a wealth of scientific knowledge, knowledge of certain moral principles, and some knowledge of religious truths. But if what passes for scientific knowledge is often not, strictly speaking, true—or might be utterly rejected in the future—may we really say that there *is* scientific knowledge? If moral principles are neither clearly grounded in experience nor plausibly regarded as a priori, on what basis can they be known? And if, as many philosophers think, there are no cogent arguments for God's existence and, in addition, God is not directly knowable through the experiential or rational sources that ground knowledge, how can there be knowledge of God?

These questions are very difficult. But we are warranted at least in giving partial answers to them. Consider the scientific, moral, and religious domains in turn.

First, while some of what is termed scientific knowledge is no doubt mistakenly so called because it is far from the truth, there may be some precisely true propositions that are scientifically known, and in any case we may speak of approximate scientific knowledge where the proposition in view is simply inaccurate, but not grossly so. Moreover, perhaps we may sometimes speak unqualifiedly of scientific knowledge, if only *of* approximations, when the truth known is not precisely formulated, but is correct within the limits of its application. The degree of inaccuracy or imprecision within which we may speak in these ways is not sharply specifiable. But particularly where a scientific proposition yields true predictions, helps to explain other apparently true propositions, and approximates a more accurate, true proposition, we may be justified in thinking we know it and correct in calling it approximate knowledge.

Second, although moral principles are neither obviously a priori nor obviously knowable empirically, each of these views is defensible. Indeed, neither has been decisively refuted despite sustained ingenious attempts to discredit them. Moreover, once we cast aside the common stereotype of scientific knowledge as representing chiefly a body of facts and laws discoverable by simple inductive generalization or provable by observations, the contrast between well-confirmed scientific beliefs and reflectively grounded moral beliefs appears at best less sharp.

It now becomes far more difficult to discredit the view that there is moral knowledge by contrasting moral beliefs with scientific ones. We should not conclude, then, that there is no moral knowledge. There is surely less reason for the non-cognitivist conclusion that there are no moral propositions to be known in the first place.

Third, even if it is true that no argument for a religious view is decisive, it should be remembered that a diverse group of independent but inconclusive arguments may, if each provides some degree of justification for a conclusion, together justify that conclusion even if none by itself does. It has not been established that this point could not apply in the case of arguments for the existence of God. In any event, discussions of the question of justified religious belief and possible religious knowledge should not simply assume the evidentialist view that such propositions can be known or justifiably believed only inferentially, on the basis of evidence. Experience might provide grounds of justification, or knowledge, or both, somewhat in the way perception does. There are many important differences between the religious and perceptual cases, however, and what we have seen does not show either that there is or that there is not direct justification or direct knowledge of religious propositions. But apparently, even if there cannot be directly justified beliefs of them, there could be direct knowledge of them.

There are powerful skeptical arguments against the view that our knowledge might have such wide scope, and even against the commonsense view that we have any knowledge of the external world, the past, the future, or the inner lives of others. When we realize that our beliefs concerning these domains are clearly fallible, we can begin to appreciate skeptical views. Even our sense that, whether or not we have knowledge, we do have justified beliefs weakens if we take seriously the possibility that what we accept as justification is no final guarantee of truth. But the common skeptical commitment to the ideal of infallible belief as central to knowledge is not warranted by careful inquiry into the nature of knowledge.

Infallibility may be a reasonable ideal for *proof*, conceived as decisively demonstrating a conclusion from rock-solid premises, such as self-evident truths and propositions about the believer's immediate consciousness. For one cannot decisively demonstrate from insecure premises, nor by making merely inductive and hence fallible steps from even the most trustworthy premises. But why should proof be our standard of the kind of justification (or epistemic certainty) appropriate to knowledge? We are not talking about what is required to *show* conclusively that there is knowledge, but about whether there is any. If we think there is, and the skeptic challenges us, we *want* to show that there is. But we must not confuse—or allow skeptics to confuse—the requirements for showing that there is knowledge with the requirements for the existence of it. Perhaps it can be shown that there is knowledge. Certainly, if we want to argue for this, we need not regard showing as equivalent to proving. But even if it cannot be shown that there is knowledge or justified belief, it does not follow that there is none.

But there surely is knowledge and justified belief. I justifiably believe, indeed I know, that that blue spruce stands before me. Those bird songs are not fantasy. My stream of thoughts is in unmistakably clear focus. Even my recollection that I planted the tree twice is clear and steadfast. I am justified in believing that I did, and surely I know this. I have a huge store of beliefs of these and other kinds. They form a structure of great complexity, with innumerable changing elements that reflect my continuing experience and thought, my actions and emotions, my learning and forgetting, my inferring and accepting, my revising and rejecting, my speaking and listening. That structure is grounded in me: in my memory, my habits of thought, my mental and perceptual capacities, my rational nature. My knowledge of the truths of reason arises within the structure itself, once I have the needed concepts. Through my consciousness of what is inside of me, and my perceptual engagement with what is outside of me, this structure is anchored, both internally and externally, to the world. That vast and various reality is at once the ultimate source and the object of my empirical knowledge.

Bibliography

SHORT ANNOTATED BIBLIOGRAPHY OF BOOKS IN EPISTEMOLOGY

Aristotle, *Posterior Analytics*, trans. by G.R.G. Mure, Oxford, 1928. A major text of immense influence. Especially relevant to Chapter 6.

Armstrong, D. M., *Belief, Truth and Knowledge*, Cambridge, 1973. A wide-ranging epistemological essay influential in the reliabilist tradition. Especially pertinent to Chapters 1, 3, and 6 through 9.

Aune, Bruce, *Knowledge, Mind, and Nature*, New York, 1965. An integrated treatment, in the coherentist tradition, of epistemology and the philosophy of mind. Bears particularly on Chapters 1, 3, 6, and 8.

Ayer, A. J., *The Problem of Knowledge*, Harmondsworth, Middlesex, 1956. An epistemological survey in the empiricist tradition. Especially relevant to Chapters 1, 2, 7, and 9.

Berkeley, George, *A Treatise Concerning the Principles of Human Knowledge*, New York, 1929 (originally published in 1710). Perhaps the most important statement of phenomenalism in the empiricist tradition. Bears particularly on Chapters 1, 3, 8, and 9.

BonJour, Laurence, *The Structure of Empirical Knowledge*, Cambridge, Mass., 1985. A detailed statement and defense of coherentism regarding empirical knowledge. Especially pertinent to Chapters 1, 4, 6, 7, and 9.

Brandt, R. B., and Ernest Nagel, eds., *Meaning and Knowledge*, New York, 1965. A large, historically informed assembly of classical and recent readings in epistemology. It bears on all the chapters.

Butchvarov, Panayot, *The Concept of Knowledge*, Evanston, 1970. A metaphysically oriented, foundationalist inquiry into the nature of knowledge; especially pertinent to Chapters 1, 4, 6, 7, and 9.

Chisholm, R. M., *The Foundations of Knowing*, Minneapolis, 1982. A collection of essays, on topics relevant to each chapter, by one of the major epistemologists of this century.

Chisholm, R. M., *Theory of Knowledge*, 2nd ed., Englewood Cliffs, N.J., 1977. A rigorous treatment of many basic topics in the field, and an introduction to Chisholm's own epistemological views. Relevant to each chapter.

Chisholm, R. M., and Robert Swartz, eds., *Empirical Knowledge*, Englewood Cliffs, N.J., 1973. A large collection of recent writings. Especially pertinent to Chapters 1, 2, and 3 and 6 through 9.

Dancy, Jonathan, *Contemporary Epistemology*, Oxford, 1985. A recent introduction to contemporary epistemological literature. It bears on each chapter.

Danto, Arthur C., *Analytical Philosophy of Knowledge*, Cambridge, 1968. A broad epistemological essay with special focus on the structure of knowledge. Especially relevant to Chapters 5 through 9.

Descartes, René, *Meditations*, trans. by W. S. Haldane and G.R.T. Ross, New York, 1927 (originally published in 1641). One of the greatest and most influential works in modern epistemology, and a powerful statement of both rationalism and foundationalism. It bears on every chapter.

Dretske, Fred I., *Knowledge and the Flow of Information*, Cambridge, Mass., 1981. A major statement of a reliabilist, information-theoretic account of knowledge. Particularly pertinent to Chapters 1, 7, and 9.

Dretske, Fred I., *Seeing and Knowing*, London, 1969. An intensive study of perception and its relation to empirical knowledge. Especially relevant to Chapters 1, 3, 7, and 9.

Foley, Richard, *A Theory of Epistemic Rationality*, forthcoming from Harvard University Press in 1987. A detailed development of a subjectivistic theory of justification. Pertinent to each chapter.

Fumerton, Richard A., *Metaphysical and Epistemological Problems of Perception*, Lincoln, 1985. A study of both the nature of the objects of perception and the way perception yields justification and knowledge. Especially pertinent to Chapters 1, 3, and 6.

Ginet, Carl, *Knowledge, Perception, and Memory*, Dordrecht and Boston, 1975. A rigorous study of these three notions in relation to each other. Particularly relevant to Chapters 1, 2, 3, 6, 7, and 9.

Goldman, Alvin I., *Epistemology and Cognition*, Cambridge, Mass., 1986. A presentation of reliabilism for justification and knowledge, with much discussion of related developments in cognitive psychology. Particularly relevant to Chapters 1, 2, 5, and 7.

Harman, Gilbert, *Thought*, Princeton, 1975. A broad study of the nature of knowledge, with much attention to defeasibility conditions. Bears especially on Chapters 1, 2, 5, 7, and 9.

Heil, John, *Perception and Cognition*, Berkeley and Los Angeles, 1983. A study of perception in relation to belief, with discussions linking epistemology to philosophy of mind. Especially pertinent to Chapters 1, 3, and 7.

Hintikka, Jaakko, *Knowledge and Belief,* Ithaca, 1962. A rigorous study in epistemic logic. Particularly relevant to Chapters 5 and 7.

Hume, David, *An Enquiry Concerning Human Understanding*, Indianapolis, 1977 (first published in 1748). A major work in modern epistemology, particularly for the topics of causation, induction, and skepticism. Especially relevant to Chapters 1, 4, 5, and 9.

Hume, David, *A Treatise of Human Nature*, Oxford, 1888 (originally published in 1739). One of the greatest and most influential works in modern philosophy, and a powerful statement of empiricism. It bears on every chapter.

Kant, Immanuel, *Prolegomena to Any Future Metaphysics*, trans. by Lewis White Beck (on the basis of the Mahaffy-Carus translation), New York, 1950 (originally published in 1783). A short presentation of Kant's greatest work, *The Critique of Pure Reason*, which is one of the greatest texts in modern philosophy. The *Prolegomena* bears particularly on Chapters 1, 4, 7, and 8.

Klein, Peter, *Certainty: A Refutation of Scepticism*, Minneapolis, 1981. A rigorous treatment of the nature of knowledge, certainty, and skepticism. Especially pertinent to Chapters 5, 7, and 9.

Kyburg, Henry E., Jr., *Epistemology and Inference*, Minneapolis, 1983. A collection of papers, of which several are especially pertinent to Chapters 5, 7, and 8.

Lehrer, Keith, *Knowledge*, Oxford, 1974. A critique of foundationalism and development of the author's own coherentist theory of knowledge. Particularly relevant to Chapters 1, 3, and 6 through 9.

Lewis, C. I., *An Analysis of Knowledge and Valuation*, La Salle, 1946. A systematic study, in the foundationalist tradition, of many major epistemological and metaphysical questions. Especially relevant to Chapters 1 through 4 and 6, 7, and 9.

Locke, Don, *Memory,* New York, 1971. A concise but wide-ranging treatment of memory and memorial knowledge. Bears mainly on Chapter 2.

Locke, John, *An Essay Concerning Human Understanding*, New York, 1928 (originally published in 1689). A major text in modern epistemology, and a powerful statement of a commonsense empiricism. It bears on each chapter.

Malcolm, Norman, *Knowledge and Certainty*, Ithaca, 1975. A collection of epistemological essays by a leading proponent of the philosophy of Wittgenstein. Especially relevant to Chapters 1, 2, 3, 7, and 9.

Mill, John Stuart, *A System of Logic*, London, 1843. The leading nineteenth-century statement of radical empiricism. Especially relevant to Chapters 4 through 8.

Moser, Paul K., *Empirical Justification*, Dordrecht and Boston, 1985. A rigorous treatment of the foundationalism-coherentism controversy which develops and defends an internalist foundationalist account of justification. Especially pertinent to Chapters 5 through 9.

Moser, Paul K., *Human Knowledge*, New York, 1987. An extensive set of classical and contemporary readings. Pertinent to every chapter.

Nozick, Robert, *Philosophical Explanations*, Cambridge, Mass., 1981. Contains a book-length epistemology section bearing on Chapters 5, 6, 7, and 9.

O'Connor, D. J., and Brian Carr, *Introduction to the Theory of Knowledge*, Minneapolis, 1982. A general introduction bearing on each chapter.

Pappas, George S., and Marshall Swain, *Essays on Knowledge and Justification*, Ithaca, 1978. A collection of recent papers, mainly from professional journals. Especially relevant to Chapters 1 and 5 through 9.

Plato, *Theaetetus*, trans. by F. M. Cornford, Cambridge, 1934. A major text in the history of philosophy. Especially relevant to Chapter 7.

Pollock, John L., *Contemporary Theories of Knowledge*, Totowa, N.J., 1986. A rigorous treatment of leading current theories in epistemology. Bears especially on Chapters 1, 4, 6, 7, and 9.

Pollock, John L., *Knowledge and Justification*, Princeton, 1974. A systematic, wide-ranging treatment of these notions which develops a foundationalist account of both. It bears on all the chapters.

Price, H. H., *Perception*, Oxford, 1932. A detailed major study of the topic, with important discussions of sense-data. Especially relevant to Chapters 1 and 9.

Quine, W. V., and Joseph Ullian, *The Web of Belief*, 2nd ed., New York, 1978. An introductory treatment of the development of commonsense and scientific knowledge. Bears particularly on Chapters 1, 4, 7, and 8.

Quinton, Anthony, *The Nature of Things*, London, 1973. A survey of problems in metaphysics and epistemology, with much discussion of the foundationalism-coherentism controversy. Especially relevant to Chapters 1, 6, and 7.

Reid, Thomas, *Essays on the Intellectual Powers of Man*, London, 1869 (originally published in 1785). An important critique of other modern philosophers, rationalist and empiricist, and an original development of a commonsense epistemology. Especially relevant to Chapters 1 through 4 and 6, 7, and 9.

Rescher, Nicholas, *Skepticism*, Oxford, 1980. A detailed critical survey of many of the arguments for skepticism. Especially relevant to Chapters 7 and 9.

Russell, Bertrand, *An Inquiry into Meaning and Truth*, London, 1940. An articulation of an overall epistemological position by one of the twentieth century's major epistemologists. Especially relevant to Chapters 1 and 6 through 8.

Russell, Bertrand, *The Problems of Philosophy*, London, 1912. An introductory survey of epistemology and metaphysics. Particularly pertinent to Chapters 1, 3, 4, and 7 through 9.

Sellars, Wilfrid, *Science, Perception, and Reality*, London, 1963. A collection of epistemological essays by a major contemporary philosopher. Especially pertinent to Chapters 1, 3, 4, and 6 through 8.

Shope, Robert, *The Analysis of Knowing*, Princeton, 1983. A highly detailed study of major kinds of analysis of knowledge. Especially relevant to Chapter 7.

Stroud, Barry, *The Significance of Philosophical Skepticism*, Oxford, 1984. An intensive study of skepticism, particularly as set out by Descartes. Particularly relevant to Chapters 1, 7, and 9.

Swain, Marshall, *Reasons and Knowledge*, Ithaca, 1981. A rigorous statement of an account of knowledge that unites justificationist and reliabilist elements. Especially relevant to Chapters 1, 5, and 7.

Will, Frederick L., *Induction and Justification*, Ithaca, 1974. A critical study of a foundationalist approach to justification, with much attention to the problem of induction. Especially relevant to Chapters 6 through 9.

Wittgenstein, Ludwig, *On Certainty*, trans. by Dennis Paul and G.E.M. Anscombe, Oxford, 1969. An important discussion of the topic by one of the major twentieth-century philosophers. Especially relevant to Chapters 7 and 9.

Wittgenstein, Ludwig, *Philosophical Investigations*, trans. by G.E.M. Anscombe, Oxford, 1953. Wittgenstein's most wide-ranging work, spanning topics in epistemology, metaphysics, and other philosophical areas. Its remarks and examples bear on every chapter.

Index

DATE DUE

MAY 17 86

ICC 1781 387

FEB 1 7 2000

APR 0 6 2002

Watzek Library
wmain
stification, and

LARK COLLEGE LIBRARY
ND, OREGON 97219

53 0652